Controlling Modern Government

Controlling Modern Government

Variety, Commonality and Change

Edited by

Christopher Hood
All Souls College, Oxford, UK

Oliver James
University of Exeter, UK

B. Guy Peters
University of Pittsburgh, USA

Colin Scott
London School of Economics and Political Science, UK

Edward Elgar
Cheltenham, UK • Northampton, MA, USA

Published by
Edward Elgar Publishing Limited
Glensanda House
Montpellier Parade
Cheltenham
Glos GL50 1UA
UK

Edward Elgar Publishing, Inc.
136 West Street
Suite 202
Northampton
Massachusetts 01060
USA

A catalogue record for this book
is available from the British Library

Library of Congress Cataloguing in Publication Data

Controlling modern government: variety, commonality, and change / edited by
     Christopher Hood . . . [et al.].
         p. cm.
     Includes bibliographical references and index.
         1. Public administration. 2. Comparative government. I. Hood, Christopher,
     1947–

     JF1351.C655 2004
     351—dc22

                                                                        2004047116

     ISBN 1 84376 629 9 (cased)

Typeset by Cambrian Typesetters, Frimley, Surrey
Printed and bound in Great Britain by MPG Books, Bodmin, Cornwall

Contents

PART III   CONCLUSIONS

Figures

Tables

Contributors

Ivar Bleiklie is Professor of Administration and Organization Theory and Director of Norwegian Research Centre in Organization and Management (LOS-senteret) at the University of Bergen, Norway.

Arjen Boin is Assistant. Professor of Public Administration, Leiden University, the Netherlands.

Hans-Ulrich Derlien is Professor of Public Administration, University of Bamberg, Germany.

Katsyua Hirose is Professor of Political Science at Hosei University, Japan.

Christopher Hood is Gladstone Professor of Government, All Souls College, University of Oxford and a member of the ESRC Centre for Analysis of Risk and Regulation, London School of Economics and Political Science, UK.

Jeroen Huisman is a Research Coordinator at the University of Twente, the Netherlands.

Oliver James is Senior Lecturer in Politics, University of Exeter, UK.

Per Lægreid is Professor of Administration and Organization Theory, University of Bergen, Norway.

Martin Lodge is Lecturer in Government and Deputy Programme Director in the ESRC Centre for Analysis of Risk and Regulation, London School of Economics and Political Science, UK.

Nicole de Montricher is a Research Scholar at Centre d'études et de Recherches de Science Administrative (CNRS and Paris 2) and Associate Professor of Comparative Administration, University of Paris 2, France.

Takashi Nishio is Professor of Public Administration at the International Christian University, Tokyo, Japan.

B. Guy Peters is Maurice Falk Professor of American Government, University of Pittsburgh, USA.

Colin Scott is Reader in Law, and a member of the ESRC Centre for Analysis of Risk and Regulation, London School of Economics and Political Science, UK.

Theo Toonen is Professor of Public Administration, Leiden University, the Netherlands.

Frits M. van der Meer is Associate Professor of Comparative Public Administration, University of Leiden, the Netherlands.

Marie Vogel is Maître de Conférence de Sociologie, Ecole Normale Supérieure Lettres et Sciences Humaines (Lyon) and Research Associate (Groupe de Recherche sur la Socialisation, CNRS and ENS), France.

Marjoleine H. Wik is a Researcher and Consultant, at Crisisplan, Leiden, the Netherlands.

Preface

Any group of academics setting out to write about institutional control is vulnerable to unkind jokes comparing them to eunuchs lecturing on the Kama Sutra, and the control of this project was both difficult and hard to analyse. To make it work we needed to develop extensive collaboration among 17 busy scholars in eight different countries over more than three years. At the same time we needed an operating style that allowed us to go back to the drawing board and refine our ideas in the light of what we discovered, rather than setting out a rigid framework in advance and getting specialists to fill in the gaps. It was a difficult balancing act, and to the extent that it was successfully achieved, it largely constituted control by mutuality.

The project started as a result of work that three of the editors had done together in the 1990s (Hood et al., 1999), in analysing a remarkable development of oversight systems in UK government over a 20-year period. We found that a period of 'reinventing government' that was being widely marketed by its advocates as a move from rules-based, process-driven administration to results-based discretionary management was in fact creating a growing industry of overseers, inspectors, evaluators, auditors and complaint-handlers. We noted that some scholars in the USA, such as Paul Light and Joel Aberbach, seemed to be saying something similar, and we were curious to know how far such developments represented some atypical Anglo-American phenomenon and how far they were occurring in other countries.

But that required developing a conversation among a group of scholars who could collectively cover a wide canvas, to arrive at a common analytic language in which 'control' and its developments could be discussed across different state and language traditions. Accordingly, we started off with a preliminary discussion in 2000, in which we discovered that the British language of public sector regulation in which three of us had been operating did not travel very effectively across the different state traditions in which we were interested, and therefore had to abandon our original analytic approach and replace it with one that seemed to be more institutionally neutral. That decision was a product of the power of mutuality and the attribution of authorial responsibility in the text inevitably underplays the contribution the group as a whole made to the development of our ideas and lines of analysis.

Much of our meeting was 'virtual' in the form of email exchanges, with the well-known advantages and frustrations that accompany that form of communication, but we met physically as a group on three occasions to refine our analysis and rework our contributions – the initial meeting which was held at the then newly established Economic and Social Research Council (ESRC) Centre for Analysis of Risk and Regulation, London School of Economics in October 2000, a further meeting in the following year in the cloistered splendour of All Souls College, Oxford, and a final meeting in London again at the end of 2002. The editors met on several other occasions and clogged up each other's inboxes with successive drafts and queries over a period of more than a year.

Mutuality as a system of control has its limits, of course, as our analysis shows, and we drew on the other basic forms of control that we analyse in this book. The necessary 'oversight' element of control came in two forms. One took the form of an organizing editor for each of the main chapters of this book – Oliver James on prisons, Colin Scott on higher education and university research, and Guy Peters on the higher civil service – each of whom produced the first draft of the introductory sections to each of those chapters and interacted with the contributors to fit the quart of material each had produced into the pint pot of a conventional-length book. The other took the form of a general editor, Christopher Hood, who devised the overall control types framework that we used as the basis of the analysis, revised the introductory sections of each chapter for overall consistency and exercised a sometimes heavy editorial hand over the other sections too.

In bringing this complex project to fruition, we have many debts to acknowledge – intellectual, financial and operational. As for the first, in addition to the contribution that the overall group made to developing and testing our themes and lines of analysis, we had further assistance from a number of other scholars who gave most generously of their time in participating in meetings and commenting on drafts. We must mention, in particular, Terence Daintith, Edward Page and Michael Power, whose ideas about a putative 'audit explosion' and 'audit society' formed part of the starting point of our study, and especially Martin Lodge, who read the whole manuscript as it was produced and offered valuable critical comments. For the second, we are grateful to the British Academy for a grant that helped to finance our initial discussions, to All Souls College for providing us with the right kind of setting to pursue our discussions, and above all to the ESRC Centre for Analysis of Risk and Regulation, which generously gave continuing financial support to help us bring the project to a conclusion. Colin Scott's contribution to the project was supported by his appointment to a Senior Research Fellowship in Public Law in the Law Program and Regulatory Institutions Network, Research School of Social Sciences, Australian National University, between 2001 and 2003.

Operational support is vital too, and we are most grateful to Michèle Cohen of All Souls College for helping to organize our workshop there, to Edward Elgar for enthusiastically supporting this project and being understanding when September turned into December for the delivery of the manuscript, and to Milena Radoycheva and Lucy Scott for valuable research assistance. Above all, we are indebted to CARR for the excellent logistical support its administrative staff gave to organizing our workshops (Louise Newton-Clare, David Black, Sabrina Antao, Abigail Walmsely, Jessica Barraclough, Liz White, Amy Eldon and Anna Pili).

Christopher Hood
Oliver James
B. Guy Peters
Colin Scott

Oxford, Exeter, Pittsburgh and London

PART I

Introduction

1. Controlling public services and government: towards a cross-national perspective

Christopher Hood

1 INTRODUCTION: FROM FOLK TALES TO STRUCTURED COMPARISONS

Schoolteachers in England swapping stories about the 'reign of terror' inspection system that was introduced in that country in the early 1990s often come up with an apocryphal tale that begins with a school gearing up for its four-yearly inspection, and going through the usual processes of frantic redecoration, clean-ups and strategy committees working late into the night drafting documents in what is hoped to be the latest and most acceptable educational jargon.

Then (the tale runs) it turns out that the teachers and students will have to deal with more than one set of inspectors, because the conduct of the inspection is itself to be inspected by a higher-level set of central inspectors. And shortly afterwards the school's harassed pupils, teachers and support staff learn they are to face scrutiny from yet another source. A team of academics based at a neighbouring university has been commissioned by the central ministry of education to question students, teachers and school administrators as part of a study designed to explore behaviour during school inspections when the inspectors are themselves being inspected. At the same time, it turns out that an international educational non-governmental organization (NGO) has asked to send two observers to monitor the process and ask some questions as part of an international appraisal of different national systems for quality control in education. As the inspectors and the various meta-inspectors arrive, a television crew also descends on the long-suffering school to film the observers observing the inspectors inspecting the inspectors inspecting the teachers and students, and to talk to the various inspectors and inspected.

Folk tale? Urban myth? Probably. The story certainly tells us something about the evaluation-obsessed social context in which it originated, which led observers such as Michael Power (1997) and Onora O'Neill (2002) to

3

conclude that the UK and other comparable countries were turning into a low-trust 'audit society' that seemed to approach a form of neurosis. But how far does the folk tale point to a general trend in the governance or control of public services and executive government today? Opinions differ. Some writers stress similarities in the way public services have changed in the recent past across different countries, with apparently common trends developing in governance and control processes. Indeed, Roger Wettenhall (2000) has even written of 'the New Public Management State', and there is a minor academic industry devoted to explaining, criticizing or justifying what is often seen as a general drift to 'managerial' controls in public services. But whereas some observers see common types of control spreading everywhere, others see a different picture. They point to the variety of historical starting points from which public service structures and processes have developed and the stickiness or path-dependency of processes of control and governance. From such a view-point common fashions in vocabulary in the internet age are one thing, but deeper institutional change is another.

Each of these views has turned into a well-worn cliché of the conference circuit. They live by taking in each other's washing and no doubt both are partly true. So the aim of this book is to go beyond the folklore and the a priori claims. We want to find out just what was common and different about the control of three public service domains across eight different countries embracing very different state traditions and how those controls changed in each case over a generation.

Making such comparisons work effectively is far from easy, for at least three familiar reasons. First, most comparisons of changes in public services are disproportionately present focused. They tell us a lot about what has happened lately but tend to be much hazier about the various points of origin. That is like comparing different travellers on a road journey by looking only at the recent odometer readings of their cars. Without knowing where the various cars started from or the route they took, we cannot make much sense of their journeys or tell which is in front or who is behind.

Second, what is considered to be 'control' can be problematic, because the word (and others like it) carries different freight in different languages and state traditions. *Contrôle* in French and *Kontrolle* in German traditionally mean accounting checks or authorization systems, in contrast to the broader sense of the word in English. We use the term here in its broader sense, but we need to avoid defining governance or control too narrowly to fit the assumptions of any one state system.

Third, while some writers distinguish broad 'state traditions' as encompassing very different assumptions about how government systems work and how they are to be controlled, others claim that particular domains of public policy – such as defence or education – often have more in common with their counterparts in other countries than with other policy sectors in the same country. So we need to examine different domains of the public sector as well as different 'state traditions' to explore how far changes or trends are uniform across different public services even in any one country.

That is what this book sets out to do. It seeks to compare control of government across time, across policy domains and across countries. It examines what happened to control systems (in a broad sense) for public services over a generation or so, in three different domains of government and public policy within eight different state traditions. The three domains are prisons, higher education and the conduct of senior civil servants, and the eight different traditions comprise Australia, the USA, Japan, France, Germany, the UK, the Netherlands and Norway.

In the final section of this chapter we explain why we selected those particular cases and what their significance is. But before coming to that issue, we need first to explain what we mean by 'control' and why it matters for the understanding of contemporary government. Accordingly, the next section sets out a four-part analytic framework for comparing control across time and among government systems, and the following one explains why change in control or governance in the public sector is important for the various and disputed interpretations of public management reform in the contemporary world.

2   GOVERNANCE AND CONTROL OVER THE PUBLIC SECTOR: A COMPARATIVE FRAMEWORK

Control in the sense used in this book is a synonym for steering or governance. Put abstractly, control is whatever keeps the state of any given system within some desired subset of all its possible states. To evaluate the existence or extent of control in that sense always involves judgement, and the existence of control can never be induced from indices of input or activity.

In orthodox constitutional theory, the two classical institutional mechanisms for making executive government accountable and keeping it under control in liberal-democratic states are oversight by elected representatives and legal adjudication by an independent judiciary. These two classical control mechanisms are normally held to have replaced the controls over government associated with earlier monarchical structures (including royal auditors, censors or procurators, inspectors or commissioners).

Such institutions vary in their independence from executive government and in the way they work, and that variation across the different state traditions in the developed democracies has often been commented on. For example, the ability of the US Congress to 'micro-manage' the federal civil service and share control with the presidency is often contrasted with the more limited opportunities for detailed intervention in the state bureaucracy by other legislatures. Moreover, the way the two classical control mechanisms operate is likely to depend on how socially close or distant legislators and judges are from those they oversee (something that is known as 'relational distance' in the socio-legal literature (see Hood et al., 1999: 60–65)). In some countries, such as Germany, the legislature is heavily drawn from career public servants (meaning that relational distance between legislators and the public service tends to be low), while in others such as the UK there has traditionally been a sharper distinction between political and bureaucratic careers. The same distinction applies to judicial office: for instance, the French administrative court system, with its traditional domination by bureaucrats within the *Conseil d'État*, contrasts with the more 'external' judicial review process in the UK where judges and civil servants often come from different professional worlds.

To bring out variety across state systems, we needed an approach to control that was institution-free, that could accommodate formal and informal control, intentional and unintentional control, and could include a range of supplementary or alternative forms of control and governance beyond the classical pair that we noted above. Any number of different ways of classifying controls over government have been put forward. For example, various authors such as Schick (1966), Schultze (1977) and Thompson (1993) have identified neo-market alternatives to 'command' systems of administration. Some have broken down the dimensions of control into the cybernetic trio of detectors, directors and effectors (see Hood et al., 1999). And one of the best-known distinctions of control styles comes from the rational choice stable in the form of McCubbins and Schwartz's (1984) well-known distinction between legislative strategies of 'police patrol' (more or less systematic review) and 'fire alarms' (concentration of attention on problem cases) in control over bureaucracy.

Most of those distinctions will be drawn on later in the book, but our starting point, following earlier work (see Hood, 1996, 1998; Hood et al., 1999), is to distinguish *mutuality, competition, contrived randomness* and *oversight* as forms of control over individuals operating in public institutions and organizations. These four basic types are summarized in Figure 1.1.

Mutuality denotes control of individuals by formal or informal group processes, whether by deliberate design or otherwise. Institutional mechanisms that make individuals answerable to a group or require them to accommodate the preferences of others are a common feature of public organizations. Processes of mutual influence can be institutionalized in various ways, from shared work space or common meal arrangements, through conventions of consultation, group decision-making processes like the Japanese *ringi* system described later in the book (in which civil servants arrive at decisions through a consensual round-robin procedure), committee or

Contrived Randomness	Oversight
Works by unpredictable processes/ combinations of people to deter corruption, or anti-system behaviour	Works by: monitoring and direction of individuals from a point of authority
Example: selection by lot, rotation of staff around institutions	*Example: audit and inspection systems*
Competition	**Mutuality**
Works by fostering rivalry among individuals	Works by exposing individuals to horizontal influence from other individuals
Example: league tables of better and worse performers	*Example: pairing police officers on patrol*

Figure 1.1   Four basic types of control over executive government and public services

board structures or their equivalents, to Madisonian systems of separated institutions sharing powers that require mutual accommodation among the various players.

Mutuality is often said to be central to control over government. For instance, mutual rating and collegiality among a like-minded elite was argued by Heclo and Wildavsky (1974) to be the central force that regulated the conduct of the British senior civil service in the 1970s, forming a controlling mechanism far more important (they claimed) than the formalities of parliamentary oversight, judicial review or ministerial supervision. Control by mutuality is familiar in the sociological literature on informal organization and the way it affects work norms (as revealed by the famous Hawthorne experiments of the 1920s (Mayo, 1949)), but as we shall see, it can work through various mechanisms and at different institutional levels. So a comparative study needs to assess the strength of traditional 'mutuality' forms of control across different state traditions and parts of the public sector, the forms those controls took and how they changed.

Competition denotes control of individuals in the public sector by processes of rivalry. Many contemporary government reformers write as if competition as a method of controlling government had only just been discovered (by them) and as if monopoly power and a sheltered life were normal features of traditional public services. But in fact rulers of all kinds have long used mechanisms that pit individuals and their organizations against one another to exert control over their executive apparatus and public service systems.

For instance, bureaucrats have traditionally been obliged to compete for appointment, reappointment, bonuses or merit pay raises, honours or medals, promotion to higher positions, even valued positions after retiring from or leaving the bureaucracy. And those who head government organizations likewise typically have to compete for good-quality recruits, budgetary allocations, valued office locations, major policy responsibilities, corporate awards or league-table rankings, reputation, prestige or position in the pecking order. Indeed, presidents and prime ministers often deliberately follow Franklin Roosevelt's classic tactic of controlling the government apparatus by making the division of tasks ambiguous and sharing responsibilities among several rival organizations. So we need to assess the strength of the competitive forces to which bureaucracies were traditionally exposed in different countries and policy sectors, the forms that such competition took, and the ways in which it has changed.

Contrived randomness denotes control of individuals in government and the public sector by more or less deliberately making their lives unpredictable in some way, as in the classic example of election or selection of public office-holders by lot. The aim or effect of such unpredictability is to make the payoffs of anti-system and self-interested behaviour (or 'rent-seeking' activity more generally) uncertain. Ways of making careers unpredictable constitute one key mechanism of this type of control, for example, by posting staff around organizations. That is a practice often adopted to limit corruption and local sympathies in traditional bureaucratic structures, and still widely used today in multinational corporations.

Other mechanisms in the 'randomness' family include random selection processes (as in jury selection) and unpredictable patterns of audit, inspection or authorization (linking randomness with oversight). Though some may see the policy environment as inherently prone to produce a large measure of randomness – in the uncertain process of agenda selection, in apparently capricious public 'mood swings', in unexpected scrutiny of dark corners of the bureaucracy by media and politicians – some elements of deliberate unpredictability are frequently found as mechanisms of control over bureaucracy, often in association with other controlling processes. Again, we shall be looking at the extent to which such controls operated in the past and what form they took in our eight countries and three policy domains, as well as exploring changes in this method of control.

Oversight denotes a fourth generic approach to control of individuals in government and the public sector, and this approach is often linked with the previous three control forms. Oversight means scrutiny and steering from some point 'above' or 'outside' the individuals in question. We referred earlier to law courts and legislatures, the two classical forms for overseeing government and public services in liberal democracies. But beyond these classic types a range of other secondary overseers can be found, in the form of reviewers, monitors, inspectors or regulators that are to some degree detached from line management or the chain-of-command structure within executive government organizations. Indeed, at least seven different types of oversight bodies can be identified outside the two classic controllers of government in liberal-democratic state theory, and they are summarized in Figure 1.2.

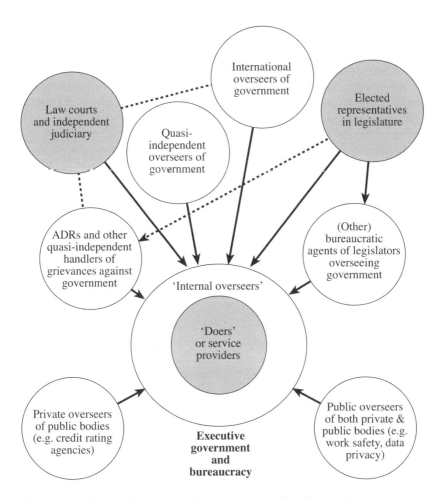

Figure 1.2   Types of overseers of government and public services

One type consists of international public overseers of government like the European Union's (EU's) fraud-busters, the World Trade Organization and bodies monitoring treaty obligations on torture and other human rights issues. A second consists of the agents of legislators, like auditors or watchdogs, or even special prosecutors. (An extreme example of the latter is the Office of the Special Prosecutor, an extraordinary office established by the US Congress after the collapse of the Nixon presidency over Watergate, to watch for any transgressions by the President. It became internationally famous through the impeachment of Bill Clinton in 1998 after the Monica Lewinsky affair, and disappeared under the George W. Bush presidency.) A third type consists of independent or semi-independent grievance-handlers and a fourth consists of officers or bodies relatively independent both of the legislature and the regular executive structure, such as bodies that police merit in public appointments or the independent commissions against corruption that developed in several states during the 1980s.

A fifth consists of arms-length monitoring and standard-setting units developed within the executive government structure itself, from traditional approval or authorization systems by central agencies or higher level of government over lower-level units (*tutelle*, in French parlance) to inspection and review, as in the classical tradition of the Chinese Imperial Censorate or the French *inspections générales* attached to most ministries to oversee their field services. A sixth consists of bodies overseeing public and private sector organizations alike, such as the now ubiquitous regulators of data privacy, health and safety at work, equal opportunities or industry-specific regulators operating in markets where there are both public and private sector providers. Perhaps we can even add a seventh category, in the form of the various private or independent overseers of government such as private audit firms auditing public bodies, international credit rating agencies or other rating organizations like Freedom House and Transparency International (Scott, 2002).

As noted earlier, the four-part framework set out in Figure 1.1 gives us a way of analysing controls over time, policy domains and countries that is relatively institution-free and not aligned with assumptions about control coming from any one state tradition. But the way those controls operate may vary across state traditions, and Table 1.1 indicates some of that variety for the five most distinctive of the eight state traditions we consider here, giving illustrative examples from each case and setting out three levels or dimensions of each of the four primary types of control identified earlier. As Table 1.1 suggests, the political systems vary in the way that oversight of public services was built into traditional forms of control, and in the form and level in which other types of control are institutionalized.

Three things can be noted from looking at control over government in this way. One is that it gives us a fresh perspective on the much discussed issue of

Table 1.1 Five selected state traditions and control styles

	Japan	France	Germany	UK	USA
1. Oversight					
By courts	Low	Hybrid	Medium/high	Low	Very high
By legislature	Low	Low	Medium/low	Low	High
By bureaucratic units units	Medium, inc. *tutelle* and administrative guidance	High, including *tutelle* and inspections	Low (no *tutelle*, few inspectorates)	High, including *tutelle* and inspections	Low
2. Mutuality					
Constitutional or system level	Low (only one veto player)	Low	High (multiple veto players)	Low (only one veto player)	High (multiple veto players)
Executive govt level	High	High	Fairly high	High	Generally low (government of strangers)
Policy level (corporatism)	High	Variable	High	Variable	Low
3. Competition					
Tiebout rivalry (among units of government)	Fairly low	Low	Medium	Low	High
Public–private	Low	Low	Medium	Medium	High
Within bureaucracy	High	High	Fairly high	High	Medium to low
4. Control by randomness					
Multiple-key features of top decision structure	Low	Variable (can be high in periods of cohabitation)	High	Low	High
Definiteness of institutional and const. rules	Variable	Variable	High	Low	High
Career unpredictability in executive government	Low	Fairly high (quasi-lateral entry)	Variable	Medium	High

11

'state traditions'. 'State tradition' is a term used by Dyson (1980) to denote different 'traditions of state philosophy' allied to different styles of public law, and the phrase is widely, though typically imprecisely, used in the literature of comparative politics. But as Table 1.1 shows, we can also fruitfully compare state traditions as constituting different approaches to control over government, notably in the form and institutional level in which they deploy mutuality, competition, randomness and oversight.

Second and relatedly, as Table 1.1 suggests, the conclusions we may reach about how different state traditions reflect the four modes of control may depend on what institutional level we look at (the importance of institutional level has been stressed by many authors, notably Weaver and Rockman, 1993). For instance, if we look at controls that operate at system-wide level as a result of constitutional or quasi-constitutional structures, we can conclude that the USA government structure is one characterized by high mutuality whereas that of the UK (in its traditional form, at least) is characterized by low mutuality. That is because the USA constitutional structure of multiple veto players (Tsebelis, 2002) builds mutuality in with the constitutional bricks in a way that did not traditionally apply to the UK system, with its single veto player. But we would come to the opposite conclusion if we looked instead at mutual controls operating within executive government, since the traditionally cabinet-centred and 'Athenaeum club culture' that is conventionally said to have produced high reciprocal influence among the various players in Whitehall stands in sharp contrast to the 'government of strangers' (Heclo, 1977) that is often said to operate at the upper levels of the executive structure in Washington. And if we go down another institutional level, to that of particular agencies or policy systems, the control profile can be different again, as we shall see later. This analysis shows that we have to be wary of grandiloquent broad-brush characterizations of state traditions, because we cannot take it for granted that the control pattern operating at one institutional level is repeated at other levels.

Third, state traditions that score high on one dimension of each of the four types of control do not necessarily score high on the other ones. Indeed, there are strong signs of compensating effects and control hybridity in each of the five major state traditions analysed in Table 1.1. Thus it is noticeable that the states with substantial 'administrative' oversight systems tend to be those where oversight of government is weak at legislative level, though that compensatory relationship does not seem to apply to oversight by courts in all cases. In the French state tradition, for instance, weak legislative oversight of government is accompanied by its famous tradition of *inspections générales*, which were formed to monitor the ramified field administration structure as part of an early nineteenth-century oversight explosion. That pattern was also introduced in the Netherlands, with its Napoleonic state inheritance, and was palely imitated for some public services in the UK a generation later in the 1830s. The functional equivalents in Germany are the courts of account which also originate in the absolutist state but became advisory to the state and federal legislatures from the 1970s, showing that the boundary line between court, legislative and bureaucratic controls can be hard to draw or easy to cross.

However, precisely for these reasons, the use of our four-part analytic scheme can help us to push beyond the commonplaces of 'state traditionism' in comparative analysis. And equally, applying that framework to a set of different states and policy domains gives us a chance to explore hybrids and variations of the four-part structure, and we shall be summing up what we found in the final chapter.

3   WHAT COMPARATIVE ANALYSIS OF CONTROLS OVER GOVERNMENT CAN REVEAL

In applying the analytic framework set out in the previous section to control over three domains of the public sector in eight different countries, we aim to answer three questions. First – going back to the issues we raised at the outset – how far can we identify general trends across developed countries in the way that individuals in the public services are controlled? Can we find truly cross-national trends, or only particular styles? Second, what light can a comparative study throw on doctrinal arguments about how to control the public sector? Can it help us to establish the scope and limits of fashionable doctrines such as 'enforced self-regulation' and more 'managerial space' in the delivery of public services? Third, what exactly was the 'old public management' like? Should we think of a single 'traditional model' of public service provision or something more varied?

(a)   Oversight Explosions? Distinguishing Cross-National Trends from Particular Control Styles

We began this chapter with a story about English school inspection that drew attention to the growth of oversight over schools and teachers in the 1990s. And several UK-based observers have written about an apparent 'oversight explosion' at that time. As we have already noted, Power and O'Neill have diagnosed the development of a putative 'audit society' obsessed with checking-up rituals on every domain of activity and undermining trust in once self-governing professionals. Michael Moran (2003) has argued that the UK saw a dramatic shift from 'club government' to formalized regulation over that period. Rather earlier, Patrick Dunleavy (1991) argued that public service reform in the UK was dominated by 'bureau-shaping' strategies on the part of senior civil servants who wanted to be released from direct management responsibilities, producing a trend towards a fragmentation of formerly mono-lithic bureaucracies into elite policy or oversight units standing at arm's length from service-delivery units. Christopher Hood et al. (1999) put some numbers on such developments. They showed that formal arm's-length overseers had doubled in size and real-term resources over two decades when the UK civil service was cut by more than 30 per cent and local government by about 20 per cent – an observation that recalls Northcote Parkinson's (1961) famous correlation between increasing numbers of clerks in the British Admiralty with declining numbers of battleships in the navy. At a time when the rhetoric of public service reform tended to stress entrepreneurialism and greater manage-rial freedom, a steadily expanding (though bureaucratically divided) army of waste-watchers, quality police and sleaze-busters was applying and monitor-ing ever more codes and procedural guidelines. Such observations have prompted discussion as to whether new public management, UK-style, far from amounting to a decisive move away from 'rules-based, process-driven' approaches to administration (the spin put on public management reform by Osborne and Gaebler, 1992), in fact amount to a more rules-based, process-driven style of executive government than ever before.

Are those 'oversight explosion' developments just a reflection of what is often seen as British administrative idiosyncrasy or exceptionalism, or are they observ-able in other countries as well? Those 'cultural' explanations that link the rise of an 'audit society' to a supposedly broad post-materialist pattern of declining deference to middle-class professionals in more educated and affluent societies, or growing distrust of big organizations in the public and private sector, might lead us to expect trends to rising oversight of government to be universal. But against such general interpretations, it could be argued that the growth of arm's-length regulation over public sector bodies in the UK in the 1980s and 1990s either amounted to a late catch-up with states that traditionally subjected their bureaucrats to more formal oversight (as with the French *inspections générales*) or to a substitute for the more effective formal oversight of state bodies elsewhere by courts and legislatures (as in the German or US traditions). So we need to explore how far the UK was extraordinary or typical in experiencing general regulatory growth over government during the New Public Management era by secondary overseers beyond the two classical forms noted above.

However, even within the UK, that growth of oversight does not seem to have been experienced to the same extent by all parts of the public sector. Though it did not escape entirely, the high bureaucracy, with its strong mutu-ality tradition of peer-group rating, was rather less exposed to a growth of formal oversight than the executive parts of the central state structure or delivery agencies at the local level such as schools, universities, health and social care, and the 'oversight explosion' also made less ground over police and security agencies. The political interpretation of such differences is that exposure to increased oversight was linked to the power of different parts of the public sector, while the technical interpretation is that activities like the achievement of test scores by school students are inherently more 'auditable' than the quality of policy advice in the high bureaucracy. Probably a mixture of politics and technical factors was in play. But to explore such developments cross-nationally, we need to compare what happened to different parts of the public sector in different countries.

(b) Assessing Doctrines of Control over Government in Comparative Perspective

If one reason for this study is to explore similarity and difference in controls over government across different societies, another is that control is central to contemporary doctrines about good governance. But those doctrines are contested in at least three ways.

One is the debate about how effective oversight, in the sense used in the previous section, can be as a way of controlling public services. Most descriptions of how government and public organizations are controlled tend to begin with an account of the formal oversight arrangements, but how far those arrangements deliver 'control' in the broader analytic sense defined above is much more debatable, and the equation of control with oversight can often be seen as a basic fallacy in the study of public administration and public law. Among those who are sceptical about the efficacy of oversight as control are James Q. Wilson and Patricia Rachal (1977), who concluded nearly 30 years ago that government could never regulate itself as effectively as it could regulate business. Another is Michael Power's (1997) view of the UK's 'audit explosion' as providing only a precarious 'reassurance' while potentially undermining an ethos of professional self-regulation. On the other hand are those who are enthusiastic about the potential of formal oversight and regulation in the public sector. Those enthusiasts include the World Bank (1999) in its claim that formal oversight regimes over the public sector are one of the critical success factors for the civil service reform efforts the World Bank sponsored over the 1990s.

That debate is connected to the debate about the feasibility and desirability of managerialism in the conduct of public services. The term 'managerial' is used in many different ways, often as a term of vague rhetorical abuse, but it is understood here to mean arrangements in which those who head public organizations have direct responsibility and some discretionary decision 'space' over the services they provide. From a control perspective, making public services more 'managerial' in that sense means relaxing process controls and *ex ante* oversight in the form of authorization, with a corresponding increase in *ex post* oversight focusing on results. Many (such as Savoie, 1994) see *ex post* control in exchange for discretion as the central theme of managerialism.

So how far and how widely has such a transformation in control arrangements taken place? For instance, how far has a reduction in some process rules (over hiring, pay, grading, contracts, financial virement, for example) meant an increase in other process rules (over matters like conflict of interest, transparency in reporting, discrimination, favouritism or bullying, or other potential managerial corner-cutting activities)? How far attempts at more 'managerial' approaches to public service provision involve a reduction in some kinds of controls and rules, and increases in others, or whether they unintentionally produce a 'double whammy' pattern in which new process rules and overseers are added without a substantial reduction of the old ones, is central to the theory of contemporary public management. Scholars like Light (1993: 17) and Hood et al. (1999) suggest that the 'double whammy' pattern is much more than a theoretical possibility.

The failings or pathologies of business regulation have long been discussed (for example, by Sunstein, 1990, and Grabosky, 1995). Commonly noted failings and pathologies include regulatory capture and accommodation, information asymmetry between regulator and regulatee, and bureaucratic-behaviour styles that lead regulators to focus on what is doable or winnable, often hitting peripheral 'soft targets' at the expense of balance or substantive goals. The perceived inability of regulators to balance the social benefits of expansion in regulatory demands against the extra compliance costs imposed on regulatees by such expansion has also attracted much debate and criticism in the context of business regulation. In principle, all these familiar problems apply equally to the oversight of government as to regulation of business (see James, 2000). Yet their analogues in the oversight of the public sector have been little discussed, and the same goes for the three other generic forms of control that we discussed in the previous section – mutuality, randomness and competition.

Nor do we know much about the conditions under which formal and external oversight can be linked to internal or immanent controls in organization. Some leading regulatory theorists, notably Ayres and Braithwaite (1992), argue for a strategy that they call 'enforced self-regulation' of organizational behaviour. But applying that sort of linkage to the public sector may be more problematic than Ayres and Braithwaite allow, because enforced self-regulation requires several quite demanding conditions to be present. It assumes a culture that can accept substantial discretion on the part of bureaucrats (a condition not present in the US federal government, according to Light, 1993). It assumes a culture that can accept substantial discretion by quasi-independent regulators over the use of enforcement powers (a condition that in the past has rarely applied to any kind of regulation in Europe). It assumes a culture in which 'big stick' threats at the top of the enforcement chain are credible because political lobbying cannot stop the sanctions escalator at that point. In earlier studies of regulation in the UK public and private sector with other colleagues, we have found all those basic conditions to be absent (Hood et al., 1999; Hall, Scott and Hood, 2000), but we lack clear cross-national comparative evidence on this point.

Our study cannot resolve all these doctrinal issues, but it can help to establish how widespread the 'oversight explosion' has been across different countries, how widely managerial approaches to control have developed, what kind of 'pathologies' or shortcomings are to be found in the four basic modes of control that we identified earlier and how far hybrids like enforced self-regulation are possible and effective.

(c)   The Old Public Management and the Pattern of Change

Third, our comparative analysis of how controls over executive government change or remain over time is designed to add to our understanding of what 'old public management' was like in different countries and what exactly is the nature of the system that has replaced it. As already noted, a conventional story told by many exponents of the idea of a general 'paradigm shift' in contemporary public sector management is that old public administration was everywhere 'rules-based' and 'process-driven', while new variants are more 'output-based' and 'results-driven' (see Barzelay, 1992; Osborne and Gaebler, 1992). While that characterization may usefully represent some of the dynamics of contemporary public management, a more subtle and varied approach may be needed to describe some of the different jumping-off points, or what precisely constituted 'old public management' in different contexts.

In some cases, as with the higher echelons of the British civil service (and several other specimens within our set), many of the key rules of the traditional system tended to be indefinite and often not formally enacted or written down at all. Examples included what exactly counted as conflict of interest and how it should be handled, just who had to be consulted over what, what were the limits of loyalty to superiors or Ministers, even apparently clear-cut matters like what counted as entitlement to a public-service pension. Rather, the culture was one that relied heavily on elite socialization and reciprocal peer-group control through 'mutuality' for such matters rather than a thick manual of enacted rules (Moran's (2003) 'club government'). The system could certainly have been said to be 'process-driven', but many of the key rules were neither enacted nor definite. A similar culture could have been found in the upper reaches of the universities, the medical world and, arguably, in business and finance too. To the extent that such structures have been replaced, it has been in the direction of writing down the rules of the game and setting up more formal structures for applying them.

Instead of the 'rules-based, process-driven' stereotype, a more plausible way of portraying the controls operating over many UK bureaucracies in the 'old public management' period was as a mix of the four generic control types introduced in the first section – a combination of mutuality, oversight, rivalry and unpredictability – not a single one. And what characterized the emerging structure, particularly at the top of the public service, was an increased emphasis on formal arm's-length oversight and new forms of competition being laid on top of traditional ones (like competition for recruitment and promotion). Whereas the older public service structure placed more emphasis on a mixture of mutuality (particularly for the top elites) and contrived randomness (particularly for the field staff and those who handled money), contemporary reforms have placed more emphasis on a mixture of oversight and competition.

As that example shows, looking carefully at the changing patterns of control over public bureaucracies may reveal patterns of historical transition that are both subtler and more varied than the conventional stereotype of old public management allows for. The aim of this inquiry is to characterize and compare those transitions across different state traditions and forms of organization.

(d)   Overall

What these three issues show is that a comparative examination of controls over executive government is not a quirky or offbeat enterprise, but can illuminate some of the central contested or unanswered features of contemporary public service reform. Some of those issues relate to the direction of historical change in different societies. Some of them concern the entailments of different conceptions of how public servants are to operate. Some of them are questions about the effectiveness or otherwise of different ways of controlling government. These issues cut to the heart of contemporary interpretations of governance reforms – what they involve, how much commonality there is across different state traditions and what the effect is of received doctrines of governance. Moreover, while undoubtedly challenging to explore, the issues are not riddles of the universe in the sense of puzzles that are interesting but insoluble. Comparative analysis cannot necessarily resolve such issues beyond a peradventure, but it can certainly help to shed light on them, as we shall show.

4   THE CASES AND THE RESEARCH DESIGN

The previous sections have aimed to show that the subject of our inquiry – how controls over executive government work in different states and in different public sector domains – raises many empirical questions that have not yet been answered. Some particular sets of overseers (notably auditors and ombudsmen) have been comparatively mapped to some extent, but not the more general picture. Nor do we have a clear comparative picture of the points of departure from which different states entered the contemporary era of public management reform.

We approached this inquiry as if it were the kind of quiz show or parlour game in which players have to choose a few questions that will produce the highest yield of information in identifying a mystery object. So our focus is selective rather than general. And, to pursue the analogy with participating in a quiz show, we needed to pose questions that were open-ended and did not beg the question by assuming any one particular answer (see Fischer, 1970). Accordingly, we set out to compare change or stasis in control over government across eight countries embracing different state traditions, in three different institutional or policy domains.

The state traditions we aim to compare cut across what have traditionally been considered 'strong' and 'weak' state forms and the major institutional and constitutional types of developed democracies. Accordingly, we examine the principal continental European models (the French Napoleonic tradition, the German state tradition and the Dutch state model that was taken by Lijphart, 1969, as the leading exemplar of consociational democracy), the Japanese state tradition that combines Confucian ideas with institutions borrowed and adapted from western countries, the Norwegian case as an example of the Scandinavian state model, the UK (and Australian) 'Westminster model', and the US case in which (as in the UK case) the monarchy lost the civil wars that the continental European monarchies mostly won in the early modern era.

As we showed in section 1, those various state traditions embrace different mixtures of oversight, mutuality, competition and randomness in their traditional institutional arrangements. We will be bringing out some of their distinct features in the remainder of the book. For instance, the French tradition has a distinct approach to oversight in the form of the famous *inspections générales* and the accompanying doctrine that (almost) every state service should have its own inspectorate, but mixes oversight with mutuality by establishing judicial oversight of the bureaucracy in a body (the *Conseil d'État*) composed of civil servants themselves. The German state tradition is often regarded as an archetype of 'legalist' oversight, with administrative courts performing oversight functions that might be performed by different institutions in other states, but embodies a structure of multiple veto players that encourages mutuality at the macro-political level.

The USA shares those two characteristics, but its courts have higher relational distance from the bureaucracy than in the German case, its bureaucracy is of the agency rather than the more autonomous German type without any distinct 'bureaucratic class' or *Beamtenethos*, and oversight of the bureaucracy is divided between the executive and legislature. The Netherlands is often regarded as a 'strong state' and a distinct hybrid of continental European state traditions, while the Westminster model UK state style (and to a lesser extent its Australian variant) contrasts with the previous ones in a traditionally lower exposure of bureaucracy to oversight by courts and judges, and traditionally embodied mutuality through a club-like social pattern at the top of the state bureaucracy, and arguably many other domains of public service. The Japanese structure has similar features, but has always been strongly influenced by German bureaucratic traditions, and has evolved within a neo-Confucian cultural tradition. Accordingly, the set of state traditions we examine cut across common-law and public-law systems, federal and unitary states, eastern and western traditions, and a different-cases design can be expected to form a sufficiently wide range of points of departure to enable us to examine how far trends in control over the public sector are truly general and uniform.

The three different institutional or policy domains that we compare are those of the control of conduct within the high state bureaucracy, the prison sector and the world of university research and higher education. These three domains are only limitedly representative of the whole range of organizations and activities within the public sector, but they do enable some degree of 'triangulation' or cross-domain inquiry. Prisons and universities are in some ways at opposite extremes as policy domains. Prisons are part of the core, traditional or defining functions of the state, involving the uniformed services of the state. They exercise the state's unique legal power to punish and in that sense apply 'sticks' rather than 'sermons' or 'carrots' as their primary policy instrument, which means that competition is possible around the edges but not in the core function.

By contrast, universities have a long history as parts of public policy (including functioning as the intellectual bodyguard of church and state in previous eras), but the instruments they employ consist more of 'sermons' and 'carrots' rather than 'sticks', (Bernelmans-Videc et al., 1998) they are far more amenable to competition and in several ways they are more akin to other policy domains that are characteristic of the modern welfare state, such as social service, health care and the rail, mail, power and water services that have been privatized in many cases in the recent past. In principle, we might expect oversight, mutuality, competition and randomness to work rather differently in those two sectors, and to product a different kind of dynamic. We might expect traditional forms of oversight to be more visible in traditional core areas of state activity and to remain at a higher level than in policy areas characterized by services and transfers.

The high state bureaucracy in some ways comes between those two extreme cases. It is also one of the traditional core sectors of the state, but its activity is more hybrid, embracing aspects of the uniformed services role but extending to more university-like activity as well. It is central to modern debates both about the reform of public management and about 'sleaze' and misconduct that are said to be a reflection of rising egalitarianism and declining trust in government in many developed contemporary democracies. And we might expect a wide range of traditional approaches to control of that structure.

Accordingly, this book aims to compare across time, across policy domains and across countries (a strategy in some ways paralleling that of Vogel, 1996). Between this introductory chapter and the concluding chapter that sets out what we discovered, the book is divided into three main chapters, each introduced by the editors and containing an account of what happened to control styles over a generation in that policy domain across the eight states. We begin with the case of prisons, move to the higher education sector and then turn to the control of the conduct of higher civil servants. In each case we seek to identify comparatively the nature of traditional controls operating a generation or so ago and to identify what changes have taken place since then. As we shall see, those questions are deceptively simple and raise some tricky issues of interpretation. Accordingly, in each of the three main chapters of the book the introductory part includes some indicative tables and is followed by an account of the distinctive features of each of the countries in the study for that domain, together with comments on the underlying politics and anything that is known about the effectiveness or otherwise of traditional or more recent controls.

Such questions by no means exhaust what deserves to be investigated about comparative patterns of control over government. And the questions are easier to ask than to answer, even for scholars who have spent a lifetime studying particular patterns of executive government or public services. Some of the answers are bound to be rough and ready, and some might certainly be disputed among different observers of the same country. But even allowing for those differences, as we shall show in the concluding chapter, we can come to some fairly firm conclusions about the development of oversight and other forms of control over contemporary government over the last 30 years or so.

PART II

Control over Government in Three Domains

2. Prisons: varying oversight and mutuality, much tinkering, limited control

2.1 OVERVIEW
Oliver James and Christopher Hood

1 Patterns of Control in Eight Countries

As the introductory chapter noted, prisons are institutions that present particularly stark issues of control, because they are 'total institutions' (Goffman, 1961) exercising drastic state power. They separate individuals from society, and monitor and shape much of their inmates' lives, including matters as basic as when and how to eat, work, sleep and exercise. They are frequently engaged in efforts to discipline, correct and rehabilitate their prisoners. The control of such institutions in a liberal democracy is problematic for various reasons, particularly because of minority-rights issues. Even in those countries, notably the USA, with comparatively high prison participation rates among the population, the experience of being an inmate is confined to a small minority of the population, as Table 2.1 shows, and indeed is typically concentrated in disadvantaged groups. So it is hardly surprising that control of prisons for purposes such as security, humanity and efficiency has been a hotly debated issue at least since Jeremy Bentham offered his famous authoritarian-rationalist blueprint for control in and over prisons in the 1790s (Bentham, 1791: letters II, VI and IX; see also Freeman, 1978; Vagg, 1994).

Each of the primary forms of control that we took as our point of departure in Chapter 1 can be found in the prison sector, as Table 2.2 shows (but the controls are often ineffective, as this table also suggests), and Table 2.3 attempts to summarize some of their applications in each of our eight cases. Competition is often difficult to apply because, unlike the high state bureaucracy and the world of university research, prison administration is typically not a career field for which there is heavy competition from the best and brightest. Prisons normally do not compete for top-quality prisoners in the way universities do for the best students, although plea-bargaining systems in some cases give prisoners some limited choice over prison facilities. Even competition over benchmarks is difficult because of unresolved conflicts over what is

Table 2.1   The background of prison control in eight countries

	Australia	France	Germany	Japan	Netherlands	Norway	England and Wales	US states (& Federal Bureau of Prisons)
Number of prisons	98	186	222	74[1]	79	43	138	1 320 (84)
Total staff/ prisoners	12 000/ 21 819	26 233/ 55 382	36 148/ 81 176	17 000/ 67 255	11 662/ 14 968	4 968/ 2 666	32 852/ 73 927	372 976/ 1 209 640[2] (33 577/ 154 000)
Approximate percentage increase in prisoners since mid-1970s	75%	70%	140%	50%	300%	40%	75%	250% (515%)
Incarceration rate (per 100 thousand)	112	93	98	53	93	59	140	417[3] (52)
Percentage of adults in contract/ private facilities	15%	0%	0%	0%	0%	0%	9%	6% (13%)
Percentage foreign prisoners	20%	22%	34%	7%	30%	13%	9%	5% (25%)

Notes:
1 Includes local detention facilities.
2 A further 665 475 prisoners are held in local facilities.
3 701 including state, local and federal prisoners.

Source: 2002 Seventh United Nations Survey on Trends and the Operation of the Criminal Justice Systems and Correctional Administrations.

the key index of 'success' and the difficulty of measuring some aspects of success, particularly rehabilitation. Elements of competition can enter into federal or regionalized systems, but that competition is not necessarily of a 'race to the top' kind, since state politicians of a law-and-order stripe may prefer to have the 'toughest' rather than 'tenderest' prisons in the country. Some element of international competition may exist too, in the sense of countries not wishing to be shamed as 'worst case' examples by international inspectors, but that competition is at a very low level compared to the university case.

In all cases, prisons compete for resources both with one another and with other potential claimants on public budgets, but this competition may also be perverse for control, in that the way to get tax resources flowing into the prison system generally or into particular prisons may be through breakdowns, riots and escapes rather than orderly or humane management. The other main form of rivalry for control is competition between public and private sector providers that was part of Jeremy Bentham's 'panopticon plan' over 200 years

Table 2.2 *Applications and examples of the four control modes operating in the world of prisons*

Basic type of control	General examples	Comment
Mutuality	Reciprocal influence among institutionally separated members of a 'prison family', for instance in prison executives and justice ministries	Tends to take the form of cosy and peaceful coexistence rather than tough scrutiny and challenge
Contrived randomness	Unpredictable career patterns around the prison system, linked with multiple-key decision-making	Often blunted by countervailing pressures of mutuality, especially but not only in small prison systems
Competition	Competition among prisons for budget resources, benchmark competition, metaphytic competition	Metaphytic competition very limited and cartelised even where it exists; budget competition can have perverse effects on control if allocation goes on best-to-worst principle
Oversight	Inspectors, auditors, visitors, courts and legislatures, line management of prison units in prison departments and 'arm's-length' executive agency arrangements	Overseers often weak and ineffective because of information asymmetry and dependence on prison sector for compliance, conflict over responsibility in systems of delegated management

Table 2.3 Control of prisons in eight countries

	Australia	France	Germany	Japan	Netherlands	Norway	England and Wales	US states and Federal Bureau of Prisons
Oversight	Varying at state level, overseers typically dominated by departments of correction, often with inspectorates	Multiple, dominated by Ministry of Justice and Prison Service, including a Prison Inspectorate at the centre	Distinct and varied *Länder* oversight systems, within a broad federal legal structure	Multiple, dominated by administrative systems with a central ministry	Multiple, with the Department of Justice and the DJI at the centre of the administrative oversight system	Multiple, with the Prison and Probation Department at the centre of the administrative system	Multiple systems with the Prison Service and Home Office at the centre plus an inspectorate and specialist ombudsman	Varied, usually centred on a department of corrections, but also including significant court activity
Mutality	Varied, with professional prison staffs	Limited Prison Service norms and local prison mutuality	Varied, but some shared norms about application of prison laws	Multiple groups at prison, bureau and ministry level, with prison level staff influential	Prison staff professionalism, especially among governors	Prison staff collegiality, especially at local level, with some other professional groups	Prison Service mutuality, but some outsiders' (ombudsman, chief inspector, private prison staff)	Varied, but high staff turnover in many states contrasting with the federal bureau 'family'
Competition	Public/private competition in some states	Limited, no public/private competition	Limited, no public/private competition for core services	Limited, no public/private competition	Limited, no public/private competition	Limited, no public/private competition	Strong public/private competition	Limited at federal level but 31 states with private prisons

Contrived randomness	Varied, some use of random inspections	Limited	Varied, some use of random inspections	Limited	Limited	Limited, some random visits by Control Boards	Limited, with some unannounced inspections	Varied, with some limited use
Changes since the mid-1970s	Varied, some change in oversight with public/private competition in some states	Limited change, some strengthening and diversification of professional groups	Limited change, much tinkering with oversight and increased role of different professional groups	Limited change, some increased court involvement and internal prison management changes	Limited change, attempts to strengthen oversight have had only limited success	Limited change, diversification of professional groups involved in prisons	Moderate change, increased public/private competition with non-trivial changes in oversight	Moderate change, increased public/private competition, expansion of judicial oversight professionalization

29

ago. This sort of competition seems to be much more thinkable as a form of control in some state systems than others, partly because the state's distinctive 'public power' to discipline and punish is often interpreted in Roman-law jurisdictions to preclude private provision of prisons. In some cases, notably the USA, Australia and England and Wales, competition between public and private providers is used for provision of mainstream prisons, but even those countries that do not contract out whole prisons make some use of competitive contracting for non-core activities.

Mutuality is also often problematic as a way of controlling prisons and those who work within them. At prisoner level, too much mutuality in the form of group control of individuals is often at the heart of criticisms of supposedly liberal prison regimes. Mutuality in the sense of dialogue between prisons and their inmates is a fact of life in prison administration, though how far it is one-sided and institutionally recognized varies (among our cases, institutionalized prisoner 'voice' in prison affairs seemed to be weakest in Japan and perhaps strongest in Norway and the Netherlands) and again it may lead to a perversion rather than augmentation of control. And at the level of prison staff, as with other uniformed state services, mutuality has often taken the form of a 'canteen culture' embracing one-for-all solidarity against outside scrutiny or criticism. How far the development of a less homogenous prison staff population in many countries – in terms of ethnicity, gender and specialism – is leading to new forms of mutuality remains to be seen, though signs of such a change can be seen in some countries, and mutuality-based professional control for prison staff was stressed by our contributors for cases such as the Netherlands and Germany.

At higher institutional levels in the prison system, mutuality takes the form of group influence over prison governors by the wider 'family' of their peers, advisers and administrative counterparts, and indeed of mutual influence between prison executives and policy departments which often function at arm's length from prison operations. It is notable that in the USA, which is often stereotypically portrayed as a land of adversarial courts and bureaucracies, there was a distinct element of mutual control within the 'prison family' of the Bureau of Prisons (as well as formal monitoring). But as our cases show, this mutuality too can easily function as a form of anti-control as much as control, in so far as it can lead to a largely autonomous world of prison administration in which more or less peaceful coexistence rather than sharp mutual checking is what characterizes relationships between prison administrators and other parts of government.

Contrived randomness is a form of control that in principle has substantial applicability to prisons, though our commentators had remarkably little to say about it. Prisons are a form of field administration, with multiple establishments across a territory, and decision-making, particularly over sensitive issues such as discipline and treatment, typically involves a number of staff, albeit within a broadly hierarchical structure. Hence there is in principle substantial scope for the classic form of contrived randomness, in the sense of posting individuals around the field system in unpredictable ways, such that it is hard for them to predict who their colleagues, subordinates or superordinates will be over time, and such devices are a traditional way of countering the conditions needed for corruption and abuse of various kinds. Prisons are also a domain, unusual in executive government structures, in which many states make use of a form of randomness in the form of military-type snap inspections or unannounced visits, and the same occurs at international level with visits to national establishments by the European Committee for the Prevention of Torture and Inhuman or Degrading Treatment or Punishment (CPT), discussed below. However, it is often difficult to use contrived randomness effectively because of the countervailing pressures of mutuality in a closed and often tightly knit professional world, particularly in small states like Norway, the Netherlands and the Australian states, with relatively few prison establishments, and the snap inspection approach is often berated as destructive of trust.

Finally, oversight figures large in institutional systems for control of prisons, though the institutional form it takes depends heavily on state traditions. In all of the cases investigated in this study, there were oversight mechanisms within the prison bureaucracy itself, with prison governors subject to review and direction from the headquarters of the prison executive (which went under a variety of titles). In most cases prison executives were semi-detached from their parent ministries or departments handling justice or home affairs policy at state or national government level, including executive agency arrangements supposedly for managing prisons at arm's length from politicians. The semi-detached organizational structures introduced another element of oversight and both departments and prison executives were, in turn, subject to oversight from central agencies in government. Indeed, the 'multiple levels' of oversight were further augmented by international overseers, including the UN Commission on Human Rights and the Council of Europe. But the efficacy of those bodies depends heavily on the internal political climate of the states they deal with.

Legislative oversight of prisons tended to consist of the well-known 'fire alarm' rather than 'police patrol' approaches, with investigations typically launched after major incidents like escapes or riots, and media coverage of prison issues tended to follow the same pattern. But legislative audit offices regularly checked the finances of prison executives, and the US Congress and German *Land* parliaments operated more extensive systems of routine monitoring. Law courts also had a significant role in overseeing prisons, particularly in Germany, France, the Netherlands and the USA, and 'prisoner rights' were given formal expression in the more legalistic systems. But the means of enforcement were often limited and in most cases prisons were subject to scrutiny from ombudsmen as well. England and Wales was unusual in having a dedicated prison and probation ombudsman. Oversight often also included lay monitoring arrangements from citizens at large, including the local Independent Monitoring Boards in England and Wales, Boards of Oversight in the Netherlands, *Beirate* in Germany and the Local Supervisory Committees in France, though the impact of those lay overseers over prisons seems to have varied considerably.

Indeed, the general efficacy of control over prisons through oversight, however well-intentioned and institutionally developed, often seems to be problematic, unless oversight is linked to some other form of control. As already noted, where parent departments functioned at arm's length from prison executives, they were often insufficiently informed to exercise effective oversight over the closed world of prison administration. For example, in Japan, the so-called 'bar class' of legally trained public prosecutors who formed the elite overseers of the system within the Ministry of Justice had career paths separate from those running prisons on a day-to-day basis and often did not appear well informed about practice on the ground. Even in France, with its famous and long-established *inspections générales*, external oversight of prisons by central inspectors did not seem to have much disposition or ability to penetrate the relatively closed world of the prison executive.

Linkage of oversight with other control forms took several forms. In some cases oversight was combined with contrived randomness in the form of un-announced military-type snap inspections, as used in many Australian states, in England and Wales, in some German *Länder* and in Control Board visits in the Netherlands. Linkage of oversight with competition took place particularly in Australia and England and Wales, which had public–private 'metaphytic' competition (Corbett, 1965) between public and private providers, thereby sharpening the incentives for prison operators to comply with the demands of overseers in the hope of retaining or augmenting their market shares. Linkage of oversight with mutuality takes place where the overseers are drawn from the prison 'family', as has already been noted for the US federal system and is also applied to some degree in England and Wales, where the central government inspectorate is normally headed by an 'outsider' but at deputy inspector level consists largely of career prison administrators. A mix of oversight and mutuality is also found where prison executives or overseers talk with pressure groups monitoring prisons, typically with concerns about promoting rehabilitation and improving prisoners' standards of care. Among the countries in this study, that mutuality–oversight combination was perhaps weakest in Japan, owing to the relative weakness of prison pressure groups there.

As cultural theorists would predict, these four types of control are hard to mix and match at will. For example, the more oversight arrangements develop in the direction of public tribunals with independent status, focusing on contract compliance and published naming-and-shaming reports (as in the case of England and Wales, but not of prison inspectors most of the other countries in this study), the more problematic frank exchange through mutuality within the prison 'family' is likely to be. Mutuality may be a form of control that is better suited to the often intangible aspects of rehabilitation, whereas quantification of performance and the language of contract compliance may be more suited to the promotion of prison security. Similar dilemmas may attend the combination of oversight with other control forms, which also present incompatible choices at the margin. For example, if inspectors mix oversight with contrived randomness through unannounced inspections as part of a strategy to break through information asymmetries, they may be destroying the trust among actors in the system that is needed as a basis for mutuality control, and the difficulty of operating those two types of control simultaneously was stressed by several of our contributors.

2   Developments since the Mid-1970s

Each of the eight prison systems examined in this book started from a different mix of oversight, competition, mutuality and randomness, and those differences relate to the differences in state tradition that are discussed in Chapter 1. It is hard to separate institutional 'noise' from signal, but looking at prison control development over a generation suggests three main conclusions about change over time.

The first conclusion is that the eight systems show little sign of converging on a single approach to control of prisons, and more generally that there is little sign of an overall oversight explosion in this field, at least at state and national government level, since the mid-1970s. Prisoner numbers may have increased in all the cases, but there was no comparable increase in the population or even staffing of oversight bodies for the control of prisons. Some countries did introduce new or expanded oversight institutions, such as a revamped national inspectorate and a prisons ombudsman in England and Wales, and new inspectorates in many of the Australian states. But little changed in the arrangements for prison oversight in other countries, such as Japan. And in other cases, notably the German *Länder* and the Netherlands, administrative overseers have both been added and removed over the course of the past three decades. But it does not credibly add up to a general 'oversight explosion' across all the state systems represented in this study.

The second conclusion is that change over the past generation seems to be better interpreted as hunting around or tinkering with forms of oversight in some cases, rather than general expansion of oversight, and perhaps the 'hunting around' theme is best represented by the German case. In some cases, overseers have made more use of performance contracts specifying bottom-line performance for prison units and prison executives, with management flexibilities granted in the use of resources locally. This trend has been most notable in the use of executive agencies in England and Wales and in the Netherlands, and delegated management regimes in some Australian states and German *Länder*, though 'process rules' over treatment of prisoners tended to grow rather than decline. In some cases, such as some of the German *Länder*, less reliance has been placed on the traditional hybrid of contrived randomness and oversight hybrid in the form of unannounced inspections (though randomness was increased in several cases at another level, in raids on cells for drug control), and in others more emphasis has been placed on mutuality, such as the introduction of quality circles in the Netherlands and increased used of professional accreditation, education and training in France, Norway and the USA as a means of professionalizing the control of prison staff. But those who believe in international arrow theories of change (McFarland, 1991) will be hard put to find a single obvious arrow in this case.

There seems to have been a divergence in the use of competition between the English-speaking systems that have introduced public–private competition for prison management and the non-English-speaking systems that have not. Indeed, within the English-speaking systems there seems to have been some convergence in control forms, with the introduction of public oversight of contracts, and spillover effects in the public systems through the development of indicators that facilitate comparison between prison facilities. Increased private involvement was a control device intended to break the traditional dominance of prison staff, and it seems to have weakened the prison union in England and Wales. But similar effects seem to have been weaker in the USA and, indeed, forms of mutuality appear to have persisted more strongly in countries that did not have an injection of private sector involvement in prison management.

A third conclusion is that there were attempts over this era to develop expanded international oversight over prison systems, though how successful such oversight has been is, to say the least, debatable. International standards affecting prisons flowed from the United Nations (UN) Declaration of Human Rights in 1948 and the conventions adopted from it, especially the International Convention on Civil and Political Rights 1966; the Convention Against Torture and Other Cruel, Inhuman or Degrading Treatment or Punishment 1984, the Body of Principles for the Protection of All Persons under Any Form of Detention or Imprisonment 1988 and the Basic Principles for the Treatment of Prisoners 1990. The UN adopted Standard Minimum Rules for the Treatment of Prisoners in 1955 which set out basic standards for prisoners. The UN Commission on Human Rights began to monitor and report on states' behaviour from the late 1960s, carrying out thematic and country studies and criticizing countries (such as Japan among our cases) over issues of treatment of prisoners. However, the UN has no effective enforcement powers and its monitoring apparatus is very limited, despite the UN Committee against Torture's attempt to establish a monitoring body in 2000, so it has resorted to shaming and moral suasion rather than juridical sanctions.

Supranational oversight of prison systems for member states of the Council of Europe also developed in the form of the European Prison Rules, which were originally derived from the 1955 United Nations prison rules. The European Convention for the Protection of Human Rights and Fundamental Freedoms also related to prisons, with a supra-national court adjudicating human rights issues under the Convention (Council of Europe, 2001). Another set of new international standards in the field was the European Convention for the Prevention of Torture and Inhuman or Degrading Treatment of 1989 (Council of Europe, 2001), which provided for a monitoring body, the European Committee for the Prevention of Torture and Inhuman or Degrading Treatment or Punishment, to visits places of detention, including police stations, army barracks and psychiatric hospitals to see how detainees are treated and, if necessary, to recommend improvements. By 2003, CPT had made 148 visits including five to England and Wales (out of seven to the UK), six to France, three to the Netherlands, three to Norway and four to Germany. It had recommended numerous changes and had been more critical of prisons in England and Wales and France than in the Netherlands, Norway and Germany.

The European Committee for the Prevention of Torture and Inhuman or Degrading Treatment or Punishment was supposed to be given unlimited access in its visits, including the right to interview people without witnesses being present, and it made some use of unpredictable mechanisms for visiting countries at short notice as well as a cycle of regular announced visits to different countries, to which governments could only object on grounds of security or safety. But CPT has no formal enforcement powers and relies on the cooperation of member governments to carry out its work effectively (Council of Europe, 2001). It can use publicity in the face of non-cooperation (its initial reports are strictly confidential, but it can and often did 'go public' with later published reports and it issues an annual published report). But, as with all such international bodies, CPT can only be effective when it is able to mobilize internal allies (for example, in supporting national prison executives in budgetary conflicts with other claimants on public budgets) and it can do little when a state does not want to comply. For example, the UK government largely rejected CPT recommendations about reducing overcrowding in the 1990s (Council of Europe, 2000a, 2000b). Indeed, at the time of writing the UK was 'derogating' on the European Convention on Human Rights on the grounds of public emergency in exercising powers of detention of foreign terrorist suspects contained in the Anti-Terrorism, Crime and Security Act 2001, and had largely rejected CPT criticisms of its activities under this legislation (Council of Europe, 2003: 15).

At international level, then, the pattern seems to be one of increasing activity, more conventions, treaties and institutions, and that certainly goes along with increasing activity by international pressure groups such as Amnesty International and Human Rights Watch (which monitor prison conditions) and Penal Reform International, which has worked with the Committee Against Torture to produce a handbook to guide countries in adopting, monitoring and enforcing prison standards (see Penal Reform International, 2001). But how far this undoubtedly increasing activity amounts to an 'oversight explosion' is debatable, given the limited formal enforcement mechanisms available to the overseers.

What remains to be seen is whether these developments can develop beyond 'conversations' between overseers and their charges. And what also remains to be seen is whether more mutuality and competition will come into play at international level. Given that an increasing number of prisoners are foreign nationals (as shown in Table 2.1), the limited monitoring by governments (and national charities) of their nationals held in other countries may be set to introduce a greater element of mutuality at international level in prison control. Governments exercise mutual control to some extent through agreements over transfer of prisoners (using frameworks such as the 1985 Council of Europe transfer convention, which now includes not only numerous European states but also states that are not members of the Council of Europe, such as the USA, Australia and Japan). It is uncertain whether such dialogue has a strong mutual influence.

Although the increasing proportion of foreign prisoners has evidently not had the same effect on prisons as the 'marketizing' impact of increased proportions of international students in universities, the development of multinational corporations in the field of prisons may have the potential to increase control through competition. The first private prison in England and Wales, the Wolds, was built with technical assistance from the Corrections Corporation of America (CCA) and other prison provision contractors have interests spanning the USA, the UK and Australia. In principle, such developments could have implications both for contrived randomness (through international transfer of staff to break up cosy cliques) and for oversight systems. Some of those corporations claim to be vehicles for the promotion of international standards (see Group 4 Falck Global Solutions Limited, 2002: 15). But so far those firms are limited to a small set of English-speaking countries and, while the firms' finance, overall corporate governance and statements of aspirations may be increasingly supra-national, the companies have distinctive contracts with the relevant public authorities in each prison system, and tend to employ staff from within the systems to draw on their local experience and to fit in with local ways of working rather than adopting a uniform way of managing prisons or developing a new class of prison officials that might standardize norms of behaviour across systems.

2.2 JAPAN: HIERARCHICALLY ORDERED MUTUALITY IN A SEMI-HIDDEN WORLD
Takashi Nishio

Mutuality, structured by hierarchical relations among different groups of staff, dominates the control of prisons in Japan. However, mutuality operates in the shadow of intermittent oversight by various administrative overseers, a combination of controls that tends to shield prisons from broader governmental and societal influence. While recent scandals have triggered increased court involvement and media interest in prisons, they have, so far, created only a small window on this otherwise largely closed world.

1 Oversight

The Correction Bureau of the Ministry of Justice (MOJ) is formally the main overseer of penal institutions, as summarized in Figure 2.1. The Prison Law has not been changed substantially since 1908 and, although bills were proposed in 1982, 1987 and 1991, it appears repressive and paternalistic by modern standards. The Ministry supervises individual establishments through the Bureau, but its capacity for oversight is limited with only 49 staff in the Bureau's central office supervising prisons. Wardens feel strong pressure to report 'no accident,' 'no mistake' or 'no problem' (Sakamoto, 2003: 173–4). The Bureau inspects prisons at least every other year, or as it thinks necessary. Visits entail one division chief (*Kacho*) of the Bureau and a few subordinates (assistant chiefs, *Kacho-hosa*), and the inspection continues for a day or two.

Oversight from outside the MOJ is very weak. Many observers see the closed and militaristic organizational culture in the traditional prison system as having only partially been affected by the post-war constitutional reforms to control government activities by the Diet or other independent organizations At this time, the Japanese government formally abandoned the pre-war, traditional style of 'transcendent' government but the new democratic institutions did not fully take root in the field of prisons. The Diet currently controls prisons through legislation, interpellations and inquiries, especially by the Judicial Affairs Committees of both houses, but the reports seldom attract the attention of the media or the general public.

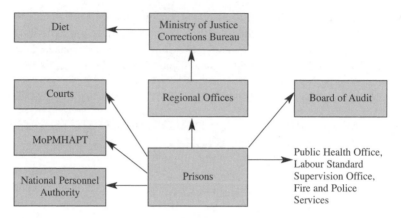

Figure 2.1   Oversight of prisons in Japan (→ reports to)

In addition, there are complaints to and inspections by public prosecutors, and judicial decision by judges. Inmates can complain to wardens, submit petitions to the Minister of Justice or to an inspecting officer of the Bureau (Kikuta, 2002: ch. 5). The enactment of the Administrative Law 1994 and the Freedom of Information Law 2001 can be new effective ways to control prisons, but the people (including inmates) seem not to be used to them yet, although there are more complaints and the courts are increasingly active. The number of petitions and suits in 2002 was about three times that of 1996; cases heard by judges have more than doubled since 1998, although inmates' demands for compensation show less of a clear rise in numbers (from 120 cases in 1998 to 150 in 2002) (MOJ figures). Petitions and complaints by inmates are said to be discouraged by prison officers and the systems are not thought to be an inmate's right (Kikuta, 2002: p. 189). In a case of serious misconduct recently exposed at Nagano prison, with five guards now on trial for abuse, the Justice Minister Moriyama admitted that prisoner grievances had been screened by prison officials and had not reached the Minister. In any case, criminal investigation and indictment by the Public Prosecutors' Office (PPO, *Kensatsu*) are an exception and the PPO is regarded as a 'family member' (*Miuchi*) of the Correction Bureau and the Ministry of Justice (legally, the PPO belongs to the MOJ but each public prosecutor is an independent public official).

There are several administrative overseers of prisons beyond the Ministry of Justice. The Administrative Evaluation Bureau of the Ministry of Public Management, Home Affairs, Posts and Telecommunications inspects the prison system every 10 years. There is no authority for enforcement but instead a custom of mutual adjustment, with the reports toned down and modest changes made. Further, the Board of Audit (BOA) reviews the public accounts to certify accounts of revenues and expenditures. However, most points the BOA has made are so trifling that they give the impression that prisons are on the whole managed legally, economically and without any serious problems. The National Personnel Authority (NPA) checks staff numbers in prisons in terms of salary grades (*Kyu-betsu Teisu*). The Equity and Investigation Bureau accepts complaints and requests from public officials about working conditions or accident compensation. The human rights of the guards, as well as of the inmates, are not necessarily respected in Japanese prisons. A former guard, Mr Sakamoto, has criticized both the MOJ and the NPA for not understanding the stressful working conditions in the prisons, even after an official died from overwork at Nagano prison in 1995 (Sakamoto, 2003: p. 251ff).

In addition to these forms of oversight, many other local public organizations check prisons, for example to oversee health and sanitation, fire safety and working conditions, but those are only the ordinary checks on a place or building where a group of people stay or work. As for non-state organizations monitoring the prison, Amnesty International publishes an annual report on Japan every year, and the Centre for Prisoners' Rights (*Kangoku Jinken Centre*) occasionally publishes books and reports on prisons and help inmates with information. Although politically they may not be very influential, they provide information about the problems of Japanese prisons. About 50 000 visitors are accepted in the penal institutions nationwide each year to see how they work. And at the time of writing, an unusually high level of media interest in prison affairs was in evidence, following a high-profile investigation at Nagoya prison by public prosecutors.

2 Mutuality

Mutuality is often the key method of prison management in Japan, with control exercised within different groups of staff that formally stand in hierarchical relation to each other. The prison is often compared to the pre-war military organization because prison administration is highly hierarchical both in staff organization and in the relation between the guards and inmates. There are clear rules concerning classification of inmates, using medical and psychological knowledge and techniques, which are applied to clarify their problems and provide them with 'individualized treatment'. However, the prisons have autonomous power to interpret the Prison Law and regulations, and there is considerable variety in procedures. Ex-guard Sakamoto notes that under certain circumstances 'each prison guard is the law' and that prison wardens can be considered 'feudal lords'. For example, one enterprising warden once held a big cherry-blossom viewing party (Hanami) in Nagano prison and gave 500 inmates light alcohol (*Amazake*), but it was reported by the media, and the practice was discontinued by order of the MOJ (Sakamoto, 2003: 172–5). Generally, the culture of mutuality inhibits the use of checks based on contrived randomness by overseers which would be seen as exhibiting a lack of trust in the prison staff.

The mutuality entailed in 'controlled prison management' includes subtle types of human relationship approach and though it is becoming increasingly problematic, it is used for management of both prison guards and inmates The MOJ emphasizes the effectiveness and efficiency of the system by pointing to the relatively small number of prison staff, low rate of escapes, suicides or deaths in prison. For example, in 1996 the number of escapes was eight and suicides six, a tiny number by comparison with most of the other prison systems in this study, and even that was the highest number for five years (MOJ, 2001). On the other hand, lawyers criticize the dignity-impairing, humiliating treatment in prisons, such as shameful orders or physical checking called 'kan-kan dance' (inmates are told to get fully undressed and then to dance to show the officials all parts of the body each morning) (Azuchi, 1988; Kikuta, 2002). Indeed, there is a shared understanding on the basic ideas of prison management by both guards and inmates. What is valued in the Japanese prisons is a 'sense of family'; a kind of 'father and son relationship' is regarded as an ideal one between the officer and the inmate. In fact, some guards are called '*Oyaji*' (Dad) by the inmates (Kikuta, 2002: 15). According to Sakamoto, some *Oyajis* in the 1960s had dignity, humanity and individuality, and were respected and even loved by the inmates, but the situation changed in the 1970s (Sakamoto, 2003: 180).

However, the administrative rules have been changed to increase the oversight and competition-orientated aspects of the system. An experiment tried at Osaka prison in 1973 has spread as 'controlled correction administration' (*Kanri Gyokei*) or 'silent prison' (*Chinmoku no Keimusho*). The system involves control and recording of inmates' behaviour and order maintenance including a system of yellow and red cards for inmates according to their violations. The system promoted competition among guards for better marks and control and gave more power to senior staff, with some officials suggesting that it inhibited the use of discretion to forge human relationships. However, remnants of the rehabilitation and discretionary concerns were not completely removed and mutuality controls remain strong.

There are distinct groups of staff in the prison system. About 90 per cent of all prison staff (17 011) are classified as prison guards, and one prison governor argues that guards are trained as craftsmen rather than true professionals. They are forbidden by law from forming a trade union, but some of them belong to the Association for Correction Education, and there is a journal entitled *Correction Policy* (*Keisei*). But that is an educational journal for prison guards rather than a strictly professional journal. Most of the articles in the journal justify the existing regulations and customs rather than discussing them freely.

The junior prison guards often have a weak sense of community or identity with higher-level officials, especially wardens and MOJ staff. The latter are part of the top elites in Japanese society while the junior staff are 'expendable' parts of the prison (Sakamoto, 2003: 225ff and 272). The Japanese civil service fast-streamer system prevents most ranks of officials from being promoted to the top positions. The fast streamers pass between the prison units, central and regional offices as often as 10 to 20 times in their career while many guards remain in the same prison unit throughout their career. Prison wardens are selected from those who pass the level 1 and the level 2 examinations plus the guard examination and usually stay at one prison for no longer than three years. In the eyes of the lower-rank officials, many of the wardens seem interested only in promotion and avoiding negative publicity. The MOJ executives are mainly public prosecutors who passed the national bar examination conducted by a committee that belongs to the MOJ and they form a sort of a 'ruling class', taking the Director and the Chief of General Affairs Division jobs in the Corrections Bureau. The administrators who passed the level 1 examination for public service cannot easily be promoted to the top central positions, making MOJ an unpopular posting for these staff. None of the public prosecutors have been appointed warden of a prison since the end of the Second World War. They seem to be more interested in control of prisons at arm's length rather than hands-on management.

The dominance of mutuality and oversight arrangements means there is no room for public–private competition for prison provision, with only a few functions, such as staff catering, contracted out to the private sector. There is a thick *Annual Statistical Book on Correction Administration* on individual prisons. But it is not generally open to the public and there is no 'league table' of prisons, although a warden may lose the career race if a serious incident is exposed in the prison. Among rank and file staff there is competition for promotion but far from being a free competition based on objective criteria, it is what Ishida called 'competition within a frame of conformity' and, as has already been shown, the personnel rules limit competition brought about by junior staff rising through the ranks.

The use of administrative hierarchy and mutuality by different groups inside the state system is combined with attempts to avoid media coverage of prisons that might facilitate broader societal control. The need to avoid media exposure has been emphasized by Directors of the Correction Bureau (Sakamoto, 2003: 192ff). However, transparency and accountability have become key words in current administrative reforms with the claim that 'what people most want to know is the real truth about what is happening in the nation's prisons and jails'. At the time of writing, one prison scandal (at

Nagoya prison) has achieved wide media exposure and has been discussed not only in the Diet's Judicial Affairs Committee but also in the high-profile Budget Committee. Indeed, a Correction Policy Reform Council, as well as an investigation committee on the Nagoya prison case, have been established. The Council consists of 15 members including a noted writer, scholars, lawyers and journalists, with open meetings, and one member of the Council has commented that if the will to know the truth is the first step of control, the Japanese people have just started controlling the nation's prisons. Whether that turns out to be the case remains to be seen.

2.3   US FEDERAL PRISONS: BUREAU FAMILY MUTUALITY IN THE 'GOVERNMENT OF STRANGERS'
Arjen Boin and Oliver James

United States prisons are run at the federal, state or local level of government. The control of prisons supervised by the Federal Bureau of Prisons (FBP) is a particularly interesting case and is singled out for investigation here because it seems to be an island of oversight/mutuality based control in a sea of randomness and competition elsewhere in federal government. While US federalism is often characterized as being composed of separate, sometimes competing, executive, judicial and legislative branches sharing control (see Fesler and Kettl, 1996), the FBP occupies a semi-autonomous niche in the system of oversight. The FBP maintains a relatively stable 'family' of staff controlled by mutuality within the broader 'government of strangers' that makes heavy use of political appointees entering and exiting with each administration (Heclo, 1977). The turnover of federal prison staff is also lower than that found in most state prison systems. Even the involvement of private sector contractors does not inject as much public/private competition into the federal prison system as might be expected, and several states make much more extensive use of the private sector.

1   Oversight

The control of federal prisons is summarized in Figure 2.2. The extensive executive oversight systems are dominated by the FBP, created in 1930 to incorporate a set of previously decentralized and independently operating prisons. Bureau oversight developed over time, especially from the 1950s to 1970s, during a period of moderate prison expansion. But recent growth of the FBP prisons has been spectacular, with prisoner numbers rising from 20 000

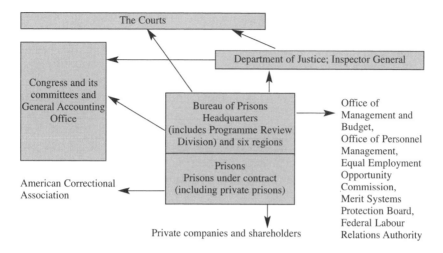

Figure 2.2   Oversight of US federal prisons

in 1970 to 150 000 in 2000. The expansion in recent decades has been associated with more use of formal, often quantified, performance information. In contrast to many federal programmes, where the involvement of multiple state, local and private organizations can substantially affect the capacity to implement policies (Pressman and Wildavsky, 1973), the FBP is an integrated, hierarchical organization that directly owns and runs most of the facilities it supervises. While 'wardens' are responsible for the management of individual prisons, they are closely overseen by the FBP central headquarters and regional management. There are centrally set prison standards for 14 correctional programmes and security standards according to the type of establishment, ranging from 'minimum' to 'super-maximum'. Monitoring of facilities is by inspection, spot checks and questionnaires for both staff and inmates. Information is regularly collected from each prison to assess performance against a battery of performance measures. Incidents of breaches of policy or law are investigated by Boards of Inquiry set up at national, regional or prison level, in consultation with the Office of Internal Affairs.

The FBP's autonomy is limited by the supervision of the Department of Justice, but the latter does not engage in much hands-on, day-to-day, oversight. The FBP's directors have not been political appointees and have traditionally nominated their successors informally; a former director said the FBP is seen as apolitical, with low public visibility and far down the Department's list of priorities for action (Boin, 2001: 109–10). The Department of Justice established an Inspector-General (under the aegis of the Inspector-General regime) to assess efficiency and effectiveness and to follow up issues raised by internal Boards of Inquiry. In addition, the FBP is subject to the various general executive-wide control systems including executive orders, expenditure and personnel controls that include those associated with senior staff's membership of the Federal Senior Executive Service. The FBP also monitors prison compliance with general societal regulations, including those relating to occupational health and safety, fire safety and environmental protection.

The FBP is subject to Congressional oversight of its overall budget as well as oversight by Congressional committees and the Bureau of Budget. Congressional committees conduct periodic investigations and hearings in which both FBP leaders and outside experts are called to testify. However, time and again, these hearings begin and end by applauding FBP's excellent performance and its responsive attitude. The FBP prides itself on its ability to accurately gauge winds of political change and act in a way that pleases Congress without upsetting field operations, using an active Office of Congressional Affairs to co-ordinate work with Congress. The General Accounting Office (GAO) regularly initiates investigations on federal prison matters, such as abuse of telephones, hospital care and alleged rape of inmates, but rarely lands a knockout blow on the FBP. A crucial change in policy occurred in the mid-1970s, shifting from a rehabilitation-orientated focus to a more containment-orientated focus. However, this change was as much the result of intra-FBP reflection on priorities as Congressional pressure on the organization's mission.

The courts are less important as a controller of federal than state prisons, though they have taken a more interventionist stance since the early 1970s. After shedding the 'hands off' doctrine in *Tally* v. *Stevens* (1965), which had effectively relegated prisoners to the status of state property, court influence has grown to such an extent that judges are now seen as juridical policy-makers (Feeley and Rubin, 1998). The number of civil rights claims filed in federal court by state prisoners rose from 2030 in 1970, to 12 400 by 1980, although after a wave of activism in the 1970s, the courts have subsequently exercised more restraint. Congress passed the Prison Litigation Reform Act in 1996 which attempted to restrict the power of federal courts over state and local corrections agencies (Collins, 1998). Even so, about one in five state facilities currently operate under court order to modify their conditions. By contrast, no federal facility was under a court order at the time of writing. The FBP largely avoids court action by pursing a co-operative strategy to avoid conflict and by using an internal Administrative Remedy Programme established in consultation with federal judges. The courts take on only those complaints that have travelled through the internal complaints procedures. Judges are regularly invited to visit prisons and have failed to rule any aspects of federal prisons unconstitutional.

2 Mutuality

The public, media representatives and judges have been invited into prisons on different programmes, to monitor activities. Several interest groups for monitoring prisons also exist, and their ability to get information about the system is enhanced by Freedom of Information legislation But the structure of these programmes is designed by the FBP itself, which can thereby keep some control over how it is monitored (Quinlan, 1990: 5). Within the FBP, mutuality is used in combination with formal oversight. The headquarters traditionally promoted mutuality as a way of developing a common set of standards across different prisons spread over a wide geographical area. This process reached its height before the 1970s and some aspects of mutuality seem to have weakened thereafter. In particular, the informal concept of a 'bureau family' traditionally placed the director in a near patriarchal position that sometimes led to the circumvention of standard civil service rules for conduct. In the past 30 years there has been more use of formal personnel procedures, which have restricted this form of control.

In the contemporary system, policy at the centre is developed in co-operation with the field; it is checked and codified by the Office of National Policy Review. While local wardens are consulted over standard-setting, FBP directors and senior management have played an important role in developing standards throughout the life of the bureau. Wardens can request waivers from the prison standards to fit local local circumstances, but central headquarters is not generous in granting waivers as they affect the cherished degree of uniformity. The headquarters has had a key role in professionalizing the prison service as a way of building its capacity to control. The bulk of federal prison staff are trained and develop careers in federal prisons over a long period. In the 1980s and 1990s the turnover of staff in the federal system was lower in each year (ranging between 5 per cent and 10 per cent) than the average for the states (ranging between 11 per cent and 15 per cent) and generally lower than three-quarters of the states in each year (Thigpen, Hunter and Thompson, 1996: 19). The FBP has worked with private sector professional organizations such as the American Correctional Association (ACA) and the Joint Commission of Accreditation of Healthcare Organizations to augment its ability to develop standards. Around two-thirds of FBP facilities were accredited by ACA in 1997 (Boin, 2001: 60). The headquarters has developed systems of both central–local and local–local mutuality to control the service.

Control over the field service involves a mixture of mutuality and contrived randomness, with staff being transferred back and forth between headquarters and the field. The rotation is strongest at more senior levels and before appointment as a warden, a stint in the national or regional headquarters is mandatory (Boin, 2001: 116). The system generally discourages outside appointments; wardens have had long careers in the FBP and the centre rather than the local institution makes the appointments. With the exception of the first FBP director, all directors and most assistant directors have come up through the agency (ibid.: 104–5). The directors of the bureau have traditionally participated in inspections and have close contacts in the field (Robert, 1994). In a tradition started in the early years of the FBP, teams of five to 10 members, taken from other prisons and from central headquarters, monitor operations in each prison. This system has been formalized in comprehensive assessments using a combination of visits, face-to-face interviews and data analysis.

There are local–local mutuality controls as well, with many staff transfers among prisons. There are often strong social links among staff, often linked to moving their families around the country (Boin, 2001: 106–7). The movement of staff 'promotes uniformity' and 'combats parochialism' (ibid.: 105). The reputations of staff for following FBP policy are monitored by the peer group in part through a weekly bulletin to staff, 'Monday Morning Highlights', which reports staff movements, promotions and other bureau news. There is peer review of institutions by warders, with wardens participating on program review teams visiting other institutions which further increases contact between staff in different prison institutions.

3   Competition

The FBP's headquarters compares federal prison establishments' performance by means of institutional character profiles, fostering an awareness of relative performance. National awards for staff and promotion procedures inject an element of competition into control systems. Moreover, public–private competition has been increasing both for federal and many state prisons. The amount of use at the federal level is less than that in several states, with about 18 per cent of inmates under the FBP's jurisdiction now being held in facilities run under contract with the private sector or state or local government (Bureau of Prisons, 2002: 56). However, rather than instigating strong public–private competition, the private prisons have been incorporated in a share of provision that now appears to be stable rather than increasing. Congress had to force the bureau to allow private parties to run prisons, and a demonstration project was finally set up in 1997 by passing the Taft Correctional Institution to the private firm, Wackenhut. The FBP has successfully argued against using more private facilities on the grounds of cost and difficulties in managing medium and high security risk prisoners who make up 43 per cent of federal inmates (House Committee on the Judiciary, 2001). In contrast, of the 31 states now using private prisons, New Mexico tops the list with 43 per cent of inmates in private facilities, and there are a further four states with more than a quarter of their prisoners held in private facilities, including Alaska, Montana, Oklahoma and Hawaii (25 per cent) (Bureau of Justice Statistics, 2002: 6).

The competitive private market for prisons in the USA involves 17 private sector providers of adult facilities, although not all currently contract with the FBP. Two of the largest private firms are Wackenhut Corrections and the Corrections Corporation of America, and such firms operate systems of monitoring and quality audit that are supplemented by accreditation by the American Correctional Association, whose standards also apply to public prisons. However, in the federal system, the companies have tended to employ wardens with experience of working in the bureau, maintaining a similarity of operating practices and preserving the 'family' traditions that seem to be the hallmark of control in the FBP system.

2.4 ENGLAND AND WALES: COMBINING OVERSIGHT WITH PUBLIC–PRIVATE COMPETITION
Oliver James

Rather than an 'explosion' of oversight, control of prisons in England and Wales has been subject to an injection of public–private competition operating in combination with changed forms of oversight, including the addition of new oversight bodies and the strengthening of legal provisions. At the same time, oversight regimes have been increasingly opened up to media interest and operated by outsiders with a background in other professions or in charities concerned about prison conditions. These trends have changed the operation of traditional forms of mutuality, in some respects weakening the influence of prison staff in the system.

1 Oversight

The backbone of the formal oversight system is hierarchical administrative control, as summarized in Figure 2.3. The Home Secretary has formal powers for 'regulation and management' of prisons including standards of treatment of prisoners, and issues Prison Rules for that purpose under a Prison Act of 1952. Prison Rules Orders provide guidance on the interpretation of these Prison Rules, and advice is regularly issued to prison governors. Different arrangements for prisons operate in other parts of the UK. In Scotland the Scottish Executive Justice Department, reporting to the Scottish Parliament, has supervised the Scottish Prison Service agency since 1999 and there is a separate Scottish Her Majesty's Inspectorate of Prisons. In Northern Ireland, the Northern Ireland Prison Service reports to the Northern Ireland Office and its Secretary of State. But it is the system for England and Wales that this section focuses on.

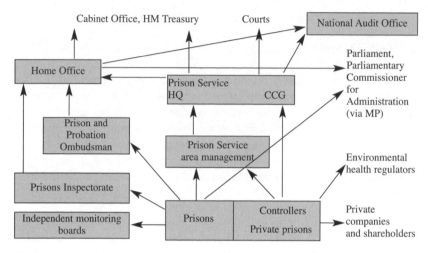

Figure 2.3   Oversight of prisons in England and Wales

In the early 1980s, quasi-contracts were instituted between individual prisons and the Prison Service. This principle was applied to the system as a whole when the Prison Service was set up as a quasi-autonomous executive agency in 1993 with a set of performance targets and budget controls monitored by the Home Office (HM Prison Service, 1999). However, as has been the case with many politically salient executive agencies, the target system has been supplemented by informal indications of shifting day-to-day priorities. Procedures for joint working were strengthened following a dispute between the Chief Executive of the Prison Service and the Home Secretary about responsibility for day-to-day operational management in 1995 (James, 2003). Within the Prison Service, individual prisons account to the headquarters for their performance, with monitoring against targets in various areas such as security, prisoner facilities and cost. The whole service is further subject to civil service regulations, especially for senior posts overseen by the Cabinet Office, and public expenditure control systems run by the Treasury. The service's key performance targets are now subsumed within the Home Office 'Public Service Agreement' as part of a recently instituted comprehensive government-wide system of performance targets monitored by the Treasury (James, 2004)

There is a limited system of oversight by semi-independent administrative bodies, which was strengthened in 1981 when the Prisons Inspectorate was separated from the Prison Department and made to report to the Home Secretary rather than to the prison administration. The Home Secretary recommends appointments to the post, but even so all three of the most recent chief inspectors have publicly criticized both the Prison Service and Home Office.

The chief inspector who retired in 2001, General Sir David Ramsbotham, argued that an emphasis on efficiency savings meant it was difficult to provide programmes designed to reduce reoffending. He also criticized performance targets for creating 'bureaucratic overload' on governors and diverting them from improving conditions (Timmins, 2001).

The inspectorate carries out thematic inspection and regular five-year inspections involving a five-day visit, supplemented by shorter follow-up visits of three days. The chief inspector has no enforcement powers to sanction prisons or the Prison Service, but inspectors have developed a 'ladder of escalating sanctions' if desired modifications are not forthcoming. The first rung on the ladder consists of informal comments to governors or directors during or after inspections. The second rung consists of recommendations in inspection reports submitted to the Home Office for publication. A further step up the ladder of sanctions is to make comments directly to the Director General or Home Secretary, although this rung is rarely reached. Serious shortcomings, such as major failings of security or very poor conditions, trigger higher-level responses straight away.

The inspectorate's statutory duty to publish reports, except where security is at issue, provides the opportunity for 'naming and shaming' prisons to influence their behaviour, which is particularly important in the absence of formal authority to sanction prisons. There is a high level of media interest in prison conditions and the inspectorate has a high media profile (Hood et al., 1999: 128–31). Broader public scrutiny of prisons is provided by Independent Monitoring Boards (formerly called Boards of Visitors), which operate as local inspectorates, being entitled to visit prisons at any time and obtain access to all areas. They monitor conditions and report on them, sometimes submitting an annual report to the Home Secretary. However, the boards do not seem to be very influential beyond pointing out divergence of practice from those set out in rules and guidance, and there is no requirement for the administration to respond to them.

Beyond executive oversight systems, Parliament monitors the system, especially through the convention of ministerial responsibility and through Public Accounts and Home Affairs Committee investigations. The heads of the Prison Service and the Home Office are 'accounting officers' who are obliged to comply with rules over financial procedures as set out in Government Accounting and reporting to Parliament (HM Prison Service, 1999: annex B). From time to time, the National Audit Office produces reports on prisons, and prisons are also subject to general regulations for food hygiene and health and safety.

Judicial control of prisons has been increasing in recent years. The Prison Rules traditionally gave the Home Secretary and governors considerable flexibility in their activities. However, there has been a growth of UK legislation affecting prisons, particularly because of European conventions that have been incorporated into UK law. The view that certain standards of treatment are privileges for prisoners has increasingly been replaced with the view that they constitute rights about minimum standards that should be met. In particular, the incorporation of the European Convention on Human Rights into English law is a major change (HM Chief Inspector of Prisons, 2001: 23). There has also been substantial growth in the quasi-judicial complaint handling system. Prisoners' grievances may be aired through local boards and two ombudsman offices. The Parliamentary Ombudsman which handles complaints referred by Members of Parliament (MPs) and the Prison and Probation Ombudsman (PPO), deals directly with complainants. The PPO has the power to visit prisons and has used it to interview staff and prisoners (Prisons Ombudsman, 1995: 12). However, the ombudsman has considerable difficulty in obtaining information from the Prison Service and lacks formal powers for enforcing recommendations (Prisons Ombudsman, 2001: 3).

2   Competition

Perhaps the most significant change to the system has been a rise in public–private competition, with the first contracted-out private prison opening in 1992. Currently, nine prisons containing around 9 per cent of prisoners have their management contracted out to private companies, with two built by the public sector and run by private companies and seven built and managed by the private sector under the Private Finance Initiative (National Audit Office, 2003: 5). There are elements of a competitive market, with four private providers, Group 4, Premier, Securicor and UKDS. The practice of clearer specification of performance standards for private prisons has spilled out into public prisons and both are now subject to similar operating standards, exposing relative performance. Some years ago the Prison Service announced its intent to subject the management of the worst performing prisons to competitive tendering. Brixton was suggested as a candidate in 2001 and four other prisons were subsequently put under consideration. Moving in the other direction, two prisons that were once run by the private sector are now being run by public sector management teams after successful bids.

   New oversight structures were established for privately managed prisons. A local prison service controller, with a permanent presence within the prison, monitors compliance with relevant statutes and contractual obligations. Controllers have formal powers of enforcement within an overall regime set by the Contracts and Competition Group in the Prison Service headquarters. Contracts include detailed specification of levels of discipline, complaints and treatment of prisoners (HM Prison Service, 2001b). In cases of non-compliance, the response is usually a default notice, followed by a financial penalty if the matter is not remedied within 20 days. In emergencies, the prison can be taken back into public hands. The threat of not contracting out further prisons to private firms, or even ending the contract, encourages private prison providers to comply with concerns raised by the Prison Service. Private prisons are further subject to public inspection and complaint systems as well as oversight by their companies' headquarters (National Audit Office, 2003: 2–3). The directors of private prisons usually have extensive experience of working in public prisons and, in the event of conflicting demands from the Prison Service and the private company, they have a key role in negotiating agreements and forging new norms.

3   Mutuality

Within the Prison Service, there is substantial movement of senior staff between establishments, and headquarters staff have often worked in the field, sharing assessments of performance. Within individual prisons, junior staff build up patterns of joint working, mutual surveillance and strong norms of behaviour. However, the 'new class' of prison officer in private prisons differs from that in the traditional public sector, tending not to have had experience working in other prisons. Annual staff turnover is higher in private than public prisons, averaging around 25 per cent (and ranging from 12 to 42 per cent) compared to just 6 per cent in public prisons in 2000/2001 (National Audit Office, 2003: 27). High turnover would appear to inhibit mutuality based control relative to formal rules and management direction. The increased competition with private providers has particularly reduced the influence of the Prison Officers' Association (POA) union that was very influential in the 1970s and 1980s in setting local working practices (Vagg, 1994: 52–4, 106–7).

Mutuality based controls extend to monitoring and influence by non-state actors. The Independent Monitoring Boards have always been composed of lay people rather than prison professionals, but the role of 'outsiders' has grown since the 1970s. The Chief Inspector of Prisons is an outsider to the prison service, though other inspectors have direct prisons expertise (Hood et al., 1999: 134–7). The current chief inspector, Ann Owers, was general secretary of an immigrant welfare body and is the director of Justice, the all-party human rights and law reform organization. The chief inspector from 1995 to 2001, Sir David Ramsbotham, was a former army general, and his predecessor, the late Sir Stephen Tumin, who held the post from 1987 to 1995, was formerly a county court judge. Similarly, the first prison ombudsman, Sir Peter Woodhead, was a former admiral, and Stephen Shaw, who took over in 1999, was previously director of the Prison Reform Trust charity (Prisons Ombudsman, 2000: 6–9). At times, the 'outsiders' have pressed for improvements to conditions that have conflicted with Prison Service staff norms and attempts to control costs. The outsiders have increased the influence of views traditionally stated by non-governmental bodies monitoring the prison system, especially the Howard League for Penal Reform and Prison Reform Trust who have agendas to 'modernize' prison conditions.

4   Randomness, Contrived and Uncontrived

The oversight system makes use of consciously designed and operated random controls. The inspectorate uses unannounced visits to gather information, but unpredictable elements also occur through the interaction of different layers of oversight and in the (uncontrived) tendency of prisons to erupt into crises such as riots or escapes. There have been several incidents of this sort over the past 15 years, including a major riot at Strangeways prison in 1990. Controllers have tended to respond by strengthening checks on 'problem' prisons and instigating special inquiries, such as the Woolf Report after the 1990 riot. The reports have led to the establishment of new overseers, reforms to structures and attempts at greater standardization of conditions across facilities (Vagg, 1994: 170–72). In 2003, the ombudsman's remit was extended in a rather ad hoc manner when he took over an investigation into a riot and fire at Yarls Wood immigration removals centre. Overall, from the perspective of those working in the system, and perhaps especially from that of an individual prison governor, prisons are subject to an unpredictable mix of multiple hybrid control systems – sometimes in tension with each other and operated by a mix of outsiders and insiders that can be volatile.

2.5   GERMANY: TINKERING WITH OVERSIGHT AND MUTUALITY IN A LEGALISTIC STATE TRADITION
Martin Lodge

Control of German prisons is dominated by an oversight/mutuality hybrid underpinned by the federal legalistic state tradition, with varied interpretations in the different *Länder*. Overall, the control systems have been characterized by stability in fundamental forms, and a stable balance between different forms, although there have been a large number of less significant reforms and some weak general trends towards decentralization and greater use of staff from a variety of professional backgrounds

1   Oversight

Oversight reflects the basic elements of the German system of federalism, as summarized in Figure 2.4. While prison directors are ultimately responsible for the operation and performance of their institutions, there are many

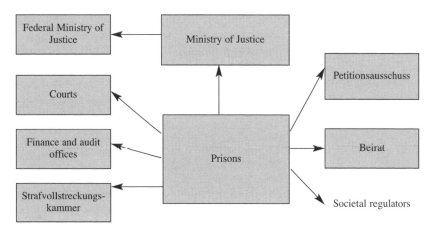

Figure 2.4   Oversight of prisons in 'typical' German Länder

constraints on their actions. There are three levels of oversight. The first of these is defined by federal legislation, the 1977 *Strafvollzugsgesetz*, that sets out the broad parameters of the way in which 'justice' is executed. Article 151 states that 'supervision' (*Aufsicht*) of prisons is to be exercised by the relevant *Länder* justice administrations. Article 2, sentence 1 requires measures that enable the prisoner to lead a crime-free and socially responsible life post-imprisonment, with security a supplementary goal. The federal ministry of justice has no formal means of administration beyond the federal legislation, although it visits prison institutions regularly and initiates consultation and information-sharing exercises.

The second, intergovernmental level entails co-operation across the *Länder*, formal and informal standard-setting in the form of 'directives', and more informal co-ordinative standardization. Federal-wide directives, agreed by the justice ministers of the *Länder*, requires the regulatory authority (or the *Aufsichtsbehörde*) to visit prison institutions as often as necessary in order always to be 'informed about the whole running of the prison', while granting the individual *Länder* the authority to regulate public access. In 2002, apart from North Rhine-Westphalia (which relies on a three-level system involving ministry, agency and prisons), all *Länder* exercised oversight of their prison systems through specialized divisions within their justice ministries (Lower Saxony having abandoned a three-level system in the early 1990s). At the same time, Article 156 of the federal law provides prison directors with substantial discretion in the running of their prisons, with the extent varying across the *Länder*.

The third level involves the oversight of prisons by individual *Länder*. There is not so much a single 'German' approach towards control of prisons, but rather 16 prison regulation regimes, broadly distinguishable by more 'social-democratic' (and 'liberal') and more 'Christian-democratic' interpretations of the application of the broad parameters of the federal law. The prisons in the former East Germany (GDR) were incorporated into the West German system and, while these systems in their traditional form are beyond the scope of this section, their incorporation into the reunified system appears to have had little effect on the West German systems. For example, in Berlin, all former GDR prisons were closed and the 'new' *Länder* have been involved in a programme of modernizing their prison system by constructing and thereby replacing many prison institutions (as well as personnel).

Direct oversight of prisons rests with the respective *Land* ministries of justice. Routine reporting requirements for prisons show substantial variation across the different *Länder*, consisting of a mixture of annual reports, operational reports and the duty to report 'unusual incidents'. *Länder* adopt different approaches towards inspection, some separating inspection regimes across operational-managerial, 'social' and 'security' issues, with the latter inspections sometimes being unannounced, or announced one day in advance, as in Saxony, or only to the prison director, as in Hesse. In the past three decades, unannounced visitations were largely abandoned in most *Länder*, although team composition has been randomly shifted in order to avoid the emergence of a stable 'inspection team' ethos, and to allow more prison staff to be exposed to other institutions.

While the federal law allows for the creation of middle-level authorities to regulate prisons, such three-level systems were only adopted in Lower Saxony and in North Rhine-Westphalia. In the early 1990s, Lower Saxony moved towards a two-level system, delegating most functions to its prisons, while concentrating supervisory functions at the ministry level. In North Rhine-Westphalia there were two middle-level authorities (one responsible for the Rhineland, one for Westphalia) that were merged in early 2003. In any case, the middle level controls were often seen as purely formal, for example the measurement of prison reports by length of entries by ruler without regard to their content. This reflected their implicit task to act as an additional buffer to deflect political pressure from the minister in the case of incidents rather than exercising ongoing control. Arguably, the traditional style of controlling the prison system was that ministries would get involved following incidents, by either directly demanding the appearance of staff 'to be hauled over the coals' ('*dann wurde denen der Kopf gewaschen*', interview, ministry officials), or by imposing ad hoc measures on the overall prison system after a single prison incident.

The regulation of prisons involves a variety of formal control elements with legal supervision (*Rechtsaufsicht*), operational supervision (*Dienstaufsicht*) and broad 'professional' supervision (*Fachaufsicht*). It is conceived as embracing advice as well as supervision and punishment. For behaviour modification, a whole range of potential measures existed, from informal exchange to the formal issuing of particular or general directives (Weisungen) and to the outright removal of a prison director. Ministries issue general directives (*Ermessungsrichtlinien* and *Auslegungsrichtlinien*) to guide and instruct prisons in their interpretation and application of the law. More specific directives (*Erlasse*) are issued ad hoc in response to specific incidents. In general, these measures are regarded as a tool to restrict the interpretation of the 1977 law (and therefore challenge its legal intent), while also constraining the autonomy of prison management. Nevertheless, at least formally, the federal law provided a central role for prison directors to use their discretion in the interpretation of the law (this substantial discretion also reduced the ability to challenge decisions). Such powers, which are differently (and increasingly differently) interpreted across the *Länder*, did not affect the legal competence of the ministry to intervene on a case-by-case basis.

Apart from the direct management of prisons by the ministry, which varies among *Länder* and is often increased by politicians following scandals, the overall prison management system is highly juristic, reflecting to some extent the predominance of jurists in the initial prison regimes (until the 1980s), and to some extent also reflecting a specific German sensitivity about the high potential for abuse in total institutions. An emphasis on legal fairness was therefore central to prison regulation. Prisoner rights were established in the 1977 federal law, although the law provided substantial discretion to prison directors. A specific court chamber deals with prison complaints, but in most *Länder* the complaint system was regarded as largely ineffective, leading to a maximum of three or four 'substantial' (or 'inconvenient') court statements per year per *Land* (about 1 per cent overall). Complaints to the parliamentary committee require a formal response by the ministry, while the committee also conducts announced visits to prisons. In most *Länder* parliamentary control is exercised by the *Petitionsausschuss* (responsible for complaints) and by the *Rechtsausschuss* (interested in legality and the interpretation of law). A largely advisory, but also oversight activity was provided by the so-called *Beiräte* (Gerken 1986; Schäfer 1997). A *Beirat* is typically composed of lay people including local members of the *Land* parliament, social welfare organizations and sometimes business representatives. While initially (in the late nineteenth and early twentieth centuries) explicitly designed to provide for external oversight institution that prisoners could address directly, this function had by the end of the twentieth century mainly turned into the giving of advice to the prison director.

The main change in oversight has been a shift in some *Länder* towards delegating managerial responsibilities to the prison institutions themselves. This shift reflected the preferences of a reform-minded 'advocacy coalition' interested in reforming the management and control of prisons. While to some extent adopting the language of managerial reform, this advocacy coalition was mainly interested in reducing operating routines that were claimed to constrain the management of prisons, without offering sufficient information of effective outside oversight. Thus, themes of decentralization and delegation of tasks (shifting certain levels of staffing policies and the like to the prison level), 'privatization' of non-core tasks to third-sector organizations, and the strengthening of the role of the prison director appealed to this coalition as one way to allow for greater diversity and experimentation, while also reducing costs and thus reducing the vulnerability of prisons to cost-cutting pressures from other interests, notably finance ministries. (See Flügge, 2001, and other contributions in the same volume edited by Flügge, Maelicke and Preusker, 2001, which is said to be the manifesto of this particular advocacy coalition.) However, the moves towards increasing formal contractual relations between prison and ministry alongside delegation of management were greeted with some scepticism by prison officials. In particular the realism of targets was disputed. For example, in one *Land*, a zero escape rate target was set for political reasons although it was widely regarded by those in both the ministry and the prison to be an impossible target. Interviewees commented that there was always likely to be political interference at times of crisis.

2 Competition

There is generally little use of competition among *Länder*, and ministries do not use comparisons between prisons as a basis for league table competition. The idiosyncratic features of different units are traditionally seen as a barrier to the use of benchmarks, and information is not presented or collected in ways that allow for ready comparisons across *Länder*, apart from information collected for international organizations, such as the CPT. To some extent this reflects differences in prison infrastructures across the different *Länder*. It also partly reflects political and administrative disagreement about which indicators are meaningful. At the time of writing, there were some attempts to develop a basis for cross-*Land* comparison, but there was also a commitment not to use rivalry across the *Länder*, to avoid blaming and finger-pointing that might reduce the capability of the prison system to withstand political pressure for immediate responses.

3 Mutuality

Since the passing of the 1977 law, there has been a general trend towards reducing the use of hierarchy towards a greater emphasis on mutuality. The *Länder* co-operate to prevent competitive comparison of performance and the relationships between prisons and ministries are very close and informal in some, especially smaller, *Länder*. Informal methods for influencing behaviour are used, with an official commenting that 'this is like being married, "love withdrawal" is the most effective instrument [of the ministry to control prisons]'. Prisons exchange information in various ways, sometimes across *Länder*, and sometimes to defend their autonomy against departments. Security-related experts of partnering institutions visit prisons and informally inspect security arrangements, often informally reporting results to build 'trust' in the system. The *Strafvollzugsausschuss* of the *Länder* heads of division responsible for the prison system co-operate across *Länder* justice ministers. Shared commitment to the legal intent of the federal law helps facilitate co-operation which extends to federal–*Länder* relationships, where officials in the federal ministry are also often recruited from the *Länder*. A further, mainly internal control within prisons, and particularly a veto position, is the work council (*Personalräte*). The work councils offer outlets for local staff dissatisfaction and, with staff unions, can be influential in shaping broader policy initiatives. However, institutions of 'internal democracy' by the prisoners themselves do not appear to exert control over prisons.

Mutuality of these kinds has been quite stable in some ways, but mutuality has been altered through more diversity in staff professional background (both at the ministry and the prison level), moving away from the former monopoly of jurists in the bureaucracy. For example, there are now more social psychologists in high-level positions and 'leadership academies' for higher-level staff to learn modern managerial skills and to adjust to increased budgetary responsibility. Inside prisons, too, the increasing share of non-jurist management meant changes in the way in which 'social' and 'security' aspects were co-ordinated, valued and evaluated.

Nevertheless, variety remains in control patterns. While some *Länder* have increased movement of staff across the different levels of their prison systems, other *Länder*, motivated by a political motivation to 'toughen' the prison regime, have moved in a different direction, opening up the control activities in the ministries to 'incomers' with a legal background in the light of what are perceived to be overly close relations in the prison domain. These divergent trends show how the legalistic state tradition is a theme that can have numerous variations when it comes to the details of control.

2.6 FRANCE: INEFFECTIVE OVERSIGHT IN THE LAND OF INSPECTIONS GÉNÉRALES
Marie Vogel

Extensive oversight systems, including several inspectorates, have only limited impact on the monitoring of prison conditions in France, and appear to have even less impact on the enforcement of standards. The prison sector rarely provokes much interest in broader governmental or social circles, despite occasional flurries of interest after crises. Despite some recent reform initiatives, little use is made of competition, and there are no private prisons, meaning that mutuality among front-line staff is the dominant form of control in practice

1   Oversight

Prisons are nominally under the authority of the Minister for Justice (a high-ranking position in the government), although prisons are not usually a pressing policy priority of the Minister. As shown in Figure 2.5, day-to-day oversight comes from the Prison Service (*Direction de l'administration pénitentiaire*) and its regional authorities (*Directions régionales*). The service is traditionally highly centralized and hierarchical, and mainstream prison staff are civil servants hired through competitive examinations and governed by nation-wide regulations. Prisons operate under the General Regulations (*ordonnance*) of 1945, reiterated by the Prisons Public Service Act 1987. There is an extensive, if not necessarily efficient, mix of in-house inspections and inspections by administrative bodies affiliated with the Ministry of Justice. In-house inspections are the most likely to be followed up in some way.

Periodic inspections of prisons are carried out by the regional prison authorities and by a Prison Service Inspectorate (*Inspection des services pénitentiaires*), which at the time of writing included five high-ranking Prison Service officials. Many of the inspectorate's assignments consist of advising the

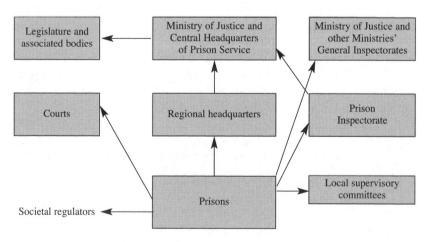

Figure 2.5   Oversight of prisons in France

Director of the Prison Service on technical matters. In 2000, for example, it performed 32 inspections: eight after being called to an incident, three as regular inspections, seven as general security reviews, five as complete searches of the premises and nine as preparing such searches. On the whole, in-house inspections play an important part in the handling of incidents and irregularities but they do not constitute day-to-day oversight of prison facilities.

The Ministry of Justice's General Inspectorate (*Inspection générale des services judiciaires*), when requested by the Minister, may conduct ad hoc inspections of detention facilities. However, it is primarily in charge of overseeing 1100 courts, with little capabilities left over for prison inspections. General Inspectorates from other ministries notionally oversee prisons with regard to matters under their jurisdiction such as hygiene, health and the safety of the workplace. But when such inspections are carried out (which is rare) they tend to apply lower standards than those applying to other public facilities (*Rapport de la Commission sénatoriale Hyest*, 2000).

Other external overseers include the courts who are formally commissioned to visit detention facilities (a mission they do not perform in practice) and local Supervising Committees (*Commissions de surveillance*), which are attached to every prison. They are composed of judges, local representatives, civil servants from the local offices of the ministries of education, health, and work, professionals, and charities. Their mission statement is all-encompassing – with the exception of matters related to the status of prison staff – and include hygiene and health, safety, working conditions, the implementation of regulations, reprimands and discipline, education and reintegration of detainees, and so on. But their efficiency is limited, as reports by various General Inspectorates have been saying for over a century. They meet once a year and exert no real control over the matters under their jurisdiction.

Last and perhaps least, parliamentary control of the prisons, although always possible, is in fact largely non-existent. The government regularly commissions reports on points of interest but reports by parliamentary special committees are almost unheard of, and committees set up in recent years to investigate the situation of French prisons have been the first for over a century. On the whole, as far as prisons are concerned, top-down and in-house direction is the dominant force, and the real impact of higher or external oversight bodies has long been almost of no account, in spite of the variety of institutions and procedures.

Most of the oversight systems, including the in-house inspectorates, have been stable in recent years and there is no sign of a recent 'oversight explosion' here. However, the extension of the detainees' rights has contributed to some weakening of Prison Service autonomy and the oversight systems have more recently come under pressure from outside with the impact of the European Committee for the Prevention of Torture visits since 1991 and publications. The statement of the European standards in the 1998 *Resolution on Prison Conditions in the European Union* has also made a contribution, and the Ministry of Justice and the Prison Service have been willing, over the last few years, to take these standards as overall policy guidelines (Administration pénitentiaire, 2002; Canivet, 2000). The activities of groups advocating detainees' rights including charities, chaplains and medical professionals involved in prisons have also been significant (Vasseur, 2000). Over the last few years, two parliamentary inquiry committees were set up, one in each house, and the Ministry began to prepare a complete revamp of prison regulations and policies, taking into some account of European advice and recommendations into account. And a law of 2000 opened the closed world of prisons by entitling MPs to visit and inspect detention facilities.

New management styles are now developing as part of a general 'modernization' of French government aiming to introduce market-orientated tools of management, but assessment of prison and probation policies remains limited. The Canivet Committee report of 2000 pointed out the weak spots of the present oversight system with regard to efficiency and implementation of European standards and outlined a possible overall re-organization, while staying within the conceptual limits of the French 'service public', following the path taken by various earlier modernization proposals (Vogel, 1998). The report stressed the importance of a clear mission statement and organizational chart and advocated a threefold organization of oversight and control into what it termed *vérification*, *médiation* and *observation*. The first (scrutiny) was to be entrusted to a centralized, independent, higher inspectorate comprising a few higher civil servants with wide powers. Conciliation would be new in the French context, roughly equivalent to the setting up of a prison ombudsman on a regional basis with a national co-ordination. The last (observation) was to be handed over to local advocacy groups. This attempt to modernize the system was still under consideration at the time of writing.

The limited impact of recent reform initiatives means competition is still not a strong form of control. Detention is a state monopoly and is managed without comparative evaluation between prisons. No significant privatization has occurred, nor a substantial move to private management methods. Some facilities from the 'Programme 13 000' originated in the late 1980s are often termed 'privately run prisons' because some services such as catering or dry-cleaning are contracted out. However, all core tasks remain in the hands of the Prison Service. And as far as staff management is concerned, the highly Weberian conception of career and status, the French administration confines competition for the most part to recruitment by competitive examination. Similarly, contrived randomness does not appear to figure large in the control system. Random or unexpected inspections, although possible in principle, do not take place in practice. Random elements come into control mainly in the form of the frequent phenomenon of crisis-based regulation – publicized incidents and sudden surges of public opinion followed by policy responses.

2 Mutuality

The ineffectiveness of formal oversight means that the management of the Prison Service is highly discretionary within a loose regulatory environment (Canivet, 2000). The Prison Service must accommodate all detainees, it may not regulate the flow and it is placed under tight budgetary control. In practice, detention has priority over rehabilitation and reintegration. Evaluation of staff and institutions mostly relies on the former criterion. The standards of good administration in the Prison Service are significantly weaker than those in other services, or in French society as a whole, and a number of prisons are derelict and understaffed. Indeed, scholars have often commented on the lack of transparency of prison management and the pressure stemming from the absolute priority on the keeping of public order.

The prison system is a closed social world (Combessie, 1994). Hence, probably, its rather unwavering operation that combines day-to-day routine with occasional, political, crisis management whenever – through escape, riot or scandal – prisons hit the news. Mutuality among Prison Service employees is shaped by the fact that they do not possess clearly valuable occupational skills in the workplace nor social prestige outside (Froment, 1998) with their identity being first and foremost built upon their status as civil servants. Therefore, union officials have been significant in the running of the prison system, especially under the one-union system that prevailed until the mid-1980s (Faugeron, 1991: 341). There is little drive for change, either, on an occupational, social or administrative basis, pressure from detainees is unobtrusive and the role of higher management positions has only begun to be highly regarded fairly recently. There has been some tendency to professionalize, focused on employees' training. Seventeen per cent of staff held a baccalaureate in 1986 as against less than 1 per cent in 1976, and they are beginning to manifest clear demands for a career, and not only a job, in the service. The professionals involved in prisons are also now more heterogeneous, and health-related functions are now under the responsibility of public health authorities (under an Act of 1994). Nevertheless, the day-to-day business of running prisons still has a low status and, in that context, prison workers and managers find it difficult to develop the standards of action and monitoring necessary for effective professional self-control.

2.7 THE NETHERLANDS: A PROFESSIONAL MUTUALITY/OVERSIGHT HYBRID UNDER PRESSURE
Arjen Boin

Control over Dutch prisons is dominated by prison professionals' mutuality, albeit operating in combination with an extensive system of formal oversight. The dominance of prison professionals has become increasingly contested, with intermittent bursts of new forms of oversight, particularly as politicians attempt to increase their influence. However, these efforts at reform have, to date, had only very limited success in wresting control from the professionals.

1 Oversight

The formal systems of oversight are summarized in Figure 2.6. The prisons, alongside institutions for juvenile offenders and some psychiatric hospitals, are part of the National Agency of Correctional Institutions (*Dienst Justitiële Inrichtingen* – DJI), a semi-independent agency in the Justice Department. The Minister of Justice maintains full responsibility and reports to parliament within a statutory framework of prison regulation. General policy goals are formulated in the Justice Department, which are then translated into policy directives and operational targets within the DJI. A body of 'pseudo law' has grown up on the basis of the way that prisoner complaints procedures developed over time. The outcome is the prison 'regime', the formal rules that govern the functioning of a prison. The prison director in the DJI allocates budgets and formulates performance indicators that are set out in the annual

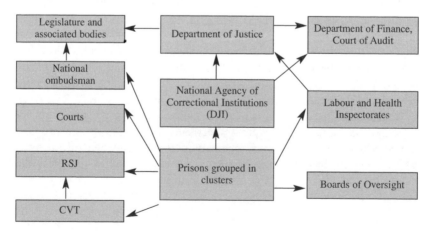

Figure 2.6   Oversight of prisons in the Netherlands

contract between the DJI and the governor of clusters of prisons. Oversight is mostly based on tracking a list of performance indicators (which has been gradually reduced from over 100 to 34), with governors reporting their performance statistics to DJI headquarters evey quarter. Formally, the Office of the Prosecutor (*het Openbaar Ministerie*) is responsible for 'the execution of detention', this office has traditionally shied away from its task and, indeed, few people even seem to be aware of it.

The contractual relation between the DJI and its 20 cluster governors is output driven: as long as governors meet their targets, DJI headquarters largely refrains from intervention. But this does not leave the governor and staff without any form of supervision. Each prison has its own Board of Oversight, a group of prominent local citizens who regularly visit the institution and make themselves available to the prisoners. They communicate their advice to the prison governor, and, if necessary, to officials higher up in the chain. In addition, the independent *Raad voor Strafrechtstoepassing en Jeugdbescherming* (RSJ), largely made up of intellectuals, judges and former policy-makers, visits the prisons and advises the Minister of Justice on the feasibility and desirability of new laws and policy directives, judged solely in the interest of prisoners. Representatives of the national body RSJ made 43 prison visits in 2000. The findings are not published, but aggregated in the annual RSJ report. The complaints procedures run by these bodies have some bite for individual cases but less in terms of general policy. Prisoners begin the process by lodging a complaint with the prison's Board of Oversight. This board makes a recommendation to the governor, who is not obliged to comply. The prisoner can appeal to the RJS, whose verdict is binding for the prison governor. This complaint procedure is well used and accepted as legitimate both by prisoners and staff (Vagg, 1994), but the policy advice frequently submitted by the RJS or the ombudsman carries far less weight than departmental or staff considerations.

A range of organizations complement this institutional structure. As one of the big spenders in the Justice Department's field, the prison sector has to deal with financial oversight both from within the Justice Department and from the Department of Finance. The audit office (*Algemene Rekenkamer*) may perform *ex-post* evaluations and the Labour Inspectorate can investigate all issues having to do with the work environment. The functioning of the prison sector is subject of regular debate in parliamentary subcommittees and, if necessary, in parliament itself. Prisons do not have their own sector-specific ombudsman but the National Ombudsman – reporting to parliament – may act on complaints from within the prison system. Ombudsman reports have been published and have received widespread attention. The courts may become involved and the National Detective Squad (*Rijksrecherche*) investigates all cases in which prison staff stand accused.

There is little intentional use of random controls, although unpredictable incidents often shape the system. The Dutch prison system has been confronted with regular, incident-driven publicity and political attention – most of it negative in tone (Baumgartner and Jones, 1993). Concerned academics – mostly criminologists and students of law – keep a watchful eye on the prisons, assisted by prisoner organizations such as the *Coornhert Liga*. The media are not so much concerned with the welfare of prisoners but are aware of the interest their readers have in prisons, and tend to magnify the scale of periodic crises. Recently this negative attention produced direct political intervention in the workings of the Dutch prison system, leading to the abolition of the one-prisoner-per-cell principle, which had been the staple of correctional quality of the post-Second World War prison system.

There is little use of competition as a control device, and no public–private competition in provision of prisons for adults, although the DJI does contract with private youth institutions and forensic institutions. While there is competition for promotion, there is little competition between prisons, for example using performance measures as benchmarks. Instead prison governors have adopted the principles and practices of the worldwide quality control movement, experimenting with audits and control circles. This approach relies on mutual auditing (governors visiting colleagues) and defines agency headquarters out of the loop. The adoption of this model makes it much harder to design central oversight back into the governing relation or to institute competition.

2   Mutuality

Prison governors have considerable discretionary powers and are largely responsible for running their prisons, within the limits of law and budget (Boin, 2001; Kelk, 2000).The governors' discretion is compounded by hands-off, long-distance monitoring by the DJI. In the 1970s the director of the prison system, Hans Tulkens, encouraged governors to be flexible in adapting departmental rules to the situation – on the condition that their discretionary freedom would benefit the prisoners. The economic crises of the 1980s brought a funding squeeze that reined back ambitions for developing rehabilitative programmes, but the relatively loose relation between headquarters and prison administrations remains. Governors visit their departmental colleagues in The Hague to discuss performance measures and other issues, but the DJI does not engage in site visits, nor do policy-makers pay regular, informal visits to their colleagues in the field. Living up to their administrative philosophy of decentralized governance, DJI policy-makers leave the management of the prisons to the prison managers. Monitoring is viewed both by governors and DJI policy-makers as a breach of trust, an unnecessary and outdated form of regulation. While DJI policy-makers will certainly castigate governors who fail to deliver on the performance dimensions or overrun their budgets, most do not stumble in this way. The governors consider non-interference as the only proof of respect for their professionalism. Mr Jägers, the DJI director, did not consider it reprehensible to admit that he had 'no idea what is going on in the prisons'. In any case, the regulations are toothless without means of enforcement. So, many insiders describe Dutch prison governors as 'rulers of their fiefdoms' (Boin, 2001).

The dominance of mutuality controls rests, in part, on a 'favourable agency myth' that a magical transformation occurred from a rather backward system in the immediate post-Second World War years to an enlightened prison system commanding the awe of both critical academics and pragmatic policy-makers all over the world (Franke, 1995). Politicians, policy-makers, prison staff and media have adopted this agency myth as an accurate depiction of the Dutch prison system and now only care about avoiding crisis incidents and keeping within budgets. But the truth is that the Dutch system is one of the most expensive in the world (Boin, 2001) and, while most prisoners have their own cells, performance is not appreciably higher than European counterparts on some key performance indicators such as escapes, suicides or health care.

Attempts to wrest control from governors have met with only limited success. During the 1980s, parliamentary majorities pushed for double-bunking of prisoners; the governors resisted this pressure, claiming the moral high ground. After a series of violent escapes in the early 1990s, the first DJI director perceived a window of opportunity to curb the power of governors and impose a minimal degree of uniformity on the prisons but was opposed by the governors (Boin and Otten, 1996). However, the DJI makes some use of control of appointments to try and augment its influence over the field operations. The ultimate sanction is removal of a prison governor (rotation is rarely used in the Dutch prison system). For instance, one recent DJI director seized on the opportunity offered to him by a media attack on a very influential governor who had been running the largest prison in the Netherlands for nearly 18 years. He was removed from his position 'in the interest of the system' and offered a position as security adviser in an office near his home town. Similarly, the DJI has used a recent clustering operation (merging the administrative offices of contiguous prisons) to select a few 'general directors' to run several prisons in their region. This seems like an obvious attempt to break the informal 'old boy network' that has frustrated central efforts to impose a minimal degree of control over the field. United in their own union (VDPI), the governors have effectively used union protection to work against policy initiatives not to their liking.

There have been other jolts to the dominance of prison professionals in the control system. The government-wide embrace of New Public Management principles in the 1980s brought changed forms of oversight, but these were adopted within the dominant framework of mutuality controls. A DJI executive agency formally came into existence on 1 January 1995 and the director attempted to pursue a more detention-orientated policy. But prison governors, who were infused with ambitious ideas about rehabilitation, refused to accept the new philosophy and did not appreciate the newly found assertiveness of their agency director. In the ensuing power struggle, the governors prevailed by negotiating their way into the policy-making process above the head of the director. Instead, the main development that kept the power base of prison governors in check was the institutionalization of the complaints procedure for prisoners, which was initiated in the late 1970s. This development gained in importance, as the prison inspectorate had been abolished in the early 1980s (although there is currently some talk about reintroducing it). The complaints procedure is well used and accepted as a fact of life by all (even in the Netherlands' only maximum security prison).

At the time of writing, the future of this mutuality dominated system is uncertain, with political pressures to make double-bunking and other initiatives mandatory for at least 25 per cent of the prison population, combined with a looming fiscal squeeze. It may be that such developments could result in a sustained effort to use control forms that do not rely so much on prison professionals' mutuality as in the past.

2.8   NORWAY: A STABLE OVERSIGHT/MUTUALITY HYBRID AMID LIMITED DIVERSIFICATION OF PROFESSIONAL MUTUALITY
Per Lægreid and Marjoleine H. Wik

A rather cosy form of professional mutuality, especially at the level of individual facilities, has traditionally dominated the Norwegian prison sector, together with oversight by a range of bodies. There is no public/private competition, and only limited use is made of contrived randomness. However, in recent decades, the traditional dominance of prison professionals has been reduced, to some extent, by the increased involvement of professionals from different backgrounds.

1   Oversight

The Norwegian Ministry of Justice has overall responsibility for oversight of prisons, with the central management of prisons organized both as a division within the Ministry and as an independent agency/directorate, named the prison and probation department. The position of the Ministry within the system of formal oversight is summarized in Figure 2.7. The department

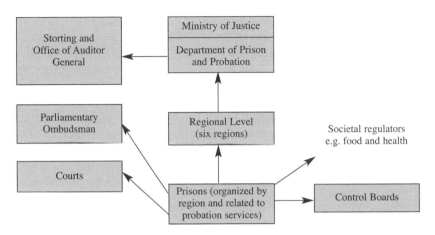

Figure 2.7   Oversight of prisons in Norway

formulates prison policy, prepares legislation and lays down the annual budget. The most recent systemic prison legislation dates from 1958 although there have been many minor reforms since then, including legislation in 2000 to bring prisons and probation together. The mixed directorate utilized in the Ministry was once a relatively common organizational structure in Norwegian central government, but during the last 40 years most such directorates in other departmental areas have been unwound, to clarify responsibilities between and within governmental units. The prison system continues to use the traditional form, but in 2001 there was a reorganization to create six regional managers, with professional and administrative management arrangements brought together at the same time, to try and improve the effectiveness of oversight.

While the central oversight system is more coherent now than 10 years ago, local facilities have discretion, and homogeneity among prisons is seen as neither possible nor desirable. Some institutions, particularly small facilities, exert considerable autonomy and some have chosen to ignore the instructions of the Ministry of Justice (Statskonsult, 2001: 41). Feedback over policy implementation has been limited and interviewees commented on 'Norwegian kindness' in the management systems, meaning that while the department issues detailed and often quantitative guidelines, no sanctions are applied when the guidelines are not followed. For example, the policy to ensure bespoke prison treatment for each inmate has been widely ignored. A former prison governor noted that he complied with guidelines but others claimed financial problems prevented them from doing so. Nor did governors criticize one another; as one put it, 'I could not be disloyal, and criticize the fact that they [my fellow governors] had newer cars than I had, but I did wonder'. The Ministry has attempted better financial management and use of performance indicators, and some larger prisons have used the 'balanced scorecard' approach. Such initiatives could facilitate central control, if the directorate set the priorities. However, the central directorate's ministerial responsibilities regarding policy advice and legislation are often prioritized at the expense of its management functions.

The Ministry of Justice uses Control Boards, made up of at least three lay members and led by someone with legal knowledge such as a judge, to visit prisons about once a month. Formally the visits are random, to obtain a realistic view of the situation inside the prison, but true randomness limits prisoners' ability to complain to the boards on visits and, partly for this reason, the visits of Control Board members are often announced one day in advance. Serious complaints are very rare, yet the whole system relies on people coming forward to complain if there is a serious problem. Complaints about 'practical, day-to-day' matters are handled by prison management, with their response sent to the Control Board and communicated to the inmate concerned. If the Control Board is not satisfied they can respond, but find it hard to assess the reasonableness of managers' excuses for inaction, particularly those based on alleged financial limitations.

Beyond the executive, administrative, systems, the Ministry reports to the Parliament, and the Parliamentary Ombudsman and courts also exercise different forms of oversight. In addition, both the media and national and international public organizations monitor conditions, injecting an element of randomness into oversight systems. However, prison managers can influence media perceptions to a large degree by only showing them parts of a prison, or only giving them the opportunity to interview certain inmates, or no inmates at all. Although there are rules about how to deal with the media, and the rights of inmates and journalists, it is the prison governor who interprets the rules. There is little use of competition as a form of control, although there is an element of competition in the recruitment of students to the prison school, with the number of applicants normally much higher than the number in each class, and competition for promotion. However, contracting out or privatization of the prison service has not been an issue in Norway, and there is no significant competition among prisons.

2 Mutuality

Mutuality mechanism are sometimes presented by those working in the system as involving prison employees monitoring and preventing abuse by colleagues. However, such processes can turn into mutual protection. The degree of job rotation is very low, and prison employees usually work in teams which can result in employees 'becoming closer than a married couple. They spend much more time together and, of course, the effect can change from controlling to protecting'. Job rotation to prevent this type of protection, and to prevent guards establishing too much power over particular inmates, is attempted. However, rotation can be difficult, especially in smaller prisons which may employ as few as 10–12 people. Mutuality additionally operates across prison units through a strongly unionized workforce, with more than 90 per cent of employees being union members. The dominant union is the Norwegian Prison and Probation Union, which organizes 75 per cent of the prison officers. This union actively works to improve the professional, social and economic conditions of its members and takes an active part in public debates and administrative reforms.

Changes in the prison workforce have altered the operation of mutuality in recent years. Three decades ago, there were almost no female employees inside the prison walls, except for some nurses. Today, most prisons employ female guards, and this has contributed to a reduction of the 'old boy network' and old norms, in which male guards 'overprotected' each other. Another change has been the employees' education. Thirty years ago, all prison guards were graduates from the only prison school in Norway. Also many of the supervisors and in some cases even the prison governors, who had started as prison guards, were graduates from this school. This of course meant that other influences did not penetrate the system much. The 'inside protection' within the small group was high, everybody knew everybody, and loyalty was often necessary in order to stay in the system and to get promoted. Nowadays, even though the prison school is still the only place for future prison guards to receive their education, there is more variation in the educational background of the students and the school itself is changing towards more focus on the role of educator and therapist, and less focus on the role of jailer and guard (Ravneberg, 2002).

Mutuality has been further altered by the move away from self-sufficiency in prisons to a model of importing goods and services. Up to the early 1970s the prisons were much more closed to the outside world than they are today. The internal staff and the prison officers themselves conducted all treatments and services. This traditional policy was strongly criticized (Christie, 1969) and the Norwegian Association for Penal Reform (KROM), founded in 1968, became a high-profile non-governmental pressure group for change (Mathisen and Heli, 1993). They argued that the prison should become an arena for rehabilitation by opening it up to external groups offering, in particular, education and medical treatment, and government policy on prisons and probation from 1977 reflected this view (St.meld. nr. 104, 1977–78). Gradually educational and medical facilities were imported into the prison system. In 1988 the responsibility for the health care in prisons was transferred from the Ministry of Justice to the Ministry of Health. Today, the biggest prisons have full-time medical teams of doctors, nurses, psychologists and physiotherapists. There are also close relations between the prisons and employment centres, rehabilitation centres, libraries, the social welfare office and the social insurance office. There has been a long co-operation with the Church of Norway that appoints prison chaplains and there is a growing social science research on the prison service system (Fridhov, 1994; Johnsen, 2001; Ravneberg, 2002) and greater media interest. These trends involving outside professionals further weaken the traditional dominance of a small group of like-minded prison professionals in shaping the system, and may be leading to new forms of mutuality.

2.9   AUSTRALIA: VARIETY IN REFORMS TO OVERSIGHT ALONGSIDE INCREASED PUBLIC–PRIVATE COMPETITION
Colin Scott

Control of correctional services varies between states within an overall national framework. There has been a trend in several states towards greater emphasis on external oversight alongside increased public–private competition, with more stability in control forms elsewhere. Where contracting out has been used, it has recast the departments responsible for correctional services as external regulators rather then line managers, and called forth institutional innovations in forms of oversight.

1   Oversight

The provision of correctional facilities falls almost exclusively within the state jurisdiction with the Commonwealth's (federal government) role in detention forming part of immigration rather than criminal justice policy. Oversight arrangements vary from state to state within an overall set of standards contained in legislation and in prison rules. Nationally agreed Standard Guidelines for Corrections in Australia were adopted by a Corrective Services Ministers' Conference in 1995 and provide a floor on which state and territory standards are built. Some states have no corrections-specific external oversight, combining operational and oversight matters within the line management functions of a government department and leaving external oversight to general regulators such as ombudsmen, while others have elaborate corrections-specific mechanisms of external oversight. The 'typical' oversight system in which most prisons operate is summarized in Figure 2.8.

Some states have separated, to a greater or lesser degree, the operational and policy aspects of correctional services. Victoria has an Office of

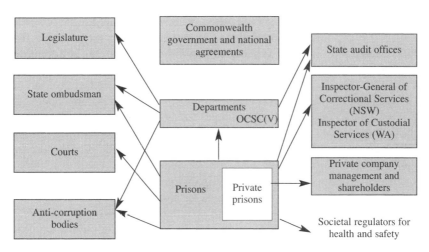

Figure 2.8   Oversight of prisons in a 'typical' Australian state

Correctional Services Commissioner (OCSC) within the Department of Justice. Queensland abandoned the independent statutory commission model in 2000 when it replaced the Queensland Correctional Services Commission with a Department of Corrective Services under the direct responsibility of a minister. New South Wales and Western Australia continue to operate correctional services within ministerial government departments. All the states and territories appoint official visitors to each prison facility with duties to visit the prisons and make independent reports to the minister or department responsible as to general conditions and particular complaints. Visitors generally have unrestricted access to prisons at all times, although specific practices vary between states (Rynne, 2001: 138). In New South Wales, the visitor system has been markedly enhanced through assigning responsibility to the Inspector-General of Correctional Services responsibility for the training of visitors (Crimes [Administration of Sentences Act] 1999, s. 213[1][d]).

Ombudsman offices are a common feature of the oversight arrangements for corrections facilities, although no state has established a specialist ombudsman service for correctional facilities. For example, the New South Wales (NSW) Ombudsman received over 4000 complaints about aspects of the corrections system during 2001–02 and visitors' facilities (New South Wales Ombudsman, 2001: 55). Each of the ombudsman's offices use the annual report to highlight the numbers of complaints against each correctional centre and the nature of the matters complained about such that the data *could* be used for regulatory investigation of systemic problems. By and large the analysis of system problems is assigned to other agencies and the regulatory role of the ombudsmen in the prisons system is restricted. Further general overseers of government cover the prison sector. In New South Wales investigations by the Independent Commission against Corruption have led the Department of Corrective Services to establish a Probity and Performance Management Branch and to redraft its ethics statement (Department of Corrective Services, 2001: 4). Similarly the Criminal Justice Commission in Queensland can investigate official corruption in the prison system, though its powers do not extend to privately run prisons (Rynne, 2001: 140). In Victoria the Auditor-General has been a leading critic of the operation of the prisons system and of conditions for prisoners, particularly as they are affected by privatization.

The role of inspection varies greatly among states, although inspectors have increasingly participated in inspections in each others' jurisdictions, introducing an element of cross-jurisdiction mutuality (Inspector of Custodial Services, 2002: 7). The state inspectorates are seeking to develop a national accreditation scheme for prisons, with the idea that failing prisons will lose accreditation with the regulator. This loss of accreditation would have no formal force, but would be a strong instrument of suasion to improve standards in a particular facility.

In New South Wales a statutory Inspector-General of Correctional Services investigates the activities of the Corrections Department, standing outside the line management arrangements and responding to complaints from prisoners (Crimes [Administration of Sentences Act] 1999, s. 213). The legislation incorporates a sunset provision such that the position expires after four years unless a positive review by the minister encourages the Parliament to re-legislate, recognizing the regulatory burden of the arrangements (ss. 222–3). The Act makes no provision for the statutory independence of the Inspector-General (IG) who requires the favour of the minister for the office to continue. Rather than using formal inspection, the IG makes much use of the department's internal records, making a confidential quarterly report to the Minister (Inspector-General for Correctional Services, 2001), and uses various means to try to overcome the department's occasional reluctance to supply information, but hitherto has never invoked higher-level sanctions such as referring the matter to the Director of Public Prosecutions or the Independent Commissioner Against Corruption (ICAC). However, the upper levels of the pyramid have not been used. The IG has uncovered high levels of non-compliance with operational rules and major weaknesses both in the management of individual facilities and in the management of the system as a whole (Inspector-General for Correctional Services, 2001: 32), but the IG has very limited powers beyond making recommendations, and no power to publish reports other than the annual report. Accordingly, suasion can only be backed up with naming and shaming once a year, and only in rather general terms.

Queensland uses inspectors to investigate specific incidents, at the discretion of the Chief Executive of the department. Where inspectors are appointed there must be at least two, of whom at least one must not be an employee of the department (Corrective Services Act 2000, s. 219), and inspectors' reports are not published (s. 223). In Western Australia the quid pro quo for legislative assent to the contracting out of prisons was the establishment of a statutory, independent inspectorate for custodial services generally (Prisons Act 1981, Part XA [added by Court Security and Custodial Services Act 1999]).The Western Australia Inspector of Custodial Services reports direct to parliament, rather than the minister (Harding, 2001: 319) and uses quite different mechanisms for collecting information from his NSW counterpart, relying more on formal requests for information, inspections, including announced, unannounced and follow-up inspections, and thematic reviews (Prisons Act 1981, s. 109T). Unannounced inspection is a sanction in itself and is deployed where there is reason to believe there is a crisis or imminent failure. The Western Australia inspector has little formal power to enforce recommendations. Departmental responses are usually prepared within about six weeks of a report, but full compliance with recommendations is not the norm.

2   Competition

About 15 per cent of the Australian prison population is held in privately operated prisons (Rynne, 2001: 131). The rules for treatment of prisoners are generally the same in publicly and privately run prisons but the forms and extent of contracting are varied. In 2001, the government of Western Australia entered into a Design, Build, Finance, Operate and Maintain contract with a private provider for a single facility, Acacia, which holds nearly 28 per cent of the state prison population. The Victoria government has been engaged in Build Operate Own Transfer contracts in respect of two facilities, holding more than 40 per cent of the prison population since 1997. By contrast New South Wales has let only a single facility, Junee, since April 1993 on Design, Construct Manage terms, holding less then 10 per cent of the population, and South Australia contracted in 1995 with a private provider simply to operate an existing facility holding less then 10 per cent of the prison population (Rynne, 2001: 133).

In Victoria, purchasing and contracting are the responsibility of the Director of Justice Policy while the regulatory role is played by the Office of the Correctional Services Commission (OCSC), both operating within the Department of Justice and answerable to ministers. Public prisons are operated by another division within the department known as CORE. The OCSC has no line management function in respect of CORE. Rather CORE reports directly to the Minister. A senior OCSC official said that while the data the office receives for public and private prisons were similar, deriving from a comprehensive incident reporting system, they paid more attention to the private prisons because this affected their performance payments. In addition to auditing the incident data, there was also an annual (in practice every two years) on-site check by OCSC. The hierarchy of sanctions for private prisons differs from that for public prisons, extending through advice and warnings, default notices and fines to the termination of the contract and the taking back of the prison into public operation. For example, a default notice was issued against the operator of Port Philip Men's Prison on 1998 (Rynne, 2001: 144–5). By contrast, CORE appear to have no 'shaming' mechanism, no capacity to fine and no mechanisms of external reporting other than to the minister.

Monitors of privately operated prisons are, in effect, dedicated regulators. They generally operate off site; in New South Wales the monitor was initially an on-site regulator in the contracted-out Junee facility, but was later moved off site (Rynne, 2001: 143). The monitor makes an annual report to the Commissioner, which is copied to the Inspector-General and incorporated into the Annual Report of the Commission in the form of a performance review (Crimes [Administration of Sentences] Act 1999, s. 242). In Victoria the OCSC has a general monitoring function but the Auditor-General has questioned whether the level of monitoring and reporting is adequate to promote effective accountability (Audit Victoria, 1999: para. 5.12, cited in Rynne, 2001: 144).

In the event that agreed standards and sufficient reliable performance information can be generated there is the potential for private and public providers to compete and for elements of cross-fertilization of best practice between public and private sector (Harding, 2001: 331–2). The OCSC in Victoria has attempted to develop comparative performance indicators for contracted out and public prisons such that the public prisons have new standards to meet (ibid.: 147). A senior official of the Auditor-General of Victoria's office was sceptical as to whether meaningful comparison over the medium-term performance of institutions was possible. The NSW Auditor-General incorporates a detailed assessment of the performance of the Department of Corrections, but in aggregate and ranked against the Australian national averages. Thus the competitive element is between states rather than between facilities (Auditor-General, 2001: 131–7). In NSW there has also been extensive learning between staff in the private Junee facility and the public sector, with most of Junee's initiatives in inmate management being later adopted by the public system as a whole (Harding, 2001: 333–4). So it may well be that metaphytic competition involves a hybrid of competition and mutuality, and that the competition is making the private and public providers more, rather than less, alike.

3. Higher education and university research: harnessing competition and mutuality to oversight?

3.1 OVERVIEW
Colin Scott and Christopher Hood

Even though prisons are often described as 'universities of crime', higher education and university research are different from the prison sector as an object of control in at least three ways. First, though universities have often been harnessed to state purposes of various kinds, including nationalism and state-building, social engineering (sometimes draconian, as with the transformation of China's universities into centres of revolutionary upheaval and the killing, imprisonment or rustication of many scholars in Mao's Cultural Revolution (Spence, 1999: 574–83)) and economic development, they are not institutions that are 'defining' at least to orthodox definitions of the state in the same way as is the administration of justice (see Rose, 1976). Second, in contrast to prisons, higher education and university-level research have traditionally been a domain of very high competition among the ambitious middle class, those seeking upward social mobility and scientists and scholars vying for prestige and discovery claims.

Third, as institutions that combine creativity and the production of new knowledge (sometimes of high political salience and sensitivity for governments and ruling regimes) with other more routine functions, this sector presents rather special issues for control. Like the medieval church in Europe, university academics in many countries successfully claimed autonomy from day-to-day oversight from the state in the nineteenth century, and academic freedom for themselves. Autonomy was interpreted to mean that control should emphasize mutuality and peer review. 'Academic freedom' was interpreted to mean not only an absence of official censorship over speech and publication, but in some versions that academic faculty should control all aspects of university governance. In most cases the idea was interpreted to mean terms and conditions for professors (or equivalent positions) that approached those associated with an independent judiciary – that is, permanent tenure after a period of probation, such that established academics could not be removed from their positions without exceptional cause (see UNESCO, 1997).

As with prisons, however, all the four primary forms of control that we identified in the first chapter can be observed in the case of higher education and university research, and Table 3.1 indicates some of the traditional ways those control forms applied. The structure of university governance in Europe, drawn from church and monastic models, as well as the larger 'invisible college' in which scientists and academics operated, heavily emphasized control by mutuality in the form of peer-group control over individuals (in the form of decision-making over publications, prizes, honours, promotion and discipline). That style is epitomized in Francis Cornford's (1908: 9–10) classic description of universities as structures designed on the principle of 'never allowing anyone to act without first consulting at least twenty other people

Table 3.1   *The four control modes operating in the world of higher education and university research*

Basic type of control	General example	Comment
Mutuality	Peer review of papers for publication, committee approval of proposals in faculties or departments	Often limited by tribalism and conventions of coexistence and mutual non-interference
Contrived randomness	Unpredictable connections from traditional conventions of moving on promotion and 'garbage-can' committee procedures	Condemned by managerialists and often weakened by overarching power cliques
Competition	Rivalry for prizes, discovery claims, budget shares, grant funding	Limited by career tenure conventions and safety nets
Oversight	Government reporting requirements; approval of curriculum and appointments in some countries	Traditionally limited by 'buffering' conventions and often formalistic

who are accustomed to regard him with well-founded suspicion'. Perhaps the purest form of mutuality is found where departments and other institutional units set and monitor their own standards, with peer esteem or shaming as the main mechanisms for monitoring and behaviour modification. But mutuality of another, albeit less face-to-face, kind can also be found within national and international scholarly communities and tribes, particularly in the peer-review system for assessing research and publications.

Competition also figured large as a control measure, as scientists battled in the race for discoveries, prizes and research grants, and as the best and the brightest vied for a tiny number of appointments and promotions (though conventions of academic tenure limited competition for those who made it into established positions to some degree). Randomness was often important too, to the extent that career progression traditionally often meant moving from one institution to another (for example in the UK and Germany), and that the identity of reviewers and decision-makers of various kinds, even within a single university, was not fully predictable. Indeed, Cohen, March and Olsen's (1972) famous 'garbage-can' model of apparently random decision-making (caused by a combination of fluid participation in decision-making, disputed objectives and uncertainty about relationship between means and ends) was largely founded on observation of university structures.

Oversight played a part as well, particularly in information collection by governments from universities, though traditional oversight structures seem to have varied substantially with state tradition. In those countries where universities were conceived as state establishments, often with explicitly state-building purposes (as in France and Germany), much of their operation ran according to civil service procedures, staff were employed on civil service contracts, and institution were subject to general administrative law courts and oversight through various forms of *tutelle*, including *ex ante* ministerial approval of appointments and budgets. But strong formal powers to direct higher education (HE) institutions were in many cases rarely deployed, and indeed the sporadic and uncertain deployment of those powers had elements of contrived randomness as a method of control. Moreover, even in those countries that adopted the civil service style of control, that approach was modified to allow for academic autonomy of the professoriat (following Germany's adoption of the 1810 Humboldtian model of the university as a set of autonomous chair-holders who combined teaching with research). By contrast, in those countries where universities were traditionally conceived as autonomous public bodies (as in the case of the UK and the Commonwealth countries) they functioned largely as self-governing bodies with limited outside oversight (and what there was tended to be of an *ex post* kind). But even in those cases, universities could be subjected to state regulation, and sometimes that regulation could be draconian, such as the legislation of 1854 and 1871 that swept away the *ancien régime* in England's oldest universities in the teeth of strong traditionalist objections.

In other cases again, notably Japan and the USA, universities were not only conceived as public or state institutions, but also could be constituted as private establishments – as in the case of Japan's private universities, many of which have traditionally been family businesses, with the university often functioning as the keystone of a larger family business conglomerate. The oversight of such organizations depends on the degree of financial leverage from government and other regulatory initiatives.

Many hybrids among the four basic control forms can be observed in the world of higher education and research, for instance in the mixture of oversight and competition with oversight. The oversight–mutuality hybrid is represented in those systems where quality is subject to overseers or auditors who are mainly drawn from the academic community (although the regulatees often perceive or portray this control as top-down oversight rather than peer review). A notable example is the USA system of accreditation of universities, a 'private governance' arrangement for quality control that dates from the 1880s. Accreditation bodies are non-governmental associations, but their decisions affect the eligibility of institutions for federal funding and student financial aid (Rhoades and Sporn, 2002: 359). Something similar was introduced into Japan during the US occupation after the Second World War (see Itoh, 2002: 10–11), though as we show later the Japanese accreditation system did not operate in practice like the US one. Even in Germany, once the epitome of the Humboldtian vision of the university as a community of autonomous professors, a mix of oversight and (relatively weak) mutuality developed in the 1990s in the form of new quality assurance mechanisms (including performance indicators and institutional profiles) set up by the German Conference of Rectors together with ministers from the *Länder*.

The world of higher education and university-level research, like that of prisons, has changed in several significant ways over the last generation. As with prisons, there has been a notable population expansion – of near-Malthusian dimensions, in the view of the many critics of this change – particularly in the numbers of students and staff, and to a lesser extent of institutions. The Malthusian analogy may be apt because in all cases in this study (except for oil-rich Norway), sharp increases in university participation rates have not been matched by increases in public funding, sharply reducing the public funding available per student and arguably creating new incentives for hard-pressed faculty to cut corners on quality. The population increase over the last generation is in many cases the latest chapter of a long-term process of university expansion encouraged by vote-seeking politicians and part-financed by the state, and it has been very noticeable in once-elitist university systems such as that of England, which have moved towards the US mass-education model, and away from earlier assumptions that all higher education and research establishments were of equal quality. Indeed, many students of higher education see significant changes in management and regulation linked to the financial and political consequences of 'massification' of higher education (see Schuetze and Slowey, 2002: 309).

As with prisons, too, student populations in many of the countries explored here have become notably more internationalized and less homogenous. And – arguably also as in prisons though in a different way – higher education and university research has been shaped by a broader set of information-age changes that have swept across the world in the past generation. Those changes are in part reflected in the growth of new service-sector and industrial processes that mimic, and in many cases have grown out of, or alongside, university research. Table 3.2 provides some summary indicators of the first two changes in workflow in this domain, showing in particular the scale of transformation in participation rates over only seven years, as well as showing some notable differences among the eight countries we are studying.

In contrast to the prison sector, there are clearer signs of an 'oversight explosion' in the world of higher education and research over the past generation. For several reasons, including ambitions to squeeze better value out of those public funds that are devoted to higher education (as shown in Table 3.2), governments in most European states and numerous other developed countries devised new mechanisms to oversee the quality and quantity of both teaching and research (see Brennan and Shah, 2000: 331). One strand of this process in Europe has been an intergovernmental attempt to create the basis for mutual recognition of degree qualifications, in the form of the 1999 Bologna Declaration on the European Higher Education Area (signed by 32 education ministers), which was designed to secure a measure of equivalence among graduate and undergraduate programmes. The 'Bologna process' is arguably as much about mutuality and competition as it is about oversight, but the European Network of Quality Assurance in Higher Education (ENQA) is a co-operative association of national agencies charged with promoting quality in higher education institutions and its objectives are to establish and spread best practice.

If many of the states included in this study witnessed a notable ratcheting up of external oversight systems that broadly fit the 'oversight explosion' hypothesis, that broad picture needs to be qualified in several ways (a summary is provided in Table 3.3). First, expansion and reshaping of oversight from government, though widespread, is not universal. The most notable exception is the case of the USA, which has seen no particular oversight explosion over the past generation, even though its university system is often taken as the 'gold standard' against which to benchmark other countries.

Table 3.2 Selected higher education indicators for eight countries 1988–95

Indicator Country	Public expenditure on tertiary education as % of total public expenditure		Rates of participation in tertiary education		Foreign students as % of all students[5]	Total number of HE institutions	Total number of students in HE
	1986[1]	1999[2]	1988[3]	1995[4]			
Australia	4.5	3.2	15.1	27[6]	12.6	44[7]	897k[8]
France	1.4	2.0	18.3	N/A	7.3	629[9]	1.71m[6]
Germany	2.0	2.3	19.1	27	8.2	363[10]	1.8m[11]
Japan	1.1	1.2	13.0	N/A	1.2	1292[12]	773k[13]
Netherlands	3.1	2.9	8.4	32	3.8[14]	63[15]	450k
Norway	2.0	4.2	14.1	25	3.2	39[16]	170k
UK	2.2	2.6	10	43	10.8	171[17]	2.12m[18]
USA	3.7	N/A	24.9	52	3.2	N/a	14.79m[19]

1 1988 figures calculated by multiplying shares of educational expenditure by sector (table P3) by public expenditure on education as a percentage of total public expenditure (table P2). Source: OECD Education at a Glance OECD Indicators (1992).

2 1999 figures. Source: OECD Education Indicators at a Glance 2002, table B3.1.

3 Ratio of the number of students of any age enrolled in university education to the number in the population in the normal age range for such programmes for 1988. Source: OECD Education at a Glance Indicators (1992), table P15.

4 1995 figures calculated by OECD as net entry rate to university level education for all ages. OECD Education at a Glance 1997, table C4.2. (except Australia).

5 OECD, Education at a Glance 2000, table C5.1.

6 1999 figures for percentage of 15–24 year olds in tertiary education. Source: Australian Bureau of Statistics Press Release 6272.0 Participation in Education, Australia (2000).

7 37 public universities, two private universities and five other higher education institutions. Source: AVCC.

8   2002 figures.

9   87 universities, 90 technology universities, 28 teacher training colleges (for non-academic teachers), 233 engineering schools, 18 private higher education institutions, 4 Écoles normales supérieures, 269 Écoles de commerce. (These figures exclude 1076 'autres'.) *Source*: Ministère de la jeunesse, de l'éducation et de la recherché, 2003.

10 2000 figures. Source: Federal Ministry of Education and Research 2002. Grund- und Strukturdaten 2001/2002; including 41 academies for the public sector.

11 Hospital and kindergarten nurses are not included; further the famous system of dual (on-the-job plus school) vocational training leads to relatively low HE student enrolment.

12 671 universities, 559 junior colleges, and 62 colleges of technology. 74.2% of the institutions and 74.6% of the students are in the private sector. All figures are from Foreign Press Centre (2004).

13 257 000 undergraduates, 216 000 graduate students, 279 000 junior college students and 21 000 students at colleges of technology. All figures are from Foreign Press Centre (2004).

14 *Source*: *Bison Monitor*, 2002: 44.

15 13 universities and about 50 higher professional education institutions (*hogescholen*). The former offer three-year bachelor and one–two-year master programmes, the latter mainly offer four-year bachelor programmess.

16 The public system comprises four universities, six specialized university institutions, two national institutes of art and 26 university state colleges. In addition there is one major private specialized university institution, a business school.

17 Universities and colleges of higher education. *Source*: Universities UK. There is one private university, the remainder are 'public'.

18 2001–02 figures. *Source*: HESA.

19 1999 figures.

Table 3.3 The four control modes compared for higher education in eight countries

Control form	USA	Japan	France	Germany	Netherlands	Norway	Australia	UK
Oversight	Low	Medium, especially over chartering/accreditation	Medium, especially over funds, appointments, etc.	Medium, but growing	Medium	Medium	Medium, chiefly over reporting	Medium with recent growth, but subject to review
Mutuality	Medium	High	High, especially over research	High, but decreasing	High, esp. over assessment	High	High, especially over quality assurance	Medium
Competition	High, central control mechanism, esp. through competition for fees from students and research funds	Increasing, e.g. for government funding	Low, but growing, esp. over recruitment of students and research funds	Low but increasing through competition for students (linked to league tables) and research funds	Low but increasing through league tables and competition for funding	Low	Medium, but increasing over student numbers and research funds	Medium and growing, especially over research funds and league tables
Contrived randomness	Low, some random elements	Low	Low	Low	Low	Low	Low, arises through sporadic interventions of state regulators, e.g. auditors	Medium through unpredictable payoffs for performance in teaching and research reviews

Second, oversight has in most cases been reshaped rather than expanded *simpliciter*, and governments and their agencies tend to shy away from the use of directive power, preferring indirect control in the form of information and incentives. Brennan and Shah (2000: 336) argue that the general trend has been towards the development of arm's-length oversight to accompany a loosening of direct controls over universities by government (at least for those countries with a tradition of treating universities as state organizations). This argument is a version of the 'mirror image hypothesis' put forward by Hood et al. (1999), which suggests that the price of loosening of one form of control in the public sector tends to be the development or imposition of another. For example, the introduction of a new system of quality assurance auditing for Australian universities has been accompanied by pressures to reduce the extent of mandatory reporting of information to the education ministry. In a number of European systems the increasing effects of competition as an instrument of control have been accompanied by a relaxation over centralized public service controls in respect of funding and appointments.

Third, the reshaping and expansion of oversight has been mixed with other forms of control, and arguably any effectiveness that the 'oversight explosion' has had in this domain can be attributed to that hybridity. In contrast to the general picture for prisons, competition in this sector has altered in a number of ways over a generation. In one sense the expansion of universities at a rate that far exceeds the general rate of population increase has reduced the overall competition for student places, faculty positions and professorships, but that change has been accompanied by a corresponding increase in 'positional competition' (that is, rivalry for what are considered to be the top places and posts). Moreover, as Table 3.2 shows, that competition has become increasingly international – at least for parts of the student body – and those university systems that have moved directly to charging fees for students and developing programmes for which fee levels are not regulated by government (for example because they attract foreign or postgraduate students or both) have become more susceptible to control through competition for students. The European Union's (EU's) funding programmes for supporting student exchanges within the EU, such as ERASMUS and SOCRATES, also enhance the potential for mobility of students and thus help to make EU universities more susceptible to control through competition for students.

Indeed, such competition has produced the basis for a new oversight-competition hybrid in the form of competitive rating by official overseers. And that official competitive rating process is mirrored or complemented by a trend towards media-produced league table ratings of universities in several countries (see Brennan and Savage, 2002: 60). The ratings produced by *Der Spiegel* in Germany, by the *Asian Wall Street Journal* and the *Financial Times* (for business schools) are interesting as a potential form of control by competition because they compare institutions and/or subject areas on an international basis. But how influential these media-generated ratings are is a matter of dispute, and HE institutions that rate badly on such rankings and ratings tend to be heavily critical of these exercises, while those who do well quote heavily, if selectively, from the rankings. Brennan and Savage (2002) argue that they fill a gap in control that neither universities nor official overseers are able to fill but, as with all exercises in control by competition, effectiveness depends on the system operating in a range below the point of mutual sabotage (or worse) by institutions or individuals desperate to get the edge over their rivals. As yet we have seen only limited signs of sabotage and 'dirty tricks', but any such system potentially invites such a response.

Part of the reason why competition may have stayed at the sub-sabotage level may be that the growth in oversight laced with competition has also been accompanied by the development of new forms of mutuality, and extra reliance on some established forms. The partial decline of the Humboldtian model of autonomous chairs in countries like Germany and Norway has been paralleled by the development of new forms of mutuality at subject-specific and cross-discipline levels, for example with peer-group decision-making in departments partially replacing the autonomous-chair model. In some cases, too, mutuality exercised through associations of university heads (rectors, vice-Chancellors etc.) seems to have played a role in shaping the sector as a whole, with national and international groupings of universities (such as the Group of 8 in Australia or Universitas 21 at the international level) achieving prominence as attempts to build cartel-like structures. Moreover, the increasing pressure for rating of all kinds (of papers for publication, research applications, fellowships and the like) has increased the demands on the peer-rating system to the point where many argue it is seriously distorted and in crisis.

Moreover, some of the new oversight regimes, such as those applying to quality assurance in Australia and the Netherlands, work by stimulating a type of mutuality in the form of dialogues within institutions to define their objectives and standards. As with all regulation demanding production of mission statements and institutional codes, the effect may depends on the culture of the institutions involved, and such cultures tend to be varied and variable. Some such regulation produces double-decker oversight systems and some produces oversight-mutuality mixes. Several observers have claimed, often on the basis of rather casual evidence, that the new forms of official oversight have tended to produce a pattern of double-decker oversight, strengthening the 'top' and central units of higher education at the expense of autonomous chairs and mutuality-based control in departments, thus fostering new managerial cultures and capacities (Brennan and Shah, 2000: 346–7). But it is hard to assess how far mutuality-based approaches, old and new, have really been displaced by the new managerial language, and the testimony of interviewees with an axe to grind has to be treated with care.

Appropriately, perhaps, randomness is the element of control that can be considered as the joker in the pack of changing controls over universities. Some elements of randomness may have weakened in systems like the UK with the decline of the traditional convention that academics moved from one institution to another to gain promotion, but that pattern is far from universal. Moreover, there are counter-trends that may well serve to foster rather than to weaken randomness as a form of control. One of those counter-trends is the growing internationalization and 'virtualization' (through information technology) of research communities, which can serve to increase the incidence of chance encounters, tripwires and unpredictable refereeing. A second is the widespread perception by middle managers and academics, particularly within the UK and the Australian systems, of performance indicators and league table regimes as quasi-lotteries (because of the difficulty of predicting weightings, scoring decisions and funding outcomes in a system where the measures are of doubtful reliability and validity and the use made of the measures is heavily dependent on the uncertainties of politics). A third is the tendency of recurring reform initiatives unintentionally to maintain, or even increase, rather than diminish the garbage-can quality of university decision-making owing to changing participation in key committees and offices and variable and disputed goals. Our contributors tended in the main to pay remarkably little attention to control by randomness, often dismissing it summarily as unimportant, perhaps because public administration scholars tend to be programmed to equate control with oversight. But it seems at least premature, as well as philosophically and linguistically problematic, to consign the garbage-can form of control to the dustbin of history.

3.2 THE USA: LITTLE OVERSIGHT, NO EXPLOSION
B. Guy Peters

The USA offers a model of higher education that is both very large (see Table 3.2) and highly diverse. A central characteristic of the governance regime is the extent to which control is exerted through competition for funds and students. Mutuality functions in a not dissimilar way to that of other systems in developing and monitoring teaching and research, but mutuality is commonly tempered by the pressures of competition. Official government oversight has played a smaller role in the controls exercised over HE institutions than applies to most of the countries in this study, and little change in this pattern is evident in recent years.

1 Oversight

The scale and importance of higher education for the American economy and society might be expected to produce a heavy regulatory involvement by government, but oversight through the public sector is not the primary instrument used for controlling the sector and is much less severe than that applying to other advanced democracies (Ikenberry and Hartle, 2000). The regulatory role of the federal government is relatively minor, although any time there are large amounts of money handed out (Titles IV and VI of the Higher Education Act of 1965) some controls naturally follow. The state governments are more heavily involved in regulation of higher education, but even they face several constraints on their capacity to regulate as directly as they, and some of their constituents, might like. The dominant control pattern found in higher education is self-regulation and the use of mutuality and peer review, along with professional values (see Dill, 2001).

The most important use of oversight over university teaching and research comes from state governments that provide significant financial resources to colleges and universities. In exchange for those resources public universities have to accept regulation. These controls vary widely from state to state, both in their extent and their impact on the core functions of universities, and the extent of regulation is to some extent a function of the level of politicization of the university systems. In some states (over a dozen) some or all of the state boards of higher education are elected, introducing perhaps greater willingness (and need) to intervene.

Although state legislatures do exercise oversight over universities, it is mediated through structures such as boards of regents that are responsible for supervising individual institutions or the entire state system of higher education. The powers and responsibilities of these organizations vary widely from state to state, as do their selection and composition, but tend to be at least partially captured by the universities and often serve as advocates for greater resources for the universities rather than stern controllers of the institutions. Boards of regents may, however, exercise more direct oversight over teaching and research, but it is generally conducted through, or at least influenced by, peer review.

So far the analysis has focused on oversight, but for private universities (and public ones to some extent), the involvement of the private sector may be as pervasive and as limiting. This is very evident in some small, religiously based institutions where the sponsoring organization often influences curriculum and personnel. That influence is to some degree mitigated by the power of accreditation bodies and the desire of most institutions to maintain their accreditation. Even if there is not a religious base to the attempts of the private sector to exercise some control over universities, the pervasiveness of a private sector conception of what constitutes good, and particularly useful, education may push colleges and universities in directions they might not go on their own.

The level of government oversight, especially by the federal government, is greatest in the ancillary aspects of higher education. That is, the federal government imposes a number of controls on institutions of higher education (and all other organizations receiving federal funding) in areas such as equal employment opportunity, gender equality in athletic funding, access for the disabled, privacy of student records, reporting of crime statistics, the use of human subjects in research, and several other areas of social life in higher education (Freeland and Hartle, 2001). These federal regulations are all worthy programmes for addressing social issues but for the most part they do not go to the heart of educational issues such as teaching and research. State governments also have some analogous regulations, including some that address less significant social issues, for example forbidding using state funds for purchasing alcoholic beverages.

2 Competition

The primary source of control within higher education is competition, and that competition is exercised across the sector, as well as within universities. This competition is manifested in a number of different ways. For example, the quality of teaching is controlled through internal competition among departments (and among individual academics seeking salary raises on the basis of their teaching assessments), as well as through competition among institutions for high-quality students. Universities and colleges invest heavily in the recruitment of National Merit Scholars and other outstanding students, and have even been known to go so far as to hack into each other's computer systems to try to 'win' in this competition.

As noted earlier, the US higher education system is highly diverse as well as large. As shown in Table 3.3, public higher education accounts for the majority of students, but nearly a quarter of students attend private institutions. And within the private sector there is also marked diversity, with institutions ranging from secular research universities (Yale, Stanford) through religiously related research universities (Georgetown, Emory) to small institutions closely affiliated with religious bodies of almost all denominations. American higher education is perhaps unique among the industrialized democracies in having some excellent private undergraduate institutions ('liberal arts colleges') that rival the major research universities in their academic standards and student quality.

In the public sector there is also a good deal of internal variation, comprising some of the most important research universities (Michigan, Wisconsin), as well as small 'third-tier' institutions providing only limited undergraduate education. All 50 states and the District of Columbia have some involvement in providing higher education, and within those states there may be different systems. For example, in California there are marked differences between the University of California system (some 10 institutions) and the California State system (another 21 institutions). But it is not only the states that are involved. Cities and counties also sponsor higher education for their own residents (City University of New York), and the federal government also directly provides some limited higher education on its own, including the four service academies and Gallaudet College for the Deaf.

Both internally and externally information is an important mechanism for making competition function effectively. Externally, there are annual ratings of colleges on the quality of undergraduate programs that prospective students use when making their choices. These ratings have no official standing but they are increasingly used in the process of selection. The colleges supplement this information with extensive advertising about their own virtues. Similarly, within individual colleges and universities the results of teaching surveys are available to students and affect course enrolments, which in turn affects resource allocation to departments. But little, if any, of this teaching quality information is made available to official overseers such as boards of regents.

Competition is also important for controlling research quality, particularly through the allocation of external research funds. This competition is personal, in that it involves individual academics seeking to advance their careers, but it is also institutional as universities attempt to augment their budgets through overheads on grants (federal grants typically pay 40 to 50 per cent of overheads), and also to develop strong research profiles to attract faculty and graduate students. More precisely, the mechanism combines mutuality – the peer review of funding proposals – with competition to control quality.

As applies to institutional quality in general, publicity is important in external competition over research at the departmental and institutional level. The National Research Council and the American Council on Higher Education publish departmental rankings that figure heavily in the decisions of prospective faculty and graduate students, and may also influence internal allocation of resources within universities. The various disciplines and sub-disciplines also generate their own rankings of programs, with each department seeking plausible ranking methods that will result in a favourable ranking for itself.

As implied above, competition also shapes faculty recruitment and retention, because departments compete with other institutions bidding for the best talent. The strong academic marketplace controls administrators as much or more than academics, many of whom benefit from having their pay and perquisites bid up. But the market is to some extent collaborative as well as competitive: for example, there is substantial information-sharing on the going pay rates for beginning assistant professors.

Control through mutuality functions in internal control over faculty, most notably in annual pay decisions. After departmental or college allocations, individual allocations are made largely on the basis of internal departmental reviews. This particular control combines competition with mutuality, given that the individual faculty members are in competition with each other over the limited amount of funds, but the allocation of funds is strongly influenced, if not always directly decided, by some peer-review mechanism.

3 Mutuality

Mutuality, especially through peer review, is a pervasive form of control in academic life, and not just in control of publication. Perhaps the most important application of control through mutuality is the way it shapes academic careers through the tenure process. The typical university provides beginning assistant professors six years in untenured positions, after which a decision will be made on whether they will be given permanent positions. That decision is largely one for faculty members, and deans, provosts and presidents rarely go against the decisions of their faculty. Indeed, mutuality extends beyond the bounds of the individual institution and, as is increasingly true in other settings, external referees from across the discipline play a significant part in the process.

Accreditation is another major instrument of control by mutuality, this time functioning externally and regulating general university quality. Accreditation organizations are organized regionally, operating as agents of the university system as a whole. Accreditation teams use extensive documentation and on-site visits to ensure that the institutions for which they are responsible meet basic standards of quality, and also make recommendations for improvement that universities take seriously. Accreditation is important because other institutions may not accept degrees from non-accredited institutions when admitting graduate students or accept transfer credits if a student moves from one institution to another. As well as ensuring quality, accreditation is used as a means of self-analysis on the part of the institutions involved

4 Contrived Randomness

There seems to be relatively little use of this form of control in higher education. The main example is the random auditing of grantees by government agencies such as the National Science Foundation and the National Institutes of Health. These audits rarely deal with research quality, which is controlled by competition and peer review, but rather with the appropriate use of funds.

The justification of overhead rates has been of particular interest to auditors over the past several years, after several major universities were caught including extremely dubious expenditures (such as maintenance of the university president's 'yacht') in their overhead calculations. At the state level state government audit organizations perform the same type of random detailed auditing of the use of public funds, although some states do not appropriate money on a line-item basis, making auditing more problematic.

5 Conclusions

Why has American higher education been able to escape centralized regulation and to control itself primarily through self-regulation and competition? Part of the answer is that this is characteristic of many aspects of American political life, with self-regulation being a common approach to the control of policy sectors. Indeed, it would be surprising if there were more official oversight. Further, the combination of federalism and multiple public providers means that potentially intrusive regulators have to consider what neighbouring states (or the private sector) are doing before acting in a draconian fashion. Finally, following the experiences of the McCarthy period in the 1950s, appeals for limiting official oversight in the name of academic freedom have more weight than might otherwise be expected, and can be used to deflect intrusions by state legislatures.

Another answer is that higher education institutions are much less dependent on the government than in other countries. The federal government provides a significant amount of money for higher education (almost $24 billion in 2000), but that is a small share of total spending on higher education. The states are the primary government funders of higher education ($45.7 billion in 2000) but that is still only 23 per cent of total spending on higher education. Further, most public institutions of any consequence have developed endowment funds or research foundations that are not controlled as closely by state laws and regulations, thus providing them the means of doing those things that state legislatures would not fund, and might disapprove of more generally. (In 2000, total endowments in colleges and universities were $194 billion [Digest of Educational Statistics, 2001].) Also, many state institutions receive significant tuition income that also is less controlled than are appropriations, even if the legislature attempts to control the level of tuition fees charged.

It follows that it is hard to overstate the importance of competition in checking what might otherwise be pressures for audit explosions. So long as there are multiple institutions with multiple modes of funding and different relationships to the public sector, any all-encompassing oversight will be difficult to sustain. As noted, even state governments find such oversight more difficult for state universities than might be expected, in part because of the 'Tiebout competition' to which they perceive themselves to be exposed.

3.3   JAPAN: ADAPTING THE AMERICAN MODEL TO CENTRALIZED OVERSIGHT
Katsyua Hirose

The Japanese higher education system is smaller than that of the USA in numbers of students, but perhaps even more diverse in terms of institutional types and with a majority of private institutions, as shown in Table 3.2. Notwithstanding similarities between the two regimes, Japan's is much more dependent on centralized oversight of HE institutions, and recent ratcheting of competitive pressures has not done much to diminish this.

National (public) HE institutions are under the general oversight of the Education Minister. Government control of national universities works basically by bureaucratic direction, and the legal basis of the government control of national universities is different from that of government regulation of private universities. Local governments are permitted by law to establish higher education institutions and there are 74 universities set up on this basis. But local government in Japan has little authority to regulate higher education, and local public institutions are treated in a similar way to private institutions under the national legislative framework.

It has been argued that the reforms to the Japanese system of the 1990s were largely directed at addressing the unsatisfactory features of the Americanized post-war system (Itoh, 2002). Reforms began with the establishment of a University Council in 1987, and since the council's influential report of 1991, various reform measures comprising 'competition and evaluation' have been proposed and developed. At the time of writing, a major change of organizational status of national universities is in preparation, with plans to reorganize all national universities into university corporations by 2004, and new professional schools at the graduate level with compulsory specialized third party evaluation. Hence for the purposes of this analysis, the control of higher education in the late 1980s can be taken as comprising the 'traditional system' and the starting point for later changes.

1   Oversight

The establishment of a national university requires the amendment of the National School Act and the establishment of a faculty at a national university is carried out by Cabinet order. By contrast, establishment of a private university or a local public university requires a charter from the Education Minister.

But the standard against which any proposed institution is judged for suitability is contained in a single Education Ministry order, and since the educational reforms of 1947 the assessment body for both national and private institutions has been the University Establishment Council (UEC).

The 1947 reform was strongly influenced by US Occupation Forces and aimed at a US-type system of higher education under which a combination of loose government chartering and strict voluntary accreditation would secure the quality of higher education while maintaining free entrance and competition in the sector. So the establishment of a reliable accreditation body independent of government was thought to be the key to successful reform. The Japan University Accreditation Association (JUAA) was established in 1947 as a voluntary accreditation body comprising the major universities. It has become conventional for half the members of the UEC to be selected by the recommendation of JUAA and it was intended that academic peers would judge all higher education institutions against the same chartering standard.

In practice, the dual system of compulsory chartering by government and voluntary accreditation by private associations never functioned according to this vision. The relationship between the chartering standard and accreditation standard was not clearly defined and as a result, while the JUAA adopted its first accreditation standard, the same standard was adopted as the chartering standard. Because of the alignment of chartering and accreditation standards the JUAA's role as an independent accreditation body became almost irrelevant, playing a very limited role, while the JUAA has some significance as an electing body of half of the members of the chartering body.

Under this system of government control of entrants to the sector through chartering, Japan's higher education was changed from small-scale elite education to mass education for almost half the young generation. In the relative size of higher education and the large share of private institutions, Japan resembles the USA, but strong government oversight at the establishment stage sharply differs from the American model. The chartering standard stipulates the basic framework of curriculum, organization of teaching staff, school facilities including land, building and size of libraries. Investigation by the UEC, with which the Education Minister had to consult before granting a charter, normally lasted for two years, examining the purpose of the establishment, the suitability of its proposed curriculum and the appropriateness of the proposed organization organization of teaching staff and facilities. It was a classic type of *ex ante* oversight.

After graduation of the first students (four years for most subjects and six years for medicine and dentistry), the faculty had autonomy to modify each teaching subject and teaching staff. But even then the framework of the curriculum and credits required for graduation in each subject might not be changed because these were written into the official chartering standard. The

requirement of general as well as specialized education was a legal requirement for any higher education institution, and could not be modified without
change to the official standard.

Government oversight of national universities was completely different
from that of local public and private institutions. National universities were
branches of the Education Ministry, which meant they were positioned in the
ministerial hierarchy, under the general direction of the Education Minister
and subject to the administrative management and financial audit applying to
all central government organizations. Wages and working conditions of teaching and administrative staff were set uniformly as for civil servants, though the
autonomy of the faculty over appointment of teaching staff was established by
law. Administrative staff of national universities were general administrative
staff of the Education Ministry, and personnel management of such staff was
carried out by the ministry.

Apart from general administrative oversight, national universities were
subject to ministerial oversight to keep them to the chartering standard, a type
of regulatory oversight that applied to private institutions. Selective on-site
inspection was the most visible tool of this type of oversight, but given that
most inspectors were university academics commissioned by the ministry into
account, mutuality also played a strong part in this system of control.

2   Mutuality

After the 1947 Education reform and even after the big expansion of higher
education, universities opposed fundamental change. Before the Second
World War universities were organized on lines that followed the nineteenth-
century German university model. This system was maintained and in national
universities and many private universities it was characterized by faculty
autonomy over curriculum, degrees and the appointment and promotion of
academic staff.

Apart from items of the chartering standard that were subject to policy
discretion, most of the academic requirements were judged by specialists from
the relevant field during the investigation process preceding the granting of
charters. As mentioned above, half the UEC's members were selected on the
recommendation of the JUAA, a voluntary association of universities, and
since almost all of those recommended persons were university academics, the
relational distance between the regulator and the regulatee in the chartering
process was low.

Both day-to-day operations and more substantial decisions over research
and teaching were carried out autonomously by faculties in most universities,
and mutuality was the basic mode of organizational behaviour. Indeed, apart
from regulation over entry into the sector by the Education Ministry and the

chartering authority, the higher education sector in Japan was basically controlled by mutuality.

3 Competition

Japanese universities and colleges traditionally compete for the best students, external research funding and government subsidies. But competition was not necessarily used as a deliberate tool of government control. Indeed, towards the end of the era of 'traditional' controls in the mid-1980s, the government policy of restricting the grant of new university charters during a period when the number of 18-year-olds in the population was steadily increasing, effectively limited the competitive pressure on the existing institutions to get good students.

Competition in the way government funds were allocated also seemed to play only a limited role as a tool of control in the traditional period. The share of annual budget of each national university relative to the total amount of public money spent on national universities as a whole was fixed rather than competitive. Financial support for private institutions was mainly on a formula-funding basis according to the number of students, but the amount of funds distributed through truly competitive processes was limited at that time.

4 Randomness

Contrived randomness has rarely been used as a conscious instrument of control here, but random selection of institutions to be visited by inspectors does provide a rare example. Moreover, the movement of staff around the network and in particular the positioning of individuals from outside the particular university concerned into key administrative posts at national universities was certainly used as a tool to prevent the capture of administrative staff by autonomous faculty in each university.

5 Recent Developments

The University Council, set up in 1987 to implement reform measures for the higher education system, has subsequently published more than a dozen reports on reform, many of which have been implemented during the last decade. While the first phase of the reform has already produced some results, many other reform measures are still to be implemented at the time of writing and there is still some uncertainty over the exact direction of those reforms.

(a) Competition

The main theme of the reform measures proposed by the University Council is the use of competition for control. The council's 1991 report, 'Improvement of University Education', proposed simplification of the university chartering standard to widen the freedom of universities to change their curricula and teaching staff organization. The report stated that given the rigid curriculum stipulated in the then existing chartering standard it was impossible for any university to adopt a distinctive curriculum. The rigid curriculum also made for rigidity in teaching staff organization and prevented effective competition among universities.

Accordingly, the Education Ministry simplified the chartering standard in 1991 and according to the Ministry almost all universities had modified their curricula by 1997. Following the simplification of the chartering standard, the Ministry also shortened the length of the investigation involved in the chartering process from two years to eight months for establishment of an institution or faculty, and from eight months to three for the establishment of a department. The resulting chartering boom is still going on, with the number of faculties established per year having risen from about 13 in the early 1990s to about 30 after 2000, and as for departments the figure has risen from about 10 to more than 60 each year.

Competition has been gradually introduced into the allocation process of government funding for research and education. For national universities, the bottom-up appropriation based on the chair system was abandoned, and the share of competitive funding in the total subsidies given to private universities has been rising significantly. For example, in the late 1990s substantial funds for development of information technology (IT) facilities were given to private universities with each allocation decided by competition among project proposals rather than by reference to student numbers. And under 'The 21st century COE plan', the Education Ministry stated that it intended to concentrate research funding in 50 institutions of excellence, judged by competitive applications. At the time of writing, there are many other public research funds that can be given to researchers or research projects at institutions not among the 50 and that made responses from higher education sector to the COE scheme less strong than expected.

Making national universities into autonomous corporate bodies separate from the organization of the Education Ministry is another way of promoting competition among universities, since it allows them to manage themselves with greater flexibility. Moreover, converting traditional budgetary appropriations into block grants is intended to give the reorganized national universities more discretion over how to spend their funds. At the time of writing these plans are still being developed but, since the association of national universities has already accepted the basic content of the reform, it seems likely that the proposed reforms will go through.

(b)   Oversight

The simplification of the chartering standard and shortening of investigation time means a clear decrease of *ex ante* oversight, giving the whole of higher education more freedom to organize research and teaching. But it was accompanied by more *ex post* oversight through evaluation of research and education in universities. Since 1991 universities have been obliged to conduct self-monitoring and self-evaluation and to publish the results. More than 92 per cent of the universities had conducted self-evaluation at least once by 2001, and 82 per cent of them published the results.

While the 1991 chartering standard only required self-evaluation, the University Council in its 1998 report proposed obligatory third-party evaluation for all universities. It argued that individualization of universities and continuous improvement of education and research required a plural evaluation system consisting of three elements (self-monitoring and self-evaluation, third-party evaluation and the utilization of the results of third-party evaluation in distribution of public funds for research and teaching. It proposed that compulsory third-party evaluation for all universities should take two forms, an evaluation of each institution as a whole that should come into operation quickly, and evaluation of each subject or discipline that would be phased in more gradually.

The report proposed a scheme for establishing reliable third-party evaluators by creating a government qualification for university evaluators, or by the establishment of an evaluation body by government itself. As the first 'third-party' institution to conduct institutional evaluation, the National Institution for Academic Degrees (NIAD), a branch of the Education Ministry, was reorganized in 2000 to conduct institutional evaluation of national universities.

A more concrete proposal for a plural evaluation emerged in 2002 from the University Subgroup of the National Education Council, and third-party evaluation is clearly now regarded as a tool of *ex post* oversight of universities by government. Legislation to oblige universities periodically to be evaluated by third-party evaluators was passed in 2002 and the government proposed to set up a new National University Evaluation Commission to conduct third-party evaluations of the new breed of semi-independent national universities.

(c)   The Attack on Mutuality

One interesting thing about the 2002 National Education Council Report proposing a concrete plural third-party evaluation system is that the word 'accreditation' cannot be found in it (though that word appeared in an earlier draft of the report). In response, the JUAA, the voluntary accreditation body of universities, claimed that the avoidance of the word 'accreditation' showed the government's intention to undermine voluntary self-regulation by universities and to place government in the position of the main overseer of higher education. At the time of writing it is reported that the Education Ministry is asking some private university associations to establish a new 'third-party evaluator' apart from the existing JUAA, with the clear intention of increasing the relational distance between universities and third-party evaluators.

6 Conclusion

In the recent development of higher education reform there is no indication of significant change in the use of randomness as a tool of control, but recent development of higher education reform in Japan shows (a) more stress on competition and *ex post* control, (b) the possibility of strengthening the Education Ministry's oversight through the linkage of *ex post* control with resource allocation and (c) increasing external pressure and widening of relational distance between higher education institutions and their overseers. The institutional setting of Japan's higher education sector as a mixture of national, local public and private institutions may have played some role in permitting government-led reforms, since it is difficult for the diverse players to speak with a single voice, and the Education Ministry could develop reform measures salami-style, by targeting only one segment of the sector at a time and thus limiting opposition.

3.4 FRANCE: MUTUALITY AND OVERSIGHT IN TENSION?
Nicole de Montricher

Control within the French system of higher education is largely built on mutuality both for teaching and research. However, some central oversight has always been a significant factor, particularly linked to financial control. After the student movement of May 1968, the *loi Fauré* introduced some autonomy at the university level over administrative, budgetary and pedagogical decisions. A second step towards greater university autonomy was initiated by legislation in 1984. However, within the reformed system the mutuality-based controls inside institutions have been changed through centralization of executive authority within universities, challenging the traditional autonomy of faculties and departments. Competition-based controls have had only a limited role in the reforms.

Higher education in France is a public service separated into three branches. One branch includes the highly selective institution of the *Grandes*

Écoles, which are controlled by the *grands corps* which their students enter. Because most of these were created during the Revolution to train high civil servants and teachers (the *École des Mines* was created in 1783, the *École Polytechnique* in 1794, and *École Normale Supérieure* in 1794), they symbolize republican ideals of equality (Attali, 1998). The second branch is research, substantially carried out within specialist research organizations, with the *Centre National de la Recherche Scientifique* (CNRS) in charge of research in general and other institutions in charge of research in specific fields. These organizations were endowed with funds of their own and given discretion over their staffing arrangements. Control is dominated by mutuality, especially peer review. The third branch is the university system. It is responsible for the provision of mass education and it may neither be selective nor charge fees.

The focus of this analysis is on the university system, which has long been isolated from external pressures because it is a public service subjected by law to principles of uniformity. The HE mission includes a monopoly on the granting of national diplomas, and when mass education became an issue after the Second World War, the geographical diffusion of universities was planned. The traditional concept of the university system excludes market constraints and local variation, because centralization is designed to generate a uniform system of higher education aimed at the construction of equal opportunity for employment.

1   Oversight

The HE sector is minutely regulated and monitored by the Ministry in charge of Education, but the oversight is heavily tinged with mutuality. Since 1965, the *Inspection générale de l'administration de l'éducation nationale* (IGAEN) has scrutinized the management of universities from a legalistic perspective. However, in conformity with the French conception of *inspections générales*, reports are not public. They are transmitted to the Minister whose decision to follow up on the results is discretionary, but top-down change is not viewed as legitimate because trust and mutuality are valued in the academic community.

Rule-making and control are centralized in various agencies within the Ministry but some of them can be classed as 'buffer organizations' because they are staffed by representatives of the academic community. Recognition of national diplomas and procedures for appointing academic staff are among the responsibilities of these buffer agencies, and this mutuality–oversight system of control was not disrupted by the 1984 law (which was aimed at creating co-ordinative authority within universities while accreditations of teachers and programmes remained centralized).

In 1984, the policy was to develop authority at the head of each institution, to balance the hierarchical power of the central state bureaucracy and challenge the power of tenured academics. Accordingly, the law provided for changes in the internal management, mainly through new participatory decision-making forums (*Conseil d'administration, Conseil scientifique, Conseil des études et de la vie universitaire*). Yet even in 2002, fragmented university governance structures were still common with the implicit agreement of top bureaucrats who negotiate directly with partners in academic organizations.

Resources remain under the control of the Minister and, despite 'one-line' budgets, the oversight type of regulation is still dominant. University boards of directors have discretionary authority over no more than 40 per cent of the funds, the major part being directly decided at national government level (salaries, fellowships, research funds, etc.). In 2002, the funding was still mostly formula driven under rules set up from the centre, mainly linked to student numbers. But some institutional authority was developing within universities and during the 1990s professional managers began to appear at university level and a pattern was emerging of professional administrators implementing national regulations through exchange of information among themselves. This mode of standard setting is aimed at monitoring individual behaviour within universities to augment the power of managers vis-à-vis the traditional power of the academics.

These developments are occurring through two particular routes. First, although they are not obliged to do so, most universities are adopting common computer systems (Guilhot, 2000). This voluntary change in behaviour is driven by the desire of university managers to bring their budgets under control by obtaining more centralized information at the university level, particularly to compare units with one another. Second the external oversight of the *Cour des Comptes* is becoming more intensive and while its mission is limited to legality, it has tended to shift from simple fiscal regularity to value-for-money issues and the 'remarks' of the *Cour des Comptes* and the *chambres régionales* have had the effect of strengthening university management.

Oversight of teaching activity emphasizes input measures. Standards are set according to agreements between top civil servants and academics appointed as experts at the national level. At the local level, decisions are taken in a collegial mode among peers within disciplinary structures. Traditionally central information was scarce and each department collected data in its own way. Teaching was not overseen, on the grounds that teachers were subject to stringent tests when they entered the civil service. Afterwards they lived under the protection of 'academic freedom' till the end of their career. Immediate oversight was left to the *recteur chancelier des universités*, who were often teachers well versed in the ways academics work and (in the classic style of the French *préfets*) tended to exercise their powers with ambiguity, making compromises to maintain good relations. But inside universities teaching activity is increasingly coming under surveillance, particularly through the computer systems that structure academic activity. This development is not compulsory, but has been frequently adopted and is much favoured by university managers (and sometimes resented by academics) because it creates central information about academic activity and performance.

Outside universities, agencies in the Ministry of Education tend to maintain their authority by negotiating directly with academics in the discipline rather than dealing with university heads, particularly for doctoral studies. The consequence is that information is still fragmented between various agencies in the ministry thus weakening synoptic oversight capacity. As reported by the *Inspection générale* (IGAENR, 2001), segmented bargaining is the rule and universities criticize the number of separate regulators because of the compliance costs they incur in responding to the unco-ordinated information demands of each regulator.

2 Mutuality

Mutuality is the second main form of control. Teachers' appointments are decided upon by a national body composed of elected peers from each discipline, the *Comité national des universities* (CNU). The same rationale has been adopted for the accreditation of diplomas which are approved by a nominated body of academics, the *mission scientifique*. During the 1990s another form of mutuality emerged when the assembly of university presidents gained a decisive role, having previously had only limited power since its creation in 1971.

Mutuality has traditionally been regarded as the most effective form of control over the HE sector. It is also the expression of academics' power to be regulated by their peers. Accordingly rules are decided, monitored and applied under the authority of the profession divided into disciplines. Since the 1990s the inflation of oversight bodies has been balanced by the tendency to staff them from the ranks of the university teachers, thus producing mutuality in another form. Performance information does not include student evaluations, instead emphasizing examination results, and teachers' evaluations tend to emphasize their research publications, thus rejecting accountability to students.

Behaviour modification also relies heavily on mutuality, persuasion being the main tool used by the bureaucracy to implement the rules, with only limited use of official sanctions and rewards. The *Inspection générale* has authority over management but not pedagogy, and its reports are conventionally presented to the president of the university, whose own view on the issues forms part of the report. In principle it is up to the minister to decide what to do in response to these reports, but typically there is no formal ministerial response. The Inspection générale publishes an annual report making general recommendations based on its inspections, but this report does not identify individual organizations and rather seeks to spread information and good practice among universities. In contrast, reports by the CNE (*Comité national d'évaluation des établissements publics à caractère scientifique, culturel et professionnel*) are individualized, but they take into account the difficulties of the job, so no sanction is considered and the reports tend to do little more than point out the constraints and highlight the issues. Indeed, in some cases illegalities are even viewed by the bureaucracy as justified, for example over unification of rules giving access to scholarships. When individuals protest asking for sanctions, central agencies promise to punish the behaviour when the next four-year contract is being negotiated. But things are changing, because students are becoming increasingly litigious, which works against internal consensus against the formal rules.

3 Competition

Control is still dominated by oversight and mutuality, although the traditional opacity of the mutuality system is declining with the increasing number of actors involved. And some desire to change towards an oversight-competiton style of control was reflected in the introduction of a new process in 1988 to monitor the public service by contract. This new tool, intended as a more efficient form of the traditional *tutelle*, took the form of four-year funding agreements between each university and the top bureaucracy (Musselin, 2001). This four-year contract system has obliged universities to change their decision styles, to set priorities on positions they solicit and on programmes they ask for (Braun and Merrien, 1999). Moreover, this change has been the lever for increasing emphasis on management information systems. During the 1990s information-gathering was greatly improved and significant data collection helped both to strengthen university autonomy and to improve management.

During the same period the relation between universities and their environment changed in various ways. Giving support to differences between institutions, this trend tends to develop institutional competition. First, although higher education does not fall under their authority, regional governments and municipalities have taken an interest in funding universities because of their crucial role in regional economic development. Second, the Education Ministry favours interrelations between firms and universities, and a law was adopted in 1999 to develop such links, which at present are restricted to large-scale firms. Moreover, universities have opened their curricula to the demands of employers by offering a new *diplôme d'études supérieures spécialisées*, a highly competitive one-year programme that recruits a small number of students at the end of their fourth year and is tightly linked with future employment.

Most authorities in the bureaucracy and in the academic world think that a managerial mode of regulation will emerge from the competition to recruit students and from the impact of globalization, because only that kind of system can get the information that the *tutelle* and inspectors cannot obtain. Hence a competitive style of control is developing under several external constraints. First is pressure from Europeanization: as stressed in the 1998 Attali report, to avoid being marginalized French universities have to adapt to European standards, with the quality of their performance being evaluated by the market, students and partner universities. Second, students and their families are becoming more discriminating consumers. Although there is no official league table of academic departments, prospective students are becoming better informed about the standing of different departments and universities, and no longer automatically go to the nearest university, as used to be the norm. Third, for the first time in 2001, *Le Monde* (18 October 2001) published an official ranking of universities. Although the criteria used have been criticized arguing that yardstick competition is inappropriate for a system in which universities cannot choose either their students or their teachers, it is the first time that differences have been publicly recognized, and the rankings were drawn up by a unit staffed by ministerial bureaucrats alone, without academics, perhaps heralding a step towards a decline of traditional mutuality.

4 Summary

Contrived randomness seems marginal as a form of control, since the rules for French higher education have been relatively stable and there is low mobility of staff. It might be argued that uncertainty as to when the central powers of the bureaucracy may be exercised injects a significant element of randomness into the system, but it is questionable whether that uncertainty is contrived. Rather, mutuality appears to be the dominant form of control within the French higher education system. It is reflected in the domination of the academic community both in 'buffer organizations' inside the Ministry to monitor public action and in agencies located outside the Ministry to evaluate the process of universities' institutionalization, to control the development of the disciplines and to measure the results of research.

Oversight controls are strong in principle, because of the formal imperatives of financial accountability and of central attempts to monitor university management. Competition is usually dismissed as a form of control, but it should not be ignored and its importance is likely to grow in the future, with increasing exposure to European student exchange programmes (giving rise to more competition than in the past), with demographic change pushing universities to seek new 'customers' as the number of 18-year-olds declines, and with the general pressures of more global economic competition.

3.5 GERMANY: GROWING COMPETITION AT THE EXPENSE OF MUTUALITY
Hans-Ulrich Derlien

Controls in German universities were traditionally built around autonomy for full professors. This feature made even mutuality-based control rather limited for the day-to-day academic activities of teaching and research. The growing number of professors, and reforms to their status, has introduced more competition, particularly for positions in elite research institutions and universities. As in France, centralization of power within the university hierarchy has put traditional professorial autonomy, as well as mutuality controls at faculty level, under pressure.

German universities are part of the state apparatus. Legally they are indirect *Land* administration in the form of self-governing public corporations (*Körperschaften*). Although there is a federal ministry of education and research, this ministry is responsible only for vocational training, for federal student grants, for allocating research funds to industry, to the 80 co-financed federal-*land* research institutions as well as to the Max-Planck institutes and the *Deutsche Forschungsgemeinschaft* (research council) and similar national academic institutions like the Humboldt Foundation or the Academic Exchange Council. Thus the federal government affects university life mainly through the power of the purse over research grants and student loans, with two exceptions. Constitutional changes of the post-1968 era assigned to the federal level both the framework legislation for universities and salary legislation for the civil service. To achieve some uniformity, in 1969 the *Länder* agreed that the federation should legislate a university framework law and pay half the costs of university construction according to investment plans devised by federal and *Land* education and science ministers (Article 91a basic law).

Still, education (including tertiary education) is an essential part of the 'stateness' of the *Länder*. All universities are run by the states, with the exception of recently founded private universities and the two universities of the *Bundeswehr* (armed forces). German professors are *Land* civil servants and *Länder* pay university staff and running costs. Universities are subject solely to legal supervision by the state ministries for cultural affairs. Article 5, Section 3 of the federal constitution grants academic freedom for research and teaching both to institutions and individual professors, so any *Land* government interference in the content of teaching and research would be unconstitutional. Nevertheless, there are various bodies of law, including the budgetary and civil service codes that bind professors (along with students, administrative and academic staff). Even more important are specific *Land* laws regulating the status of universities and their staff. And for degree courses universities are obliged to draft *Satzungen* (by-laws that have the status of secondary legislation) that set out curricula and examination procedures, thus granting students rights vis-à-vis the university.

Traditional oversight thus relies on ministerial powers of appointment of professors (on the suggestion of the individual university), budget constraints and incentives, and approval of curricula. Otherwise, the system is based on mutuality of professors and controlled through reputation, apart from a modicum of contrived randomness in the form of occasional inspection by *Land* public auditors. (And given the juridical emphasis of the German state system, there is surprisingly little litigation over matters such as academic appointments.)

Nevertheless, Humboldt's 1810 ideal of 'loneliness and freedom,' of unity of research and teaching (Schelsky, 1971), has been challenged since the 1960s. As with schools, universities have been exposed to 'permanent revolution' (at least from the perspective of traditional observers: others might see it differently) in the aftermath of the 1968 student revolt. What started as participatory reforms ended in the management of scarcity 10 years later and, owing to the explosion of tertiary education, all the rules mentioned above are continuously being adapted. For instance, the 1976 federal university framework legislation was reformed in 1985, 1987, 1998 and 2001, inducing various adaptations of *Land* university laws as well as university by-laws. The laws regulating salary schemes and the status of university personnel have also been amended, and the by-laws concerning teaching arrangements are also frequently reformed, albeit on the initiative of individual faculties. These incremental changes are accelerating, and recent reform attempts by the federal government may turn out to introduce further major changes, this time aiming to improve university teaching. Many see research, traditionally the foremost function of German universities, as being downgraded in the process, and this is important, because in the German system (in contrast to France) there is no functional specialization of teaching in universities and research outside the university. These changes obviously have implications for the traditional control system of German universities that was based on individual autonomy, intrinsic motivation, reputation, professional self-control and mutuality.

1   Oversight

The post-1968 reform was revolutionary in that it introduced tripartite participation in university decision-making: students, non-professorial academics and administrative staff are represented on university senates and faculty boards. Previously only full professors, all of them on the faculty board, decided university affairs, and only a full professor could be elected rector of a university. The deanship of faculties traditionally rotated among full professors, with deans carrying on their normal professorial duties, though with a slight reduction of teaching obligations.

The 1976 framework law provided for the possibility (optional) of replacing the traditional rector (elected by the professoriate for a four-year term) with a US-type president, who had to be elected but did not need to be a member of the university. Since 1998, some *Länder* added to the senate, traditionally the highest collegiate decision-making body of the university, a university board, comprising members from other organizations such as firms, cultural institutions and other universities. There is a tendency to give such boards more power than the senates in shaping university profiles and budgets. In a parallel development, deans (traditionally professors elected by the faculty board) were to serve up to four years instead of the traditional two, and a separate office of student dean was created in 1998 to monitor teaching obligations and to evaluate curricula and courses.

German universities are thus experiencing a sharp increase in oversight, reflecting what Light (1993) observed for other institutions in the USA. In Bavaria, evaluators have been installed to check on teaching quality, with professors elected for this job by each faculty and their reports sent both to university senates and *Land* ministries (though the only sanction available to those authorities is to reallocate the resources given to a professor). In a move to harmonize university degrees across Europe, the traditional German four-year degree courses ending with a diploma or 'state examination' (for lawyers, teachers and physicians) are to be replaced by three-year degrees followed by master courses, borrowing from other countries. Several accreditation institutes have been established to certificate new courses, and curricula are being modularized in all subjects.

Each university has an institutional budget (part of the *Land* ministry's budget) with items for fixed staff costs, new building and equipment costs, and running costs. To these are added funds raised elsewhere like research grants. *Land* ministries sometimes set up special grant programmes for which the universities are invited to compete, such as 'overload programmes' to pay for more teaching staff to help first-year undergraduates improve on the basics they did not learn at school (like mathematics and proficiency in German), or introduce special programmes to improve career chances of female staff or to keep young researchers in the system while they wait for a professorship. Sometimes a window of opportunity opens for a university when the government identifies a serious problem to be solved by building new research capacities. On the other hand, the ministry can close down institutions, basically by prohibiting vacancies to be filled (but the resources released often remain in the university for other purposes).

Some *Länder* changed university budgeting from line-item budgeting to so-called global budgets, ostensibly to enable universities to set priorities by reallocating their resources. However, the total amount of money available did not grow, so – predictably – the level of conflict in university senates increased, while politicians and ministerial bureaucrats could keep off the battleground. It is in this environment where the above-mentioned trend towards stronger executive leadership backed by an externally recruited university council is gaining significance: it is hoped that the strong rector or president will overcome professorial resistance in faculties and senate to re-allocate resources. Another innovation, introduced in North Rhine-Westphalia and Berlin, is contract management, which has some parallels with French developments described in Section 3.4 above. Ministries and universities negotiate goals/outputs and resources (for example, promising that resources would be stable for several years for a university that agrees to shut down a degree course), but ultimately such contracts are not legally binding. Indeed. some *Land* ministers have negotiated pacts with all universities in the state, guaranteeing a level of total spending on all universities for a couple of years while enabling them to reallocate funds among universities.

2   Competition

It is now explicit policy of federal and *Land* science ministers to increase competition in the university system. But that is far from pure market competition, because universities are not allowed to be selective in admitting students or to charge student fees. And degree courses are fairly standardized across the country, meaning that universities are competing primarily in terms of teaching and research profiles: the number and kind of programmes they are offering. What is their reward? More students? More money? More administration? It is not yet clear.

Although individual universities may be overcrowded, they still want to attract more students. The incentive to do so is the indirect profit they might gain by showing *Land* governments their importance in the competition for public funds. So it is ultimately a motivation to improve universities' infrastructure rather than just to preserve their existence. Also, by becoming more prestigious, individual university departments may create a situation where they can select students once a *numerus clausus* can be established on grounds of excessive demand for their courses. This, too, may improve departments' positions in the competition for public funds.

As in other countries, competition has also manifested itself in the search for international accreditation in, and the emergence of, university rankings published by the media on the basis of student surveys, but it is not yet at a comparable level with competitive benchmarking in countries like the UK. Published rankings began in 1990 when *Der Spiegel* published the first ranking, followed by *Focus* and *Stern*, targeting students as potential customers.

The indicators used in those rankings are of questionable validity and do not necessarily accord with expert judgements (although some attempts at more sophisticated rankings have been made, for example by the *Zentrum für Hochschulentwicklung*, Gütersloh). Inside the system, individual and (aggregate) institutional performance indicators include numbers of students and degrees awarded, amount of grant funds acquired, results of annual student satisfaction surveys and number of publications. Goal displacement is bound to occur under such a regime, because it does not take account of the quality of research and other professional activity by academics involving the creation of 'academic public goods'. At the time of writing, Chancellor Schröder's second government promised to introduce an official system of university ranking, a task likely to be given to the *Hochschul-Informationssystem*, a national public institution that since 1969 has provided universities with computer systems and student surveys. Such developments may possibly lead to more serious benchmarking activity in the future, particularly after the humiliating experience of various Organisation for Economic Co-operation and Development (OECD) benchmarking studies indicating the mediocrity of the German education system.

3 Changes in Mutuality

To see the reforms in context, readers need to understand the working environment of German professors. There are basically two categories: those with no staff ('naked professors'), who earn less than a full professor but are tenured. The full professor or *ordinarius* (still the official title in Bavaria) has at least two staff, has no probationary period and is appointed until retiring age. Assistants have fixed-term contracts for up to 10 years, to enable them to qualify as professors, so the incentive of an academic career is to make it to professor and improve salary and working conditions through successive 'calls' to other universities (something that, combined with the traditional convention that academics did not apply for professorial positions in the universities where they gained their *habilitation*, introduces an important element of randomness into the system).

The federal government's most recent reform proposals aim to introduce junior professors on a six-year term after their doctoral dissertation, with performance evaluation after three years (Enders, 2001). The overall number of positions and the resources made available to faculties were to be kept constant. But to make the junior professorial positions attractive, their pay had to be set above that of the traditional assistant, and as the whole scheme had to be cost-neutral, the base salaries of professors had to be reduced (while allowing them to recompense their losses through performance-related bonuses).

4   Conclusions

Owing to universities' status as self-governing corporations with autonomy protected by the constitution, the substance of research and teaching is free of oversight and is controlled, if at all, only by various forms of mutuality. But indirectly the universities are under the oversight of ministries that decide on organizational arrangements, personnel structure and appointments on the basis of their power of the purse. Rules and compliance costs proliferate in the generation of paperwork, but monitoring of conformity is weaker. Mutuality in its traditional form has suffered, and is limited to the external peer reviews and more recent ethics appeals.

Inside a faculty, competition among professors creates pressure to meet prevailing quantitative indicators. An indication of how problematic traditional mutuality has become can be seen in the institutionalization of research ethics commissions in all universities after some cases of fraud in medical and genetics research. Many scientific associations also established ethics commissions to monitor fairness and non-discrimination as well as ethical problems of research. Mutuality is found among colleagues of the same discipline, but those colleagues also compete and status differences are growing, so everyone guards their fiefdoms. But mutuality still functions as a control system in inter-university networks, and these networks are also influential in various peer-review activities.

If the traditional mix of controls over higher education in Germany stressed autonomy and mutuality, with oversight from ministries over administration but surprisingly little court intervention, the mix has moved recently in the direction of controls that place increasing stress on rivalry and oversight, particularly linked to the power of the purse. Up to now, there was no official ranking of universities or departments in Germany, and evaluations of all kinds are only indirectly fed back to funding ministries, though centralized quality assurance mechanisms may well develop in the future. In addition to the workings of the career system there is an element of contrived randomness through the unpredictable way that ministries now offer resources.

3.6   THE NETHERLANDS: A MIXED PATTERN OF CONTROL
Jeroen Huisman and Theo Toonen

Up to the early 1980s, control over higher education in the Netherlands was a mixture of oversight and mutuality. The oversight stemmed in part from the statement in the Constitution that 'education is subject to the continuous attention of the government' and from prevailing political views about education as one of the building blocks of the state (de Vijlder, 1996). The constitutional imperative gave some leeway for different forms of control, but the Dutch government favoured regulation by oversight, quite often rather detailed in character. However, that oversight took place in the context of a particular kind of mutuality, in the form of corporatist practices in a traditionally 'pillar-ized' society, because of the sensitivities of the different religious denominations (Leune, 1981). Pillarization has withered in recent decades, but that has not changed the corporatist policy style (van Wieringen, 1996: 99).

Three interrelated developments changed the pattern of traditional controls. First, greatly increasing student numbers have produced a less orderly, more difficult to steer public sector. That increase also had an impact on the state budget and raised the question of whether the government should or could continue to be the sole funder of higher education. Second, from the 1970s to the early 1980s there was considerable doubt about the government's ability to continue to plan and steer the public sector (in general) through detailed oversight. Third, there was a growing awareness at the Ministry of Education and Sciences that higher education's environment was becoming more complex and dynamic, requiring more leeway for higher education institutions to adapt. So the Ministry of Education and Sciences' 1985 White Paper, *Higher Education: Autonomy and Quality*, paved the way for more institutional autonomy and competition, and control in Dutch higher education nowadays is a mixture of oversight, mutuality and competition.

1 Oversight

Official oversight of Dutch higher education currently takes several forms, for instance in obligations on higher education institutions to supply reports and information to government. Oversight can best be illustrated by looking at the regulation of university programmes, university governance and employment conditions for personnel in higher education.

The 1985 White Paper promised more freedom for the institutions over the supply of programmes and the introduction of new study programmes. But Parliament feared an explosion of new programmes, something that was taking place in the higher professional education sector that had already been granted greater autonomy over programmes. So the Minister had to change the proposals and set up a national committee (Advisory Committee on the Supply of Programmes, ACO) to oversee the supply of programmes from 1993, from the perspective of 'macro-efficiency'. Although the Minister maintained that institutions had gained more autonomy, the involvement of a quasi non-government agency (ACO) and government involvement in setting rules and criteria for starting new programmes meant more oversight than had been promised (see also Huisman, 1997; Huisman and Jenniskens, 2000). The ACO encountered considerable criticism and resistance by higher education institutions and after almost 10 years of existence it was abolished, with the evaluation of 'macro-efficiency' becoming a direct responsibility of the Minister of Education, Culture and Sciences. It is interesting to note that the reintroduction of this form of oversight was induced by Parliament, with the silent and sometimes overt support of the university sector. The idea was that the distributive and redistributive issues involved in macro-efficiency policy could not be handled by the higher education sector itself – due to its heavy reliance on processes of mutuality – and that it should not be decided by uncontrolled competition either.

Institutional governance structures may not seem the most obvious element of government control, but changes in such structures have devolved several formerly governmental responsibilities to the universities themselves, with significant consequences for the control of academics and support staff. As in Germany, from the 1970s Dutch university governance structures involved democratic representation of academic staff, non-academic staff and students in councils both at university and faculty level. Democratic representation implied that the University Councils had considerable power vis-à-vis the Executive Boards, for instance over budgets and the introduction of new study programmes.

A new governance structure introduced in 1998, strengthened the Executive Boards relative to the University Councils, whose decision-making powers were replaced by an advisory role. Deans of faculties were also given more power and a new overall governing body – the Supervisory Board, appointed by the Minister – was introduced at the central level. Its main tasks were to approve major plans of the university, to appoint the Executive Board, and to resolve disputes between the Executive Board and the University Council (de Weert, 2001).

The increasing power of Executive Boards and deans signifies a shift from traditional academic decision-making towards a more managerial and less collegial approach to governance, allowing the university to act more like an entrepreneurial organization than a professional/collegial bureaucracy. But those new regulations concerning the governance structure were largely a codification of emerging or existing trends towards stronger executive leadership in universities. It is too soon to give a definite judgement on such changes, but there are signs of a shift of control within universities from a traditional form of mutuality in the form of collegial decision-making to more emphasis on competition and oversight (for instance in the form of performance-based allocation of funds, individual assessment of academics).

Until 1989, the central government Ministry of Home Affairs determined the basic salaries and working conditions of all public sector employees. After that, the Minister of Education and Sciences and the labour unions bargained over employment conditions (though pensions and social security rights remained within the remit of the Ministry of Home Affairs) and in the 1990s personnel matters were further decentralized. The former principle that staff terms and conditions were determined, unless stated otherwise, by the Minister was turned around, universities became legally able to determine all employment conditions that did not come under the Ministry (de Boer and Huisman, 1998) and, by the late 1990s, terms of employment were almost fully decentralized. Since 1997 the employers' organizations of the universities and *hogescholen* have negotiated (separately) with trade unions over almost all terms and conditions of service, to produce collective, national agreements. But bargaining also takes place at the level of individual universities, since universities have some leeway to determine their own conditions. While central government is not a direct player in the bargaining process any more, it still shapes that process by determining the total budget available for employment.

2 Mutuality

Control by mutuality is most evident in the Dutch system of quality assurance. The 1985 White Paper introduced a new quality assurance system in which higher education institutions themselves would be mainly responsible for maintaining and improving quality. Although the government saw a role for performance indicators in quality assurance as well as important powers for the Higher Education Inspectorate, the higher education institutions in fact managed to avoid the use of performance indicators and to limit the power of the inspectorate. In essence, the quality assurance system implied a change from *ex ante* oversight systems, approving rules and procedures in detail, to *ex post* evaluations. The assurance system consists of periodically external evaluations of university teaching at the levels of disciplines or sub-disciplines, combining self-evaluation, peer reviews and a report by a visitation committee. The outcomes are published and government can apply negative or positive sanctions in the light of the results. The Higher Education Inspectorate's role is essentially one of a meta-evaluator, reporting annually on the evaluations performed and judging the efficacy of universities' quality improvement measures: if the inspectorate considers the responses inadequate, the Minister may decide to stop funding the study programmes in question.

Recently, the Dutch government introduced an accreditation system (to fulfil the requirements of the Bologna Declaration) on top of the existing quality assurance arrangements. A National Accreditation Agency was to be responsible for accrediting programmes, and it was to use Validating and Judging Institutions (national, foreign or international) to judge whether programmes meet the standards. The umbrella organizations for the universities and *hogescholen* were to count as such institutions, and after having developed the procedures and set the criteria, the National Accreditation Agency was intended to be merely a guardian of procedure.

The 1985 White Paper also introduced a new planning mechanism for the higher education system that involved further strong elements of control by mutuality. The White Paper proposed a continuous dialogue between government and higher education institutions based on institutional development plans and a biennial government planning document, *Higher Education and Research Plans* (HERPs). Each institution's development plan would set out its future activities, based on an analysis of external trends and higher education developments, including government policy, while the government's HERP would set out overall frameworks for further development. But over time the degree of mutuality in this process seems to have weakened. Ministries have become less preoccupied with detailed policy proposals, instead focusing the HERPs on the general state of the art, external developments and the future policy agenda. Second, the communication function of the planning documents changed, and in so far as concrete policies are mentioned, these quite often have already been discussed with (and more or less accepted by) the main players in the policy arena.

3   Competition

From the 1980s, the government tried to increase competition, notably by implementing a research funding mechanism (conditional funding), in which quality played a role in the reallocation of funds. But that policy failed and competition is now most visible in funding mechanisms and rankings.

Funding mechanisms changed from input-orientated measures (based on student numbers or historical funding for research) to output-orientated ones, and government tried to increase competition in research by allowing universities to set up research schools. Such schools were initially intended to contain only the highest quality researchers, but over time it became clear that in most disciplines a large majority of researchers were members of those schools. Competition for research grants did not change so much and quality is still the most important criterion applied by the Dutch Research Council (NWO) in allocating funds (although government and research council are challenging the universities to develop grant proposals in specific prioritized areas). A final element of competition is the growing expectation (both from government and the universities themselves) that departments and universities acquire funds from sources other than the state budget.

For a long time rankings were not accepted in the egalitarian Dutch society, although there were some hidden or perceived quality differences among the different higher education institutions. But, as in Germany, from the 1990s Dutch newspapers and weeklies published rankings, based partly on the results of the quality assurance system, but also partly on opinions of students and staff. The rankings show some differences between the higher education institutions, but the differences are not large and there is no sign that these real or perceived differences are significantly shaping student choice up to now.

4 Contrived Randomness

Examples of contrived randomness are hard to find in Dutch higher education. Audits (as part of the quality assurance system, including visits of the Higher Education Inspectorate) are always announced. The apparent lack of this type of control seems to be best explained by the reliance on mutuality and oversight in control. Government still has substantial regulatory power over higher education, but the corporatist policy style means that higher education institutions are well aware of government thinking and intentions of the government, and so are unlikely to be 'surprised' by unexpected behaviour on the part of executive government. Government actions are mostly predictable, and most of the unpredictability stems from unforeseen consequences of policies when they are implemented and of unexpected negotiating outcomes.

5 Conclusion

In the Netherlands, competition has gradually been introduced as a form of control, in addition to the traditional forms of oversight and mutuality. Contrived randomness appears to be lacking, and oversight changed from detailed *ex ante* approval to more general, less pervasive *ex post* evaluation. Most of the new initiatives have been mixtures of forms of control. For example, in the quality assurance system, the process is co-ordinated and carried out by the higher education institutions (mutuality), but government sets the conditions (oversight).

Development over time indicates two features. First, because of the corporatist nature of the Dutch policy style, government intentions to introduce more competition and market-type mechanisms have been tempered – if not blocked – by those involved in those processes (see also Huisman, 2003). Second, unintended consequences of policies based on the notion of competition have sometimes forced government to rethink its policies and implement policies based on other forms of control. So the Dutch system has followed a decidedly winding path towards control by competition.

3.7   NORWAY: HOLDING BACK COMPETITION?
Ivar Bleiklie

Traditional control of Norwegian universities amounted to a classic 'Humboldtian' contract in the sense that universities in principle were given the right to organize teaching and research as they pleased provided they saw to it that the state's needs for qualified bureaucrats and professionals were satisfied (Ben-David and Zloczower, 1991). That contract brought together oversight and mutuality in a peculiar way. First, freedom of research and teaching was combined with detailed oversight of matters of importance to government, such as introduction of academic degrees, curricula, establishment of new academic positions and fields of study, and hiring of academic staff. Second, oversight was often combined with or based on mutuality in the sense that government decisions on such matters were usually based on recommendations by academic bodies. Third, universities were hierarchical organizations, dominated by a small collegium of professors, leaving little room for other members of the university community to influence decisions and the way control was exercised (Neave and Rhoades, 1987: 283ff).

Since 1970, higher education has gone through several changes. First, all forms of oversight have become more formalized, standardized and top down as the system has increased in size. Second, institutions have become internally democratized in that they are directed by bodies representing all members of the university community as well as society at large. Third, competition and performance evaluation has increasingly been directed towards institutions as well as individuals. Nevertheless, apart from incentive based funding, peer review has remained the dominant form of evaluation.

This means that although oversight and mutuality still are dominant forms of control, the way they work and the level at which they operate have changed. These changes need to be understood against the backdrop of two developments. One is the steep growth of the higher education sector that has made the higher education system less socially exclusive, more politically visible and its costs more susceptible to public scrutiny. The second is ideological, represented by the rise of so-called New Public Management (NPM) and implies that the ideas about the mission of higher education institutions and how they ought to be managed have changed in a fundamental way (Bleiklie, 1998). The following analysis of the development of control forms (based on Bleiklie, Høstaker and Vabø, 2000; Bleiklie, Byrkjeflot and Østergen, 2003) traces out a particular manifestation of that ideology.

1 Oversight

An important feature of Norwegian political life in comparative terms, is the rather withdrawn part played by the court system. Disputes over controls are in practice the exclusive domain of the legislative and executive branches, namely Parliament and the Ministry. And except for occasional direct interventions from Parliament, the Ministry of Education and Research is the main traditional regulator of university affairs. But the organization of oversight has changed in several ways. Until 1989 most universities were regulated under their own separate laws, which laid down the governing bodies, regulating degrees, curricula, hiring procedures and so on. There was a considerable bottom-up element in the way control was conducted because many regulations were based on close informal contact between Ministry officials and university leaders, in the context of a small system. In addition to legislation, budget decisions were equally important as instruments of oversight. As part of annual national budget procedure, funds were traditionally allocated by specifying the number of positions that were funded in the various disciplines, what kind of equipment might be purchased in each disciplines, and what funding was available for building maintenance and so on.

In 1990 common legislation was introduced for all universities and specialized university institutions, and in 1995 it was replaced by a law covering all higher education institutions. The law was said to increase university 'autonomy' (in the sense of institutional autonomy, not the autonomy of individual researchers and teachers in the traditional Humboldtian sense) because numerous decisions, such as the hiring of senior academics, were transferred from the Ministry to the institutions. Changes in funding procedures also meant a similar transfer of decision-making power to the institutions, as funding came as a lump sum for each institution to allocate it as it saw fit – in principle, at least.

Funding criteria were also changed, with the emphasis moving from an exclusive reliance on input criteria before 1990 to a gradually increasing reliance on output criteria. Until 1990 the estimated running costs of a university department were based on the number of tenured academic staff. Increased student numbers would only affect the budget indirectly, and depended on the ability of departments to convince faculty and university bodies that they needed to be given more academic positions. In 1990 a limited use of incentive criteria was introduced, and from 2004 an estimated 40 per cent of university budgets will be incentive based in some form. Whereas teaching incentives are mainly based on output measures (number of examinations and graduates), research incentives are based on input measures (such as number of doctoral degrees and funding from external sources). These measures serve as performance indicators, but other measures are used as well, in particular indicators on research productivity in the form of publication statistics. The use of such performance indicators for teaching and research performance is obligatory and standardized for all higher education institutions, with annual reporting to the Ministry, but the results have no specific economic consequences for individual institutions or academic staff within them.

There are no 'buffer organizations' between individual institutions and the Ministry that allocates funds and regulates higher education, but two bodies are about to become more important, the Norwegian Council for Higher Education and the Norwegian Agency for Quality Assurance in Education. The former, a continuation of the national Rectors' Conference, was established in its present form in 2001 and has now become a co-ordinating body for all higher education institutions. The latter is an independent government body under the Ministry of Education and Research, established in 2002 to oversee (through accreditation and evaluation) quality control in higher education. At the time of writing it is still developing its criteria and systems.

2   Competition

How dominant the public higher education system is compared to the private sector depends on how the balance is measured. Only one major institution, accounting for about 10 per cent of all students, is privately owned, compared to the 38 institutions that make up the public system. From a funding perspective, public dominance is even more overwhelming as public money also goes into the private institution through research funds and student grants and loans. Moreover public–private competition is confined to one academic field, whereas other professional schools and academic disciplines face no such competition at national level.

Traditionally, higher education institutions have tended to recruit both students and faculty locally, but there are now some signs of developing competition for students. Those signs first emerged in the 1980s when student numbers were stagnant and institutions tried to attract more students by creating 'vocationally oriented' study programmes, notably in business administration (Vabø, 2002). At that time incentives to compete for students were limited and, as student numbers started to rise sharply in the late 1980s, the need to compete for students tapered off. Tuition fees are still insignificant, except for the private business school, but incentives to compete for students will be increased with a new funding model due to be introduced in 2004. The only 'league table' for higher education in Norway is an annual survey published by a group of major newspapers where students rate institutions and departments/study programmes in terms of teaching quality and quality of life.

Until now there has not been significant competition for academic staff. One reason is that salaries (as in the rest of the civil service) have traditionally been uniform across institutions. Recruitment of academic staff has tended to be local, with jobs for life within a single institution and low mobility between institutions. Over the last decade, there has been some modest differentiation of salaries as a means for institutions to attract research talent, mainly in fields, such as medicine, law and business administration where graduates can obtain better salaried jobs outside academia. A system of performance pay was introduced in the 1990s, but individual wage hikes have until now been rather small.

3 Mutuality

Tenure in the American sense does not exist in Norwegian higher education, but full-time academics have a functional equivalent, in the form of a degree of job security that protected the autonomy of teaching and research. Until 1990 full professors and readers enjoyed the traditional protection that pertained to all top civil servants (*embetsmenn*, modelled on the German *Beamter*). Top civil servants were appointed directly by the government (formally by King in Council) and the only way they could lose their job was by being convicted of some criminal act. When the appointment of professors was decentralized to individual universities, they lost their senior civil servant status and have now the same protection as general civil servants, meaning that in principle they may be dismissed on grounds of redundancy. That has not happened up to the time of writing, but the removal of their former legal protection and privileged status is seen by some observers as symbolizing a decline in academic freedom.

The academic community has traditionally dominated both standard-setting and decisions over such matters as teaching evaluation, examinations, the award of doctoral degrees, hiring decisions and allocation of research funds. Decisions are traditionally made by or on the recommendation of committees of academics often with a majority or the committee chair from another institution. External academic representation on the committees has been a way of trying to prevent institutionally based power structures from undermining quality standards in a system with little competition and low mobility. There are two exceptions to this form of academic control. One is teaching evaluation, which is usually based on student surveys within each department, and is used to provide feedback to individual teachers rather than provide information to students, institutional leaders or the public at large on teaching performance. The second exception is the decisions made by the Research Council on research funding, whose decisions may be affected by the views of politicians, bureaucrats and other non-academics. This non-academic influence that has been wielded particularly by the Ministries was singled out as a potential threat to the quality of research in Norway in a recent evaluation report on the Norwegian Research Council.

A system of external monitoring has been built up in the form of evaluations of disciplines, of faculties and of institutions. The Norwegian Research Council organizes the evaluation of individual disciplines, with a peer-review panel evaluating the research performance of the institutional units engaged in teaching and research in the discipline. In addition, the units involved write self-evaluation reports and provide written documents on their performance. Furthermore, the Ministry from time to time may request institutional evaluations of entire universities that assess their administrative functions as well as their teaching and research. Finally, universities have evaluated individual faculties on their own initiative. A common feature of all such evaluations, however, is the emphasis on peer review, as well as the use of multiple data sources and the complex and laborious nature of such exercises. Moreover, the results of evaluation exercises are rarely used as a basis for hard sanctions against the institutions being evaluated, but rather as sources of advice and information.

4   Conclusions

The Auditor-General's Office scrutinizes higher education institutions, like other parts of the civil service, and the public auditor has become more active in general, but the increase in activity does not entail more control by contrived randomness and there is no evidence that the Auditor-General has become more active in scrutinizing the higher education sector (Bleiklie et al., 2002). Generally speaking, contrived randomness has not played a significant role in controlling Norwegian higher education and there are no indications that this is about to change.

Overall, the changes described above do not represent changes in primary forms of control and the important changes lie in the way the existing control types are used. For oversight, more detailed scrutiny over a limited area has been replaced by less detailed scrutiny over a wider array of issues. And oversight has shifted from process (rule-following) to outcome (goal attainment). Traditional mutuality has been weakened in university governance but has taken a new form with the spread of peer-review evaluation of disciplinary and institutional performance. Competition for academic positions and research funds has been a long-standing form of control, and with an increasing share of university budgets funded by competitive research grants, competition has become more important. Institutional competition for students, though still not very prominent, has also showed signs of increasing importance, albeit on a smaller scale than some of the other countries in this study.

3.8   AUSTRALIA: LINKING OVERSIGHT TO MUTUALITY AND COMPETITION
Colin Scott

Higher education in Australia has traditionally been controlled mainly by mutuality and peer review, with government oversight restricted to reporting requirements. Increasingly, those requirements have been linked to control through competition for funds, both for research and teaching, producing a hybrid control regime. Arguably, the recent proliferation of regulatory controls over Australian universities stems from the high degree of autonomy they traditionally enjoyed, and a review of higher education policy in 2002 elicited widespread complaints from universities that they were overregulated. But problems caused by commercialization of university functions in teaching and research have also been perceived, and recent moves to reform university governance in Victoria (Kosky, 2002) were triggered by concerns about the commercialization of universities expressed by the state Auditor-General. Investigations by the Independent Commission Against Corruption into universities in New South Wales have also drawn the federal Department of Education Science and Training into participating in state regulation of universities (Independent Commission Against Corruption, 2002a). At the time of writing the federal (Commonwealth) government was also seeking to influence state regulation of universities through floating the idea of a national protocol (Illing, 2002).

1   Oversight

When higher education funding was transferred by the states to the federal level of Australian government in 1974, the function was given to a 'buffer organization' the Commonwealth Tertiary Education Commission (CTEC), broadly similar to the funding bodies currently operating in the UK (Nelson, 2002b: 14). The CTEC's abolition in 1987 (Niklasson, 1996: 11) made the ministry responsible for higher education in the Commonwealth government both the central policy-maker for, and regulator of, the newly unified sector (Nelson, 2002a: 5; Higher Education Finance Act, 1988). Since 1993, universities have been funded directly by the Commonwealth rather than through state and territory governments (Nelson, 2002b: 5), and officials feel themselves under constant pressure to elaborate on the accompanying regulatory regime, partly because problems discovered in particular institutions are frequently raised in the Senate. At the time of writing the Higher Education Group in the Department of Education, Science and Training (DEST) comprised only about 100 staff, most without direct experience in higher education, even though it had to cover a wide range of functions, including funding, information and analysis, and innovation and quality.

Because education is a function of state governments under the Constitution most HE providers in Australia are creatures of statute which are subject to a panoply of state and territory oversight mechanisms including ombudsmen, auditors-general and anti-corruption organizations. (Universities are also subject to a complex web of regulations over matters such as establishment of companies, investments and borrowing, land use, acquisition and disposal and employment (Phillips, 2001).)

The DEST collects information from higher education institutions mainly by imposing reporting requirements. Higher education institutions are statutorily obliged to supply annual educational profiles to the DEST in a form determined by the Minister (Higher Education Finance Act 1988, s.14). A recent Minister acknowledged the burdens placed on universities by these requirements, admitting that the DEST 'requires of universities onerous reporting and acquittal data, not all of which I am convinced are necessary for quality education'. He further added 'Armies of university administrative officers collect and remit this information, frequently having to provide it in a different form and at a different time to their State or Territory government' (Nelson, 2002b: v). The response to a recent review of the Australian Vice-Chancellors' Committee (AVCC) made much of the need to develop more streamlined reporting arrangements to both levels of government (Australian Vice-Chancellors' Committee, 2002a: 9).

Responsibility for checking the detail of the profile is diffuse. State auditors-general audit the financial statements and loadings of student places filled and used are cross-checked against records of the Higher Education Contributions Scheme (HECS) held by the Australian Taxation Office (ATO). Details of research income can be cross-checked against the records of the Australian Research Council or other funders' information, but the planning and forecasting elements of the profile are not audited.

The DEST operates an 'enforcement pyramid', starting with private suasion, moving through publicity (for instance, in the form of league tables) and moving up to financial instruments, mainly taking the form of carrots rather than sticks, but the application of financial penalties for failure to meet conditions of grant is also possible. Accreditation of universities is within the jurisdiction of state and territory governments, although subject to national protocols. These accreditation arrangements are additionally audited by the Australian Universities Quality Agency, an intergovernmental body. Accordingly, the DEST does not have the power to close a university and cannot withdraw funding completely – it is obliged to fund even failing institutions.

2 Competition

Competition is the main instrument used to control research quality in Australia. The total budgets of the two main public research councils exceed 10 per cent of the total public spend on higher education and the allocation of core grants for research by the DEST is determined in part by reference to information supplied by universities about their performance in attracting research students (30 per cent), in raising research income (60 per cent), and the 'quality and output of publications' (10 per cent). The DEST has been aware of the crudeness of this data as indicators of research quality. The initial scheme involved counting of all publications and offering funding per publication, a policy that predictably generated a 'massive increase in numbers of publications'. The scheme was revised to weight most of the funding for publications of books by respected publishers and in refereed journals, but the perverse effects of this change included a rush by journals to designate themselves as refereed and the downgrading within the scheme of outputs in other respectable forms of professional activity such as book chapters.

A central requirement of a system which links research funding to research outputs is confidence in the accuracy of returns made by universities. Recognizing this the AVCC has established an audit of research publications claimed, which it contracts out to a commercial company. The audit combines a full check in some categories of submission in which the entries are relatively small but the funding implications high (books, patents and refereed designs) and a sample check for other categories of research output (Australian Vice-Chancellors' Committee, 2002b). Where inaccuracies are detected on a scale to warrant action the powers to apply financial sanctions, discussed below, are retained by the DEST.

There are no widely used or trusted league tables of higher education institutions in Australia. No comparative audited data on key indicators such as teaching quality and research performance exist to make up such a table. *Asiaweek* magazine has in the past published an annual survey based on information voluntarily supplied by Asian and Australian universities, which showed Australian universities struggling to compete with the top Japanese, Korean and Hong Kong institutions. The *Australian Financial Review* publishes an annual ranking of business schools, based on survey returns from the universities.

3 Mutuality

By contrast with its British counterpart, Universities UK, the AVCC is a much more active self-regulatory body for the higher education sector. In addition to its policy role it publishes guidelines across a wide range of areas including teaching, research practice and ethics, accreditation of universities and gender equity. It thus represents a form of control through mutuality in articulating core standards for higher educational practice, and it has also established itself as the audit body over universities' declared research output, as noted above. The importance of the AVCC in policy and regulation is reflected in the assertion by the influential *Australian Financial Review* in 2002 that the five most powerful players in education in Australia are the Commonwealth education minister, the senior bureaucract of the DEST, the chair of the Australian Vice-Chancellors' Committee and two other vice-chancellors.

Responsibility for quality control over teaching lies mainly within universities themselves. The DEST has for many years been the key external regulator, operating through the Higher Education Council and later through the Committee for Quality Assurance in Higher Education (CQAHE), a non-statutory ministerial advisory committee (Candy and Maconachie, 1997: 10–11). The CQAHE engaged in the first systemic external audit of universities in 1993, with reports prepared on each university, and recommendations made to the Minister on the allocation of substantial sums in 'special incentive funds' over three years (Candy and Maconachie, 1997: 14). The second audit focused on teaching at all levels, and the audit reports were published with league tables of institutions against set criteria. More recent government policy has sought to reduce the amount of discretionary federal funding to the HE sector and to lay more emphasis on building up the capacity of the institutions themselves (Candy and Maconachie, 1997: 16).

In 2001 a new intergovernmental organization was established in the form of a company limited by guarantee in which each of the state, territory and Commonwealth ministers was a subscriber. The Australian Universities Quality Agency (AUQA) is responsible for auditing higher education institutions' quality assurance arrangements and publishing its reports. Information is mainly based on self-review documents provided by universities in quinquennial audits, followed up halfway through each period. A senior official claimed there was a 'philosophy of dialogue and openness' fostered by the low relational distance between the agency and senior university officials. Most AUQA staff have had substantial experience working in HE institutions and 100 or so audit staff came mainly from serving university professors. AUQA can be seen as a 'meta-regulator', checking and steering the self-regulatory mechanisms that universities themselves have established. Thus the new regime represents an application of the classic 'steering at a distance' technique. And while AUQA's establishment represents a new layer of regulation over HE institutions, it may in the future provide the occasion for the reduction in reporting requirements to the DEST (Nelson, 2002b: 13).

4 Contrived Randomness

The impact of state governments overseers as regulators of higher education appears to be rather sporadic and may thus be considered an element of randomized control. In New South Wales the Ombudsman has reported an increase in its scrutiny of universities. This activity has included one major investigation, using Royal Commission powers and receiving evidence from 27 witnesses in hearings, concerning the way examinations were conducted for a particular candidate given special considerations at the University of Sydney. The report of the investigation included 'model special consideration guidelines' which the office suggested be used in future and the recommendations were circulated to all NSW universities (New South Wales Ombudsman, 2001). Thus the Ombudsman's office has set itself up as a standard-setter over university examining, though without powers to ensure its recommendations are followed.

The Auditor-General for NSW, in addition to providing annual financial audits of the NSW universities, makes occasional performance audit reports on particular matters affecting universities. For example, a report on a performance audit found that the costs of administration at the University of Western Sydney were excessive (Auditor-General, 1998). Still in New South Wales the Independent Commission Against Corruption (ICAC) was sufficiently concerned about its findings arising from individual cases of corruption at particular universities that it launched a general risk assessment of corruption in the university sector. It was highly critical of a complacent attitude to risks across a wide range of university operations (Independent Commission Against Corruption, 2002b).

5 Conclusions

The Australian regime for regulating higher education places considerable emphasis on self-regulation both by individual institutions and by the AVCC. This is particularly true for teaching quality and related quality processes, but less so for research where traditional controls based on mutuality have been rapidly displaced by control based on competition for funds. The complexity of governmental oversight over HE in Australia derives largely from the multiple and overlapping jurisdictions of state, commonwealth and intergovernmental regulators.

3.9 THE UK: HYPER-REGULATION AND REGULATORY REFORM
Colin Scott

The UK tradition of university autonomy has been maintained to some extent by the retention of 'buffer institutions' for allocating funds to higher education, though that allocation process has been much modified through the introduction of new controls over research and teaching quality which, though based on peer review, are portrayed or perceived by many universities and academics as 'hierarchical oversight'. These changes are partly a response to the ending of the 'binary divide' in the UK, which meant that former polytechnics and some higher education colleges (previously subject to tight centralized oversight through the Council on National Academic Awards), were given similar autonomy to the traditional universities. The changes also reflect the funding pressures associated with a shift from elite to mass higher education.

1 Oversight

The Universities Funding Council, which succeeded the former University Grants Committee, was replaced with the ending of the binary divide between the polytechnic and university sector in 1992 by separate funding councils for England, Wales and Scotland (Niklasson, 1996: 12). Those funding councils had wider statutory functions than their predecessors and one of the new functions was to 'secure that provision is made for assessing the quality of education provided in institutions for whose activities they provide, or are considering providing, financial support' (Further and Higher Education Funding Act, 1992, s. 70(1)(a)). Initially the funding councils conducted teaching quality assessment themselves, while the institutions developed mechanisms of institutional audit through the Higher Education Quality Council. However after a major inquiry into higher education in 1997, both functions were taken over by a new non-statutory company, the Quality Assurance Agency for Higher Education (QAA), which was to provide both subject and institutional audits to each of the three funding councils in Great Britain. Alongside the QAA several professional bodies, such as the General Medical Council and the Law Society and Bar Council accredit courses as meeting professional standards.

A senior Higher Education Funding Council for England (HEFCE) official reported that foreign visitors are amazed by the autonomy of the HEFCE and the universities from government. That autonomy is symbolized by the HEFCE's location in Bristol, well away from the centre of government and ministers rarely give HEFCE statutory guidance. But ministers clearly retain power over the sector because of their power to make changes through legislation, and their ability to make the grant of funds to the funding councils dependent on conditions they specify for the higher education sector as a whole. The funding power has been used chiefly over pay and related issues, with funding for pay increases linked at various times to wage restraint, staff development, and increasing the proportion of the population in higher education. Ministers have also frequently intervened in other ways, notably in attempts to secure wider and more equitable access to higher education, and in one celebrated incident to resolve an impasse between the higher education institutions and the Quality Assurance Agency over the scope of the latter's audits.

The Higher Education Funding Council for England is a statutory agency, accountable to the Secretary of State for Education and to Parliament. But in practice it occupies a position at least as close to the universities as to government. Its chief executive is traditionally a senior vice-chancellor, typically with leadership experience in Universities UK and its predecessor, the Committee of Vice-Chancellors and Principals. So one might assume that the regime operated by the HEFCE would emphasize mutuality, and it does seem that its reporting requirements, while onerous, are viewed rather less as top-down impositions than their equivalents in Australia. But, in common with Australia, regulation has come to rely heavily on control through competition. There is some competition for limited numbers of funded student places, but the fiercest competition is for research funds and for rankings in league tables produced by the media on the basis of information published by the HEFCE.

The HEFCE sees the monitoring and maintenance of the financial health of HE institutions as central to its functions. Ultimately, the HEFCE can withdraw funds from an institution, but its lower-level sanctions include warnings to governors, the issuance of financial memoranda about particular institutions and the placing of an institution into 'category 1', meaning that it has to produce half yearly updates and financial reports. The possession of the big funding stick enables the HEFCE to speak softly (Ayres and Braithwaite, 1992). The HEFCE makes extensive use of financial incentives in research funding, using research selectivity for allocating the annual research budget. The HEFCE also uses financial penalties, not over teaching quality, but to encourage institutions to meet their student recruitment targets. In 2002–03 these penalties applied both to those who overshot their targets and to those who undershot in particular fields (Higher Education Funding Council for England, 2002). It has been argued that the absence of a link between funding and assessment of teaching quality deprives the latter of any 'teeth' (Stiles, 2002: 728).

The 'audit' of English universities became the responsibility of the non-statutory Quality Assurance Agency in 1997. The QAA mission was to develop national standards, mainly for teaching, across the HE sector, and to provide the mechanisms and procedures for institutional audit and subject review. In carrying out these functions the QAA was supposed to regulate with 'a light touch'. Its main standard-setting instrument is a Code of Practice that deals with matters such as external examining, student appeals, assessment of students and programme approval, monitoring and review. Additionally, the QAA has devised a uniform qualifications framework intended to ensure the consistent use of qualification titles (for example, setting out the minimum level of achievement to obtain a bachelors degree or a masters degree). Drawing on panels of senior academics in each subject area, the QAA has also set down subject benchmark statements setting out the minimum knowledge and skills expected of a student for each level of a degree in a particular broad subject area.

The QAA's new methods of institutional and subject review were heavily criticized by universities. The QAA claimed that to fulfil its responsibilities it needed to continue with on-site reviews of every teaching department in every subject. Further, whereas earlier reviews of teaching quality had only been concerned with assessing provision against a department's own statement of objectives, the new QAA subject review would also assess provision against national standards which the QAA (and not departments) had set in the Code of Practice, the Qualifications Framework and the Subject Benchmarks. While these standards were said to be reference points only (Quality Assurance Agency for Higher Education, 2000: app. E), institutions inferred that they would be criticized if they did not follow them. So to universities the new regime looked more like heavy-handed inspection than light touch regulation. The chief casualty of the dispute between vice-chancellors and the QAA was the first QAA chief executive who resigned following government intervention to restrict subject review to a maximum of 40 per cent of departments.

The QAA later abandoned even the more limited subject review and folded all reviews into a single institutional audit, though that change raised concerns among professional bodies that they might have to inspect departments themselves if the QAA did not do it (Law Society of England and Wales, and General Council of the Bar, 2002: 3–4). Universities remain concerned that institutional audit may reintroduce compulsory subject review by the back door, notably the requirement for discipline audit trails and detailed inspection of about 10 per cent of courses (Better Regulation Task Force, 2000: 28). This light-handed approach will be coupled with new requirements on HE institutions to publish key performance indicators on their websites (Better Regulation Task Force, 2000: 29), in an attempt to increase the information available to prospective students and thus substitute retail competition for official inspection.

At the time of writing the burdens placed on universities by regulation were coming under closer scrutiny in England. An early indicator of the stresses came when the HEFCE was judicially reviewed by a dental school over its rating in the 1992 Research Assessment Exercise. The HEFCE itself commissioned a report from consultants on the burdens of accountability (PA Consulting, 2000). That report noted that the regulator could not control how HE institutions would respond to particular regulatory measures, which might generate unintended consequences and staff stress. The theme of excessive regulation was subsequently taken up by the Blair government's Better Regulation Task Force (BRTF, primarily designed to evaluate regulatory burdens on business), which recommended that more be done to cost the burdens of regulatory initiatives on the HE sector (Better Regulation Task Force, 2000). The BRTF's investigation mapped all the regulatory relationships affecting HE institutions, identifying over 100 public agencies and departments, charities and professional bodies to whom the universities are answerable for some aspect of their performance on the basis of statute or contracts (ibid.: 8–9).

2 Competition

The UK regime stresses competition for grants from the various research councils. Most public funding for research comes in the form of central grants to institutions determined largely by research performance, and the key mechanism for assessing research performance, and thus 'research selectivity' is the research assessment exercise (RAE, conducted in 1986, 1989, 1992, 1996 and 2001). One evaluation of the RAE suggests that academics have succeeded in sustaining 'academic values and academic control', but that it has nevertheless created a 'profound disturbance' (Henkel, 1999: 105–6). Institutional funding for research is based on a formula which multiplies the number of research active staff by a multiplier determined by the grading of the department. And there is a substantial element of randomness in the control process since the funding formula is liable to change each year, as is the quantity of funds available.

Competition among universities is also linked to student numbers, and is shaped in part by national league tables (of universities and departments) produced by *The Times* and the *Guardian* newspapers using data published by the Funding Councils. The tables use large amounts of data including teaching quality and research quality scores, staff–student ratios, availability of student accommodation, library and IT expenditure, grading of students on entry and exit and employment prospects. They are widely read and disseminated among both prospective university students and staff.

3 Mutuality

As noted above, the regulation of both research and teaching are hybrids of oversight and mutuality, with elements of competition. Institutionally, the buffer body, the HEFCE, has elements both of mutuality and oversight. It 'calls the shots' on devising scrutiny of research quality, but much of the actual assessment works through peer review, and a similar relationship between oversight and peer review applies to the regulation of teaching. But even though most of the monitoring (though not standard-setting) is carried out through peer review, the regimes are not widely perceived as mutuality based within the HE sector.

The position of academic staff security in universities has been affected both by statutory changes to academic tenure in 1988 and by a process of casualization, with more staff appointed to temporary contracts. Before 1988 tenured academics could only be dismissed from their posts for misbehaviour, but reforms to university charters in that year added provision for dismissal on grounds of redundancy. This change was a response to the problems experienced by universities in trying to downsize their staffs in the early 1980s in response to government funding cuts, and the heavy costs they incurred in creating incentives for tenured staff to retire early. Casualization of academic posts is a linked trend since it gives universities greater control over staff budgets in the medium term, and although casualization has largely taken place below professorial level, major research universities, with large numbers of research-only staff, are liable to have fewer than half of academic staff on permanent contracts (Association of University Teachers, 2001).

4 Contrived Randomness

Contrived randomness plays only a limited role in the regulation of the sector. No use is made of unannounced audits or inspections. Most of the uncertainty comes from the difficulty of predicting the payoffs for good or bad performance in research and teaching. The HEFCE frequently only determines the payoffs after the assessments have been completed and, in the case of the 2001 RAE, ministers introduced another key element of randomness by intervening to change the scheme of research funding which the HEFCE had devised. In addition, individual academics face uncertainties over the payoffs for particular activities in their careers, since processes of promotion and setting of pay are notoriously unpredictable and vary from one university to another.

5 Conclusions

Control of UK universities has rapidly moved from individual and collective self-regulation to more formal oversight that emphasizes both external rule-making and inspection, particularly for quality. Competition for research funds and students has also increased, and published competitive performance indicators have been introduced. The weight of contrived randomness is hard to determine and so is the issue of whether it has grown, declined or remained constant in the brave new world of university controls.

4 Higher civil servants: neither mutuality implosion nor oversight explosion

4.1 OVERVIEW
B. Guy Peters and Christopher Hood

1 Varied Patterns of Control and the Puzzle of Invisible Randomness

The control of higher civil servants is an issue in every political system, and for several reasons. One is the political importance of securing loyalty, honesty and competency from those in sensitive high-level positions in the state. There is a voluminous literature examining higher bureaucracies as a principal–agent control problem, with elected politicians cast in the role of principals and the bureaucrats as the agents who are the objects of control. Important as that approach undoubtedly is, higher civil servants in many countries are to a greater or lesser extent part of a constitutional system of mutual checking, exercising autonomous powers at least for some purposes. Even in the UK Westminster model, civil servants have such a constitutional role in handling transfers of power from one elected government to another, in personally accounting for the expenditure of public money and in preventing the apparatus of executive government from being used for electoral campaigning. Moreover, some higher civil servants have direct statutory powers vested in them. So in many cases higher civil servants are part of a web of control in a broader sense. They are not just on the receiving end.

The main focus of the analysis here is on the control of individual conduct of civil servants rather than the control of public bureaucracies as organizations, for example in budgeting or resource allocation. Admittedly, the two cannot be separated at the margin and numerous reformers have aimed to bring them closer together. Controls over the behaviour of civil servants take different forms across political systems, but all the four primary types discussed in the introductory chapter can be identified in a general way, as Table 4.1 illustrates. In the public administration literature there is a long-running debate about the relative importance of external oversight and mutual peer-group checking processes in the control of higher civil servants. That debate is epitomized in a famous exchange between Herman Finer (1940) and Carl

Friedrich (1940) over 60 years ago, but it originated long before that and it is still evident in contemporary discussion. Indeed, oversight and mutuality have traditionally taken varied forms and received different emphases in different state systems, as Chapter 1 showed.

Oversight of higher civil servants by the legislature has traditionally been weak in most parliamentary systems compared to the often-remarked 'micro-management' of the federal civil service by the US Congress. And equally the evocations of peer-group control in traditional images of higher civil services

Table 4.1   Types of control and the higher civil service

Type of control	Example	Comment
Mutuality	Conventions of consultation, committee working or multiple-key decision or authorization systems, informal mutual rating, influence and moral suasion	Powerful requisite-variety capacity, often institutionalized to some degree, but with familiar weaknesses (groupthink, positive illusion, relational distance bias)
Competition	Rivalry for position, prestige, promotion, influence, honours in some systems, jobs after office	Often takes place 'in the shadow of hierarchy'; can degenerate into mutual sabotage in hyper-competitive bureaucratic cultures
Contrived randomness	Unpredictable postings and transfers around the government system linked with other 'garbage-can' ingredients; conventions of moving on promotion	Conventionally seen as most effective for controlling corruption and sabotage rather than for positive motivation
Oversight	Inspections, security vettings, adjudication by courts, tribunals and ombudsmen, audit, inquiries and hearings	Often linked with randomness and competition (for example in traditional UK Treasury control); commonly fails for requisite-variety reasons and vulnerable to gaming through information asymmetry

as a gentleman's club (the stereotype of old-style Whitehall) or band of samurai warriors sharing a common ethic of knightly self-restraint (the stereotype and self-image of the Japanese civil service since the Meiji era) have not normally been applied to the control of the 'government of strangers' Washington bureaucracy. But one of the main conclusions we drew from this exploration was the different forms that mutuality took in different contexts. Germany has its own particular form of mutuality for higher civil servants, with mutuality – perhaps characteristically – written into the official rules, as Hans-Ulrich Derlien notes in this chapter. Hence Germany is a case of enacted rather than spontaneous or immanent mutuality that contrasts with the Japanese type. And France shows a different pattern again, in the form of a special combination of mutuality and oversight, with a distinctive form of mutuality operating through the *grands corps* structure and civil servants in one part of the state structure sitting in judgement on civil servants in another part of that structure. The oversight structures, such as the *Conseil d'État* and *Inspection des Finances*, exercise *ex post* and *ex ante* checking functions and follow a 'legalistic' style. But those impressively judicial-seeming oversight bodies are largely populated from the small world of the higher civil service elite itself, and the legal determinations are made by those civil servants rather than by relationally distant judges of the type found in the Westminster system or even by the semi-distant administrative law judges in the German case.

However, although mutuality and oversight are the forms of control that have been most commented on by observers of higher civil service systems, the other two primary forms of control that we identified in Chapter 1 can also be readily detected in these cases. Competition has played a notable part in shaping civil service behaviour in many states, particularly in the traditionally elite civil services of Europe and Japan where the best and the brightest once vied with one another for entry-level positions and then competed to scale the bureaucratic heights, though once in post – and often before that – it tended to be 'competition in the shadow of mutuality'. And the logic of that combination is easy to understand, since within a bureaucracy fully 'unshaded' competition between individuals can mean mutual sabotage rather than peaceful coexistence, let alone the positive cooperation and teamwork that is often seen as a desideratum in government work. Arguably, competition is most effective as a control over competency (and over at least some dimensions of loyalty) than over ethics and honesty, and, as in business life, 'cut-throat competition' can tempt individuals to look for short cuts to gain advantage.

As with the other public sector domains examined in this book, many of our contributors downplayed contrived randomness as a form of control and paid more attention to what they seem to have assumed were more powerful forces of oversight and mutuality. But that assumption is far from unchallengeable. Indeed, the equation of control with (often ineffective or tokenistic) oversight or easily degraded mutuality can be considered as the same sort of fallacy as the proverbial drunk looking for the lost keys under the street lamp because that is where the light is. But if we look beyond the light of that beguiling street lamp, randomness can certainly be found as a force that shapes and restrains the individual conduct of civil servants.

For example, Napoleonic bureaucracies of the French type have traditionally moved people around their ramified field structures in ways that are far from fully predictable, and this is arguably one of the few defences in such systems against the ability of a small group of 'old friends' to arrange matters as they choose ('A bunch of old friends, that is our Republic!' as a French mayor once put it (Becquart-Leclercq, 1978)). The practice of moving higher civil servants to a new posting every few years, like Methodist ministers, was also deeply entrenched in the traditional British and Japanese systems. In numerous civil service systems, promotion has traditionally tended to mean a move from one place or unit to another, producing an element of uncertainty even within a closed-career corps structure, while in other civil service systems (such as Norway) lateral entry to higher positions produced an element of uncertainty in another way.

Randomness at the top is produced in another way in bureaucracies with a party-spoils tradition, as in the different party-spoils systems of the USA and Germany. In those cases, the intersection of career and political administrators produces a less than fully predictable set of colleagues and reproduces many of the features of Cohen, March and Olsen's (1972) famous 'garbage-can model' of decision-making at the top of the bureaucracy, in ways that make the payoff matrix for the various players in the game highly uncertain. Moreover, some element of randomness is often linked to oversight controls, for example in random security checks or financial audits, and it can appear in competition systems too, for example when the competitors cannot be sure of exactly what it takes to win prizes such as promotion to the top.

In short, randomness in the control of higher bureaucracies is all too often invisible to conventional analysis, but elements of it, albeit in different forms, can be found in most of the state systems examined here and it is of great theoretical significance for the understanding of control of senior civil servants. It is significant because making the payoffs of activity less than fully predictable is one of the most important ways to limit the scope for bureaucrats to play the system by the sort of simple strategies (exploiting built-in information asymmetry) that were stressed by early New Right rational choice analysts of bureaucracy, notably William Niskanen (1971).

2 Patterns of Change: Arrow, Circle or Brownian Motion?

The 'New Public Management' era has been an age of 'arrow' theories

(McFarland, 1991: 257) of change in civil service systems, and it has produced numerous grandiose claims about changes in control over upper-level civil servants. Many commentators, from Aucoin (1990) to Maor (1999) and Rhodes and Weller (2001) detect an 'arrow' pattern of tighter oversight and direction from elected politicians over higher civil servants in the parliamentary countries – changing higher civil servants from self-controlling 'mandarins' to 'valets', according to the latter. And much has been said about the frequently voiced aspirations for more competitive and tightly managed public bureaucracies in the contemporary era, implicitly less subject to garbage-can processes and random controls. (Much less has been clearly established about the success or otherwise of those aspirations.)

However, our observations about control of higher bureaucracies in this study do not sustain a dramatic 'arrow' theory of change, with all the countries clearly heading for the same reform nirvana. Rather, what we see are some 'arrow' patterns, some cycles, something approximating 'Brownian motion' (irregular oscillatory movement) and some sheer stasis, in spite of all the reform hype. Table 4.2 presents some summary indicators of how the higher bureaucracies in the countries in this study were traditionally controlled and how those controls have changed, within the framework of the four polar types of control presented in Chapter 1. Any indicators of this kind must necessarily be imperfect, and should be treated as first approximations, but they provide a starting point for comparisons across countries and over time.

The indicators for oversight amount to a count of some familiar structures and procedures in government designed to control civil services. Indicators of mutuality are intended to show how far members of the higher civil service have procedures that allow them to assess each other's conduct in office, control entry into the service and advancement through the ranks. To some extent competition is indicated by the inverse of such measures, including the extent to which there are external pressures on civil service careers coming from non-career entrants, and the extent to which competition inside organizations is linked to competition between organizations. Finally, one of the indicators for contrived randomness relates to the extent to which governments attempt to break up established structures and patterns and expose civil servants to unpredictable scrutiny from outsiders.

(a) Oversight explosion?
In many countries there have been numerous political pressures over the last generation for more oversight of government in general and of the public bureaucracy in particular. Some of these pressures came from political activists outside government but they also came from political elites who wanted to exert more leverage over policy and administration (Peters and Pierre, 2001). Indeed, all the countries in our set added some means of oversight over their high

Table 4.2 Some summary (and approximate) comparative indicators of control at 2000 (equivalent data for 1970s in parentheses where available)

	France	Germany	Japan	USA	Norway	UK	Netherlands
Oversight							
1 Presence of specialized oversight organizations (approx. number)	22(24)	4 (3)	3 (2)	4 (1)	1	4 (2)	3 (2)
2 Presence of formalized code of conduct	Y	Y	Y (N)	Y	N	Y(N)	Y
3 Presence of code of administrative procedure	Y	Y	Y (N)	Y	Y (N)	N	Y
4 Presence of committee system for legislative oversight	Y	Y	Y	Y	Y	Y	Y
5 Number of other legislative institutions for oversight (ombudsman etc.)	1(0)	3 (1)	1 (0)	1 (0)	1	1	1 (0)
Mutuality							
6 Percentage of civil service covered by closed career system	100	100	99	100/5[1]	75 (89)	85 (100)[1]	90 (100)
7 Role of civil servants in promotion and retention decisions for top three levels	Y	Y	Y	Y	Y	Y	Y
8 Presence of a *corps* structure	Y	N	N	Y	N	N	Y
Competition							
9 Use of competitive exams	Y	N	Y	N	N	Y	N
10 Success rate in competitive exams if known	9	N/A	42	N/A	N/A	1	N/A
11 Use of league tables for control of higher civil service	N	N	N	Y (N)	N	Y (N)	Y (N)
Randomness							
12 Percentage of higher civil service spending 80% or more of career in same organization	40	85	70 (85)	80 (85)	50 (70)	40 (80)	N/A
13 Presence of randomized audits	N	Y (N)	N	Y (N)	N	Y (N)	N

Note: 1 100 per cent for civil service per se; much less if political appointees are considered.

bureaucracies during the last 30 years or so, and in some cases those additions seem to have been significant. Some, like Japan, were starting from a low base of oversight-intensity, since Japan, like the UK, had traditionally relied heavily on mutuality and a shared samurai ethic to control its higher bureaucracy. But over the last 30 years Japan added one specialized institution for oversight, strengthened procedural requirements and also activated an element of legislative oversight that had hitherto been dormant since the Meiji restoration. Others, like the USA, were starting from a high base of oversight-intensity, but the USA added to its already substantial investment in oversight by setting up yet more oversight institutions such as the Inspectors-General of the Carter-Reagan era (Light, 1993).

Whether that amounts to evidence for a generalized oversight explosion for individual conduct of higher civil servants, however, is at best debatable. After all, most of the expansion in oversight machinery and institutions was in the form of waste-watching, quality policing and policy-checking of one kind or another, as in the case of the general rise of value-for-money auditing, and thus was more concerned with control of public service organizations rather than the individual conduct of higher civil servants. Moreover, such oversight increase as took place – and that was arguably much less than that faced by those in some other domains of the public service, such as the universities – seems (see Hood and Scott in Section 4.8) to have been largely 'part of an unintended backwash or boomerang effect from oversight systems aimed primarily at other parts of the public service'.

It is true that in the post-cold war era of heightened consciousness of 'sleaze' and misconduct, more attention in many countries was paid to the honesty and probity of individuals in high public office. But much of the attention was directed to elected politicians as much or more as on senior bureaucrats. For bureaucrats, much of the sleaze-watching was conducted through more intense use of existing organizations (notably public prosecutors) rather than new organizations, and where new organizations were established, in all our cases but one (the former East Germany) they tended to constitute the palest shadow of the sort of draconian oversight represented by the Special Prosecutor's Office established in the USA after the Nixon presidency and abolished under the George W. Bush presidency after having over-reached itself politically under the Clinton presidency. Many of the new codes of ethics and the machinery for developing and applying them were an extension of traditional 'internal' modes of discipline.

Moreover, any increased intensity of anti-sleaze operations took place in an overall context in which some kinds of oversight of individual behaviour were being wound back. Examples include the relaxation of traditional penny-pinching oversight of procurement decisions to allow senior civil servants to use government credit cards with lighter procedural requirements than those applying previously (as in the USA and Australia), the relaxation of traditional classified civil service pay and grading controls into a regime that allowed the pay of individual civil servants to be set without close oversight from central agencies, and in some cases, such as the UK, an apparent loosening of the rules and conventions about communication up and down the chain of policy command in the bureaucracy (Foster, 1996), as revealed by the increasing importance of – largely unregulated – special advisers and the 1996 Scott Report on the Sale of Arms to Iraq (Scott, 1996). And though our contributors found it hard to document, for obvious reasons, it seems likely that the hidden oversight systems of security vetting and the like may have waxed and waned with events (such as the cold war and the attacks on the USA on 11 September 2001) rather than describing any single 'arrow' pattern. Changes in oversight seem to have been by no means a one-way street.

(b)　Mutuality implosion?

In an era often said comprise growing scepticism about 'government', we might expect oversight to be increasingly substituted for mutuality in the control of higher bureaucrats. But this study produced rather little evidence that mutuality has suddenly disappeared as a mechanism for regulating individual conduct in the higher state bureaucracy, though in several cases (notably Japan and Germany) it seems to have been reshaped and to have weakened somewhat in its traditional forms.

Nevertheless, Japan and Germany have up to the time of writing maintained a wholly closed-career system in the civil service (with the expectation of peer-group control as a key element of control over senior bureaucrats). France's personnel system remains closed at the beginning of the career, and lateral entry at mid-career tends to be in the outward direction – to the private sector – rather than into the higher reaches of the bureaucracy. Likewise in most countries the civil service remains a key player in the selection process for posts at the highest levels in the service. Indeed, in two cases – the USA and the Netherlands – the creation of a senior executive service has been in effect the creation of a new corps structure that is able to exercise a certain amount of control over its own members.

The one area in which there has been some apparent loss for mutuality in the control of the higher civil service is the opening of higher-level positions in some states to outside recruits on permanent or temporary contracts. Again, some countries took this route from a low base, and perhaps the most dramatic opening of this type over the period we are examining here took place in the UK, where a closed career system was replaced by a significant amount of lateral entry recruitment for higher positions, especially in the executive agencies that were created during the Thatcher and Major governments. The Netherlands also changed in the same direction, though not to the same extent as in the UK. But other countries always had a significant amount of lateral recruitment. For instance, the upper level of administration in the USA has been open to outside political appointments for the entire time period, though there was some 'thickening' of government (in Light's, 1995, term) as ever more political appointees were added to the upper echelons of government. In Norway, too, lateral entry has been a traditional feature of civil service that contrasts with closed-career systems, and that seems to have increased some-what during the time period we are investigating here.

3   Conclusion

If the domain of higher education and research presents a picture of sharply growing oversight in most of our countries and the case of prisons shows less dramatic change at the domestic level (albeit with a growth in international standards activity), the individual conduct of higher civil servants looks like an intermediate case. Competition declined in several cases as the attractions of alternative career paths directed some of the best and brightest away from closed-career civil service systems during the boom years of the 1980s and 1990s, and the competitive element had to be injected in rather different forms, notably in pay-for-performance systems and lateral entry in some closed-career bureaucracies. The international feature of control in the other two cases (manifested as a weak form of oversight in the case of prisons and mainly as mutuality and competition in the case of higher education and research) is markedly less prominent in senior civil service systems. Despite the quasi-Maoist permanent-revolution reform hype that became normal in many countries over the last decade or so and numerous claims of world-historical change sweeping across the world by 'arrow' theorists of change, traditional systems of control over individual conduct of higher civil servants in most cases do not seem to have changed out of recognition over this time period and deeply entrenched institutional differences remained in the specific ways that the four main types of control played out in detail in each civil service system.

4.2   THE USA: HIGH ON OVERSIGHT, LOW ON MUTUALITY?
B. Guy Peters

What do we mean by 'the higher civil service' in the USA? Several alternative conceptions are available, but some possible groups will be excluded here for reasons of analytic tractability. First, I will discuss only the higher civil service at the federal level. The bulk of US public employment is at the state and local levels but, unlike Germany, the systems are hardly integrated at all, and attempting to deal with the wide variations in formal and informal regulations across the 50 systems would be monumental, tedious and in many ways unproductive.

Even restricting the analysis to the federal level, there are tricky issues about how to treat presidential and secretarial political appointees, because several thousand political appointees hold senior positions equivalent to those held by career civil servants in many European countries (Heclo, 1977). The typical executive department has four or more layers of political appointees above career civil servants. Those careerists may have responsible jobs and often manage substantial budgets and staff numbers, but they are supervised by political appointees, who have the real responsibility for policy and programmes. Likewise, policy advice coming from within the bureaucracy is usually through political appointees before reaching the cabinet secretary, or even the agency head. From our analytic viewpoint, these birds of passage add a substantial element of randomness to controls over the bureaucracy.

While these political appointees direct the career bureaucracy, they are themselves controlled in several ways. They serve at the pleasure of the President, and/or other political officials, and can (subject to political constraints) be dismissed and disciplined easily. The lack of elaborate regulation to control these employees may also reflect the strength of the mutuality controls to which they are subject. Since they belong to the party or profess the ideology of the incumbent administration, others in the party continually monitor their actions and assess their prospects. Favourable evaluations by such peers are important for those whose career may involve successive moves in and out of government. Moreover, they are subject to mutuality controls from a second reference group. As Heclo (1978a) argued, political appointees are members of policy communities that shape policy regardless of which party is in office, and political appointees now need to have substantive expertise and connections in the policy fields they are working in, rather than just partisan affiliation. That means that while they may want to shape policy in line with their party's ideological preferences, they also need the respect of their fellow experts within the relevant 'epistemic community'.

The regulation of the career public service, on which the remainder of this section focuses, follows a rather different pattern. Presidents often feel that their first task as managers in government is to gain some control over the career officials who are meant to be their official helpers (Aberbach and Rockman, 2000), but political control over such officials is problematic. Career civil servants enjoy protections associated with the tradition of a politically neutral civil service with associated protections, and presidential control is also difficult because of the separation of powers and the independent role of Congress in making personnel policy and in oversight of the administration (Aberbach, 1990).

I will now discuss the various controls available to both President and Congress when they deal with the higher levels of the permanent bureaucracy. To these controls must be added others that are exercised within the civil service system, and by other actors in and out of government. The various controls address a range of issues, including prevention of 'fraud, waste and abuse' and abuse of power. For elected and appointed political leaders the crucial control question is how to ensure that they are actually in charge of the organizations that make and implement policy. But there are countervailing concerns about the politicization of the civil service, and perhaps an excess of control instruments available to the political level of the administration.

1   Hierarchical Controls: Direction, Regulation and Oversight

The Constitution gives the President the duty 'to ensure that the laws be faithfully executed', a seemingly innocuous phrase that has spawned a federal bureaucracy of about 2.8 million employees, with some 7000 members of the Senior Executive Service at the upper levels (as well as a few people still employed in the General Schedule 16–18 grades). This relatively small group is meant to manage the rest of the civil service as well as providing some policy advice to the political appointees who come and go.

The federal government's personnel system is a mix of political appointment and a highly legalistic merit system for the career civil service that goes back to the 1887 Pendleton Act. Over time more categories of federal employment have been subject to the merit principles first developed in this Act, which built a civil service primarily recruited and managed through detailed regulations. The regulations determined how bureaucrats were hired, promoted, disciplined and (if necessary) fired (there are a significant number of dismissals for cause each year, though few are at senior levels). These detailed regulations made management of federal personnel very inflexible and served as a straitjacket for managers.

Another of the 'traditional' regulations governing the civil service is the 1939 Hatch Act, formally titled 'An Act to Prevent Pernicious Political Activities'. This Act imposes severe restrictions on political activity by civil servants, and was originally interpreted to prohibit civil servants from any form of political activity except voting. Since then the courts and Congress have gradually expanded the political rights of civil servants, though civil servants are still prohibited from political activities such as running for office or taking major roles in political campaigns. Yet, as will be argued below, the dangers of politicization of the higher civil service may not come primarily from the more overt political activities of civil servants.

The first major departure from the traditional pattern of regulation came when the Carter Administration created the Senior Executive Service, to which most senior civil servants now belong, through the 1978 Civil Service Reform Act (CSRA) Ingraham and Ban, 1984). The CSRA's purpose was to create a mobile management cadre following the (assumed) model of the European higher civil services. It also split the former Civil Service Commission into two independent organizations. One, the Office of Personnel Management (OPM), managed the federal personnel system, including testing, hiring, promotion and discipline. The other, the Merit System Protection Board (MSPB), monitored the work of OPM and handled complaints from federal civil servants about violations of merit principles. A third smaller organization – the Office of the Special Counsel – was created soon afterwards to process allegations of the most egregious violations of merit principles.

The Senior Executive Service (SES) has been called 'Carter's gift to Reagan', because the CSRA gave the president more powers over the higher civil service (see Savoie, 1994). It permitted up to 10 per cent of general management positions in the SES to be appointed politically, further increasing the already substantial grip of the President over top-level staff in government. Many of those appointed to the political positions were career civil servants willing to forsake the protections of the merit system (especially tenure) for the opportunity of a more interesting position. The CSRA also loosened the tenure protections of senior civil servants (political or not) so they risked being fired for poor performance. The political appointees risked being dismissed simply because they had lost the confidence of their political masters, and would almost certainly lose their positions following a change in administration.

The Carter administration added another important overseer of the public bureaucracy at all levels, the Inspectors-General, assigned to each major organization in the federal government. Their task is to guard against 'fraud, waste and abuse' and they are linked to the chief executive of their organizations, but also report to Congress and possess a range of instruments to detect and punish malfeasance (numerous instances of which normally appear in their annual reports).

Of the other more recent legislation governing the conduct and conditions of the higher civil service, one of the more important concerns pay and perquisites. Older legislation had contained a commitment to pay equality between the public and private sectors, but that commitment collapsed in 1989 as government pay for senior level positions fell well behind the private sector and government then attempted instead to keep federal pay raises in step with price inflation. The main barrier to pay equality, apart from cost, is the political requirement to set executive salaries equal to, or below, Congressional pay, which is limited by pressures of political competition. The annual pay raises are also politicized in that Congress and the President have to agree on them (for instance, in 2003 President Bush approved a raise 1 per cent less than that recommended by Congress, to help pay for the 'War on Terrorism').

Finally, the senior civil service is regulated by many of the same acts that impact all members of the civil service. In addition to the Inspectors General Act mentioned above, the Whistleblowers Protection Act and most importantly the Administrative Procedures Act all regulate the behaviour of civil servants. Some of this legislation is intended to control organizations more than individuals, but it imposes particular constraints on senior civil servants because of their responsibility for programmes. To some extent these provisions depend for their effectiveness on mutuality (in the sense of civil servants whistle-blowing on one another) rather than pure oversight.

As well as formal powers of oversight and direction available to President and Congress these officials, and especially the president, can set a tone within government that can shape behaviour. For instance, the George W. Bush administration brought with it a corporate culture and sought to manage government from the top down, in contrast to the more participatory, bottom-up style of the previous Clinton administration. It sought to mix hierarchical direction with control through competition, and a more general development of a managerial 'results orientated' culture placed increasing demands on senior civil servants for reaching performance targets.

2 Control through Competition

Traditionally, control through competition occurred at entry into the civil service. Most civil servants were recruited through formal examinations and, for higher grades, entry was secured through educational qualifications and appropriate university degrees. But, given that the civil service was not a prestigious career, the level of competition was actually rather slight. The one exception was the Foreign Service, entered by a rigorous examination and interviews. However, after entry into the civil service, the main competition was for promotion. Pay followed a rigid grid system, with different pay rates only possible if a position was uprated. Traditional tenure arrangements, preventing dismissal without substantial proof of malfeasance or nonfeasance, also reduced competition, but competition was greater at the top of the service, given the continual interaction with political leaders.

The 1978 CSRA introduced several competitive mechanisms for controlling the senior civil service. The most important was a limited pay for performance scheme for the SES. The implicit deal underlying the 1978 Act was that members of the SES would trade job security for the opportunity for increased rewards. Those rewards were to take the form of bonuses for outstanding performance, rather than permanent increases in base salaries, because the latter route might violate the political principle of keeping civil service salaries below Congressional salaries.

Implementation of this bonus scheme has been problematic almost from the start (GAO, 1987). At least initially bonus payments were severely limited, and measuring performance of senior managers in any serious manner is difficult. The USA has been relatively slow to move to performance contracts or similar agreements for senior managers, although some were introduced as a result of the Gore Commission's 1993 National Performance Review. The absence of agreed criteria for judging performance has permitted use of political and/or personal loyalty criteria rather than job performance in a strict sense in the assignment of bonuses.

The Clinton administration discontinued performance bonuses for political appointees in the SES, believing it was inappropriate to reward individuals who were in government for only a short time in the same way as career public servants, but the George W. Bush administration reinstated bonuses for some appointees, notably non-career SES members. Critics feared that this plan would place more pressures for political conformity on appointees and the civil servants with whom they worked (Lichtbau, 2002), displacing the public interest or efficiency criteria intended in the CSRA. The George W. Bush administration also sought to use competition to enhance political control over the civil service by proposing to 'privatize' approximately 850 000 federal jobs, in the sense that selection of employees and administration of the reward system would be managed outside the existing civil service system (Krugman, 2002), extending a principle already applied to about 100 000 employees when the Department of Homeland Security was created (Congressional Digest, 2002).

The 'results oriented' government promoted by the Management Agenda of the George W. Bush administration also involved a new mix of competition and hierarchical direction in control over the civil service (see Peters, 2002). The 1993 Government Performance and Results Act primarily addressed the organizational rather than the individual level of control, but to the extent that individual civil servants were associated with a programme, the application of the principles of the Act also shaped individual behaviour (Wye, 2000).

The Management Agenda was in essence a performance management document, but it required the reduction of civil service protections to give the control system the 'teeth' that the President and his staff at the Office of Management and Budget wanted. This change can also be considered as a way of using competition among employees to enhance performance, but the changes were being implemented in the absence of a clear performance management system, raising a real possibility of abuse and the use of political criteria in recruitment and management.

To increase competition among civil servants and their organizations, the

OMB began in 2001 to publish an annual 'Executive Management Scorecard' rating departments and agencies on their achievements in five areas selected by the President (Human Capital Management, Competitive Sourcing, Financial Management, E-government, and Budget/Performance Integration). On the first round of ratings, published in 2001, most organizations failed in all the categories and there was only one completely satisfactory rating. Evidently it was not the kind of race where everyone is a winner and all get prizes.

3   Control through Mutuality

As with any elite group, the higher career civil service in the USA operates some self-regulation, but perhaps to a lesser extent than do their counterparts in other industrialized democracies. The relative absence of effective self-regulation is partly a function of the higher civil service not being considered a true elite in the USA, reflecting general public scepticism about government in general and bureaucracy in particular. The capacity of bureaucrats to regulate themselves is also limited by career paths that keep individuals within a single department or agency for their entire career. There may be some mutual control within that structure, but not for the service as a whole.

If anything the capacity for control through mutuality is being reduced by contemporary changes in the federal government. The changes in personnel management, and the chief executive officer (CEO) style of governing are reducing the stability of the public service and further diminishing any sense of their being an elite group. The 'thickening' of government (Light, 1995) is also directing many issues upward in the organizational hierarchy and making the system more politicized. Ironically, this development has followed the reforms of the Gore Commission that sought to increase decentralization and emphasized the importance of lower echelon employees in defining issues and even managing organizations.

4   Summary

As shown above, the US higher civil service is heavily regulated by a myriad of laws, covering traditional issues of 'merit', political activity and prevention of 'fraud, waste and abuse' and extending more recently to the promotion of managerial values and behaviour. Rather obviously, the accumulated body of legislation is at times contradictory in its purposes and creates confusion for public sector managers that may amount to a form of randomness.

Although there is a strong legal and hierarchical basis for regulation there are several other types of control in operation. At the time of writing the George W. Bush administration was emphasizing competition and more market-based controls, and the emphasis increasingly was on performance and results for both individuals and for organizations. That emphasis may bring control of the US higher civil service more in line with other countries, but may also politicize the civil service through the back door. Emphasizing competitiveness has come to mean greater latitude in hiring, and with that a potential decline in merit principles, particularly for the higher civil service.

4.3   JAPAN: WHERE MUTUALITY REIGNS SUPREME?
Takashi Nishio

1   Introduction

Despite the fact that the Japanese government has eagerly transplanted Western systems for more than a century, and the Japanese lifestyle has become increasingly westernized, most observers, both at home and abroad, find strong elements of the traditional culture in seemingly modern, western-ized government institutions in Japan. The persistence of traditional values can be seen in the way the higher civil service is controlled. Mutuality, as contrasted with competition, oversight or contrived randomness in the cultural theory (Hood, 1998; Thompson, Ellis and Wildavsky, 1990) remains the basic pattern of control over (and within) Japan's high state bureaucracy, with egal-itarian mutual adjustment at all levels of governance. But it links with a notably hierarchical structure.

Given the strength of mutuality, oversight is relatively weak in Japanese bureaucracy. Observers have identified some lack of accountability of the government and weakness in external oversight of the bureaucracy. But that goes along with strong elements of hierarchy in Japanese administration, applying not only within organizations, but also in inter-organizational rela-tions. What is called 'exalt the officials, despise the people' (*Kanson-minpi*) thinking epitomizes this cultural tendency.

Competition is also a prominent phenomenon of organizational life in Japan. The highly competitive nature of the examination for the Faculty of Law of Tokyo University, of the examinations for fast-stream positions in the national civil service (the level 1 examination for career officials) and of the race for permanent secretary positions in ministries, are all well-known. Political scientist Takeshi Ishida saw both competition and conformity as key concepts to understand the Japanese political culture. 'Every society contains, to a varying degree, elements of conformity and of competition. What is unique about Japan is that these two elements are so closely intertwined within its social and cultural context', and 'in a conformity-conscious society like Japan, competition takes the form of competition to prove one's loyalty,

whether to the emperor or to the state . . .' (Ishida, 1983: 23, 31). Such competition is not necessarily connected with the Western style of individualism, but
it nevertheless works effectively as a management tool to maintain order in
Japanese government.

Finally, contrived randomness, associated with fatalist view of organizational life, also features strongly in Japanese bureaucracy. Each official sees
the promotion and transfer process as nothing but random or irrational because
of the way the Personnel Section of the Minister's Secretariat deal with the
assignment of hundreds of career bureaucrats to Tokyo headquarter positions,
to local branches and offices overseas. On average fast-streamers move from
one position to another once every one or two years, and such changes of posting often mean physical transfers and house moves. Such moves are a test of
loyalty to the ministry for each official, and obedient acceptance is required.
A person who refuses the decision of the Personnel Section, which sometimes
happens now, drops out of the race. Such a pre-modern style of loyalty is associated with 'a sense of calm trust in Fate, a quiet mission to the inevitable',
something that Inazo Nitobe (1969: 1) thought Buddhism had contributed to
the Japanese conception of chivalry (*Bushido*).

Indeed, control patterns in Japanese bureaucracy form a complex mixture
of Japanese and Western, pre-modern and modern, naturally developed and
artificially designed elements, and includes all of the four primary forms of
control analysed in this book. Further, the persistence of immanent cultural
influences does not mean that the Japanese government has not tried to change
control styles. Rather, many post-war constitutional reforms were aimed at
democratizing the traditional bureaucratic culture, including features such as
official privilege and administrative compartmentalization. Recent administrative reforms, beginning in the early 1980s, also aimed to mitigate the highly
centralized, closed governmental system. Those reforms have comprised
deregulation, privatization of the three main public corporations (for railways,
telecommunications and tobacco) in the 1980s, decentralization (2000), enactment of an Administrative Procedure Law (1994) and a Freedom of
Information Law (2001), reorganization of central ministries (2001) and ongoing civil service reform.

2   The Point of Departure: The Importance of Mutuality

Mutuality is dominant in modern Japan's governance. Since the 1868 Meiji
Restoration, the concept of 'family' (*Ie*) has been important for nation-
building, institutional and organizational development. As the Japanese word
Kokka (state) literally means 'a house of the country', the ideal state was seen
as an extended family with the emperor as father and the people his children
(*Sekishi*). An old Japanese phrase *Hakko Ichiu* (to put all places under one

roof) was a national slogan during the Second World War and symbolized the idea of forming the nation-state as a family. The same idea applied at the level of companies or ministries, where harmony (*Wa*) without conflict was the ideal. In a sense, separation of the government and the people, compartmentalization within government, and the lack of co-ordination among ministries, can be understood as following from the latent ideal of making an organization like a family. This mixture of egalitarianism and hierarchy continues, but the degree of the former seems to have increased with post-Second World War democratization and economic growth.

An account of the *Ringi* system, administrative guidance and factors lying behind the weakness of Cabinet co-ordination can help to bring out the dominance of mutuality in Japanese government. The *Ringi* system, a distinctive form of collective decision-making, is a typical form of mutual adjustment within government. When it was first introduced it was used to show that policy proposals are originated by the lower level of administrators and written up in a specified form (*Ringi-sho*) for approval by higher officials. Proposals are circulated in sequence to all the officials under whose jurisdiction the question falls, finally reaching the person at the top empowered to give it final approval (Abe and Shindo, 1994: 37).

Administrative guidance (*Gyosei Shido*) is another reflection of the culture of mutuality in Japanese government. It is an informal custom by which administrative agencies attempt to make specific individuals or organizations do their bidding over the application or execution of law, but in which, without any basis in law, spontaneous agreement and co-operation is elicited from the other party by setting out what the administrative agency hopes or wishes to see done (Abe and Shindo, 1994: 35). It involves rich communication between the administration and other actors, each of which is dependent on the other for information or action.

This custom is linked to the 'descent from heaven' (*Amakudari*) pattern, in which bureaucrats retire early to take up senior posts in companies related to their ministry – a practice which has attracted criticism and was a theme raised by the opposition party in the 2003 general election. Administrative guidance is both cause and consequence of intimate relationships between administrative agencies and their clients, but these relationships are far from transparent and no one can tell which party is more powerful. Guy Peters has described the movement of people between the sectors as 'the colonization of the society by bureaucrats or, conversely, the colonization of the public service by representatives of certain interest in the society' (Peters, 2001: 98). For instance, top bank employees may stay in close touch with the Ministry of Finance (MOF). Without them the banks cannot know the subtle content of the MOF's policy or administrative guidance and the MOF cannot regulate the banks effectively (Ishizawa, 1998: 145–7).

Weaknesses in the Cabinet also reflect mutuality. The Cabinet, first established in 1885, suffered from weaknesses in co-ordinating power until the defeat after the Second World War. The problem originated in leaders' excessive efforts to balance the powers of two dominant clans (Choshu and Satsuma) in the Meiji era but, later, over-compartmentalization and the absence of civilian control over the armed forces exacerbated the problem. As a result of the post-war constitutional reform, reflecting the fact that Japan had gone to war because of weak political leadership, the authority of the Cabinet was formally strengthened. The Prime Minister became a substantial political leader, not just the *primus inter pares*, being empowered to appoint and dismiss other ministers. The change of the status of the emperor, and the abolition of the military force, which had been another independent power centre before the war, also helped the Cabinet to increase its authority.

3　The Changing Mix of Controls

One of the most important post-war reforms concerned the nature of public officials. Before the war they had been called the 'officials of the emperor' and were not responsible to the people at large, but the new constitution of Japan redefined the relationship between officials and people, declaring; 'the people have the inalienable right to choose their public officials and to dismiss them. All public officials are servants of the whole community and not of any group thereof' (Article 15). Reflecting that notion, ministers' powers over the civil service are only nominal and political appointment of higher civil servants has been very limited. The autonomous nature of personnel management within each ministry was justified by the logic of administrative neutrality and rationality. A significant feature in the history of Japanese personnel administration was that an old absolutist system was shifted to a new rational system without experiencing a political spoils system. There have been a few, rare cases in which ministers promoted or dismissed higher officials against the will of their ministries, but such instances were not usually regarded as a form of democratic control.

Another important post-war reform was the establishment of the National Personnel Authority (NPA), Japan's first independent public personnel organization. The NPA was given a wide range of quasi-legislative and quasi-judicial powers to prevent party politics from jeopardizing the rationality of personnel administration. The history of the NPA has been one of constant struggle and compromise with forces opposed to its autonomy, in which the NPA has lost some of its formal powers one by one (Nishio, 1988). In a sense, the NPA gained stability and an accepted position within government in exchange for giving some ground on its original mission and independent status.

Thus, the NPA's role in shaping the high bureaucracy is now limited. But when many scandals involving higher officials came to light in the 1990s, most of which concerned companies 'treating' those officials, the NPA was expected to respond. Having failed to tighten discipline inside ministries, the government decided to enact an ethics law for the civil service in 1998, enforced by the National Public Service Ethics Board. But the enforcement of this law has turned out to be unpopular because it prevents officials from having contacts or collecting information necessary for policy-making.

Another organization overseeing the bureaucracy, the Board of Audit (BOA) is highly independent, with its status guaranteed by the constitution. The BOA audits the public accounts every year and reports to the Diet. Although each administrative section becomes sensitive before the BOA visits its office to examine the accounts, the BOA is not regarded as an effective controller of the bureaucracy. Rather, it is seen as an organization that relies solely on its formal, autonomous status without being involved in difficult mutual adjustment processes with other organizations.

Finally, the Administrative Management Agency (AMA) was established in 1948, originally to conduct administrative inspections and later to oversee staff numbers. Although the AMA claims that it conducts inspections as a 'third party', it is criticized on the grounds that the results of its inspections are revealed only after 'mutual adjustment' by the AMA and the ministry or agency in question. The AMA's oversight of staff numbers seem to have real effects, but this must be understood along with the increase of public corporations, which are also checked by the AMA. (The AMA's functions were absorbed in a new Management and Coordination Agency in 1984, and re-organized again in 2001.)

In short, the organizations charged with overseeing the bureaucracy cannot help being involved in mutual adjustments with those they oversee. Since the custom of *Amakudari* also exists in the oversight organizations, they need help from the ministries they oversee to find posts for themselves outside government, because the oversight bodies usually do not have client companies of their own. In addition, there are several key positions in those oversight organizations that are 'occupied' or 'colonized' by the MOF or other powerful ministries.

4 Analyzing the Contemporary Pattern

In the mid-1990s, most people began to feel that no organization could reliably control the bureaucracy. Only the Public Prosecutors Office (PPO) was active in prosecuting 'unethical' bureaucrats (including a permanent secretary), as well as corrupt politicians. The PPO's activities were built on formal oversight authority, relatively free from the pervasive bureaucratic culture of mutuality. In contrast to the PPO's power and independence, the Diet does not use its formal authority to control the bureaucracy. Although 'each House may conduct investigations in relation to government, and may demand the presence and testimony of witness, and the production of records' (Constitution, Article 62), it is rare for either House to conduct investigations of the bureaucracy, for at least two reasons. First, ministries and civil servants can reject investigations on the grounds that the information required is a matter of national security. Second, the Diet depends on the bureaucracy for information and staff work on legislation. It is ironic that ordinary Japanese citizens have a right to know the content of government activities through the 2001 Freedom of Information Law, while the Diet still lacks authority or information.

Judging from the above facts, the Japanese bureaucracy is accountable only to those people or groups that are relatively independent of ministries and have a culture of 'defiance'. In a society where the culture of mutuality is dominant, formal rules for administrative accountability would not work because the overseers have a mutual relationship with their charges. Since the bureaucracy has been regarded as a source of money, information and power, very few organizations and people, including politicians, have tried to be independent of the bureaucracy, or tried to oppose it. So the borders between the public and private sectors, between bureaucrats and politicians, and even between central and local governments, have been blurred.

5   The Effectiveness of Controls over Government

What are the conditions for transplanting individualist or hierarchist approaches to control into a soil with such a rich culture of mutuality? First, there are numerous experiences of hybrid organizational models being created in the private sector. Many companies have been successful in developing egalitarian styles of organization under strong leaders such as Mr S. Honda or Mr A. Morita in very competitive markets. So it is ironic that the Japanese government seldom tried to borrow ideas from its own private sector, while other countries have been more interested in learning from Japanese business customs.

Second, hierarchical relationships have been the social basis of modern Japan. The present situation, in which no one seems to respect authority, is regarded as a transitional stage from an unenlightened world to a more rational, democratic civil society. As the nature of authority changes from a mysterious one (in which the Emperor is conceived as a god) to a more down-to-earth one, oversight as a type of control over government may become more acceptable. In addition, rising fiscal pressures may make the costs of co-ordination in the traditional way too high, with more need for fixed rules and regulations, rather than mutuality or negotiation.

Third, civil service reform may be more important than structural change of the ministries, but will only be effective if it can bring about cultural change in the bureaucracy. Changing the deep-rooted bureaucratic culture of mutuality would need to be based on a selective strategy of change. The important thing is to change mutual relationships from a closed policy community into a more open policy forum, and promote the diversification of the civil service. And it is possible that local rather than central government may be the key driver of such a change, because (since Japan adopted a presidential system at the local level after the Second World War), governors and mayors, directly supported by the people, can exert stronger leadership than the Prime Minister and many such figures are experimenting on a trial-and-error basis with various reform ideas, reflecting changes in popular culture.

4.4 FRANCE: HIGH MUTUALITY, SOME RANDOMNESS, WEAK OVERSIGHT
Nicole de Montricher

1 The Traditional System of Control

Mutuality, centred on *grands corps* staffed by career civil servants recruited through competitive exams and trained in prestigious *grandes écoles*, was the heart of the traditional system of control. Among these *corps*, *inspections générales* have traditionally functioned as overseers to assist in monitoring the long chain of command from the minister to field services (Ménier, 1988), but their function is exclusively information-gathering rather than standard setting for the bureaucracy. The scope of their supervision includes administrative, financial and technical questions, it is not limited to error detection because it comprises a critical examination of institutions, and can be exerted concurrently with specialized oversight (Degenne, 1975). Most *inspections générales* are within ministries but the prestigious *Inspection générale des finances* supervises accounts across government. Above all the civil service is ruled by mutuality, balanced by a culture of self-control and political loyalty to the minister.

By tradition equality is the glue of the *grands corps*, based on the elitist recruitment of these individuals (Dreyfus, 2000). They are trained to stay in the public service for a career and still monopolize the top positions in the bureaucracy (and in politics, since most top political positions are held by high civil servants, including the current President, Jacques Chirac, who is from the *Cour des comptes*). Standards are set by peer groups and control over individual behaviour is exercised by the *grands corps* themselves. The *Conseil d'État* is the model, recruiting an average of five people per year through a competitive exam at the end of the *École Nationale d'Administration* (ENA) course. The successful candidates either stay in the institution, with their career determined strictly on seniority, or elect to go outside and get involved in competition to be appointed to top positions, in a ministerial *cabinet* for example. Marie Christine Kessler (1986) notes that young members of the *grands corps* are subject to intellectual autonomy in their work and moral socialization by senior individuals.

The expertise of some *corps* members gives them a monopoly over some positions: the *Inspection générale des finances* monopolizes positions in the finance ministry, as does the *corps des ponts et chaussées* in the ministry of public works. Some *grands corps* dominate a specific policy field, such as the *corps des mines* over nuclear policy and the *Conseil d'État* over the media, the railways and the Paris transport system. Nevertheless there is strong institutional competition within the bureaucracy for new areas of influence (though desire for influence does not mean that the *grands corps* have substantive positions on public policies (see Suleiman, 1974; Thoenig, 1987)).

Although mutuality dominated for individuals inside the state structure, the traditional system had competitive elements at several points, notably entry into the *grandes écoles* and *grands corps*. There was also, as in Japan, competition over opportunities to move from government into the private sector, and into lucrative positions in government and quasi-governmental corporations. Some degree of oversight came from the parliament and the strong *grands corps* such as the *Conseil d'État*, and the rotation of staff around the ramified field administration structure, particularly for officers such as *préfets* introduced some key elements of randomness into a closed-career elite system that was seriously vulnerable to cliques and cronyism.

2   Developments since the 1980s

After 23 years of Gaullist rule the 1981 elections produced a socialist majority which undertook several changes, notably decentralization. Privatizations in 1986 and rapid changes in political majorities changed the context in which higher civil servants worked and produced new career opportunities for them. The classical roles remained, but the substance of their jobs changed through politicization, and there was more competition and more randomness, with the average stay in each position being two or three years. Mutuality through the *grands corps* still dominated the control system, but a new breed of 'entrepreneurial civil servants' emerged, moving from the top of the ministerial bureaucracy to positions in public enterprises and eventually in private firms. Although leaving the civil service for a second career is a traditional feature of French public administration, its incidence increased and it now takes place earlier in the career. By the mid-1990s, 45 per cent of France's biggest firms were directed by an ENA or Polytechnique graduate (Bauer and Bertin-Mourot, 1994). The practice was formally regulated in 1991 by setting up a board to advise on possible conflicts of interest, but little change took place in practice because each group is advantaged by permitting departures: individuals gain a new career, the *grands corps* extend their influence over society and private firms gain access to the bureaucracy.

The monopoly over the education of French top civil servants by the ENA and Polytechnique has been criticized, and the partial move of ENA from Paris to Strasbourg (and proposals to move it wholly to Strasbourg) has been seen by some as a threat to its position. Nevertheless, competition from other institutions is limited (Suleiman and Mendras, 1995) and though the competitive examination to enter ENA has been made more open to those with management skills than in the past, public law and the ideology of public service constitute the core of education for higher civil servants. Since 1983 a 'third track' has been instituted to staff ENA with professionals, but their number is limited. The same can be said of the procedure for recruitment *au tour extérieur* which allows a spoils system of political nomination of members of the *grands corps*, but the quotas for such nominations are very limited and the *corps* own advice has to be taken before any decisions.

Reforms designed to debureaucratize the government by limiting the number of ministerial directions eliminated numerous hierarchical grades and set up numerous national services with national authority, but such changes have not introduced any new competition within the higher civil service. On the other hand, a survey conducted in 1991 by Luc Rouban (1994) demonstrated the willingness of higher civil servants to be evaluated according to results, with 48 per cent agreeing and another 25 per cent expressing qualified agreement (Rouban, 1994). In fact, some of the *grands corps* are already partly paid on performance. Other competition-augmenting developments include allowing private firms to bid for some of the work of the smaller *inspections générales* (but not the most prestigious ones like the *Inspection des finances* or *Inspections des affaires sociales*), which, as noted earlier, gather information not only as error detectors but also as management auditors (Joncour, 1999).

Since the 1980s oversight of the activity of the higher civil service has increased to some extent. Legislation in 1979 required justification for unfavourable decisions affecting individuals and various later regulations transformed mutuality by allowing democratic discussion prior to the making of decisons. Over the last 20 years several independent agencies have been created (Chevallier 1986) to oversee the behaviour of the bureaucracy, including the higher civil service, though such bodies are more engaged in standard setting and information-gathering than changing behaviour. There is a distinct element of contrived randomness in the way such bodies operate, and they also limit the traditional form of mutuality by providing more information on high civil service conduct. Other independent regulatory bodies have been set up under EU pressure to set standards under professional norms, separated from political preferences.

3   The Dynamics of Control

The control system contains some elements of contrived randomness for standard-setting, for information-gathering and for behaviour modification, derived from the mixing of politics and administration in France where top civil servants have always been involved in politics. The *cabinet ministériel* (Suleiman, 1974) is symbolic of this composite milieu, since high civil servants play the role of political advisers in such *cabinet*s, meaning that a mix of mutuality and oversight interactions develops between the *cabinet* and the rest of the bureaucracy, while the unpredictable workings of the political process results in constant changes in personnel in the *cabinet* in classic 'garbage-can' fashion (Cohen, March and Olsen, 1972). In such circumstances, standard managerial formulae for evaluating top bureaucrats by corporate 'results' are hard to apply, and the institutional configuration makes the control of higher civil servants essentially a mix of mutuality and randomness.

Information used in oversight is patchy and variable. The *Cour des comptes* and the European Court of Auditors make the provision of some information obligatory, while the *Inspection générale des finances* uses unannounced visits, and routine information gathering is the job of *inspections générales* that are slowly modernizing their operations to supplement their traditional approach based on rule and rote. Independent regulatory agencies can ask for information over specific cases: for example the freedom of information regulator, *Commission d'accès aux documents administratifs*, received numerous individual requests involving refusal of central agencies to deliver documents about individual careers in the civil service. But such activity rarely results in dramatic behavioural change and overseers normally recommend changes rather than adopting a tough prosecution-based approach.

4   Conclusion

Mutuality is at the centre of any new development in public policy in France because top civil servants select specific interest groups and give them access to the bureaucracy. Mutuality is also induced by the fragmentation of the government structures that requires inter-ministerial co-ordination (Jobert and Muller, 1988). The quintessential example of mutuality, epitomizing the operating style of the French bureaucracy, is the role of the prefect who is constantly negotiating with representatives of local governments (Montricher,

2000). Standards set by other authorities are ignored unless they are seen as an order coming from the the Prime Minister or a political demand from the presidency (and the latter is not even possible during periods of *cohabitation* when the President is a member of the political opposition).

That is the background against which the politics of modernizing public administration plays out. Numerous boards and services set standards to improve the public service, including attempts to reorganize central agencies in line with the demands of decentralization and Europeanization, and monitoring activity is highly developed for the field services. But that is not the case for central agencies. The *Cour des comptes* instigates some investigations, and *inspections générales* and private firms also occasionally gather information aimed at reform. But as a rule there is little systematic monitoring of the activity of higher civil servants at the apex of government, and the general practice is that of 'network communication' both inside ministries and between them and their professional counterparts. Even evaluation is conceived as mutuality at this level, with top civil servants usually being involved in any projects to scrutinize activity within their own own institutions (Monnier, 1992). Behaviour modification occasionally occurs as a response to some hierarchical overseer, but more often it is the result to mutual influence, even though behaviour modification of any kind is very difficult to obtain unless ministers themselves are clearly involved in the changes involved.

4.5   GERMANY: VILLAGE LIFE BECOMING MORE COMPLICATED
Hans-Ulrich Derlien

Hierarchy and mutuality have traditionally been central to the control of the senior public service in Germany and remain so. Indeed, of all the administrative systems considered here Germany at federal level has probably been the least changed by managerial reforms over the past generation (Derlien, 1996). Only under fiscal stress resulting in part from German unification in 1990, did such reforms gain any ground, and then mostly at the local and *Land* levels. So new forms of control have not replaced traditional forms of oversight and mutuality, but rather have been laid on top of them, to produce a more 'redundant' pattern of control.

The federal structure produces strong mutuality in control over civil service policy-making. The federal government only 'oversees' the *Länder* in exceptional circumstances, for instance when there are conflicts between the two levels of government over nuclear power plants and waste disposal. Otherwise, mutuality rules in the implementation of federal policy through *Land* governments, in the conduct of both ministers and bureaucrats, and producing particularly strong 'vertical brotherhoods' of expert civil servants produced by common professional background, mutual departmental policy interests and frequent interaction in joint decision-making. Mutuality also applies to co-operation among the 16 *Länder* and EU bureaucrats are also often included in the vertical brotherhoods.

1 Hierarchy, Mutuality and Competition as Controls over the Bureaucracy

Mutuality influences policy-making activity within a federal civil service that is comparatively small, given that federal ministries are separated from operations and implementation. The higher civil service is also relatively homogenous in that most of the 25 state secretaries and 120 division heads are jurists and recruitment to top positions comes mostly from those already working in ministries or from 'politically friendly' *Land* ministries. Inter-departmental mobility is low, but control over policy-making works through bargaining as policy initiatives work their way up the chain of command from policy experts at section level to cabinet level (where the unresolved conflicts are usually settled 'out of court' by last-minute deals between ministers rather than 'shootouts' in cabinet). Mutuality extends across federal ministries and agencies, in spite of varying administrative cultures. Indeed, collegiality is an explicit norm, in that the government manual obliges civil servants to co-operate with one another and it is the duty of any superior to see to it that this norm is observed. Mutuality as a form of control works on the basis of common professional training and administrative culture, but it is also laid down in a legal code and functions 'in the shadow of hierarchy'.

Controls over the activity of civil servants within each ministry involve a combination of mutuality and hierarchy. The mutuality includes 'dialogue' over policy judgements between ministers and civil servants (Mayntz and Scharpf, 1975) and negotiations among colleagues of equal rank. The hierarchic element comes from the way that most activities of civil servants are formalized or subject to legal constraints laid down in the government manual, the civil service and budgetary laws (codes), and ultimately the constitution and the established body of law. Hierarchy is also reinforced by the fact that the topmost civil servants can be put into temporary retirement if they are not politically compatible with the government in office, a fate that has hit roughly half of the 145 topmost civil servants following changes of government since 1969 (Derlien, 1988; 2001).

Hierarchical control inside ministries is not matched by strong external oversight by central agencies, because the so-called *Ressort-Prinzip* (principle of departmental responsibility) enshrined in Article 65 Basic Law leaves the day-to-day running of government departments to their ministers and is interpreted as forbidding centralized personnel policy by the Chancellor or his office. However, there is a federal civil service code, adjudicated by a quasi-independent federal personnel commission set up in 1953 (Engels, 2001). The commission is preoccupied with deciding exceptional cases brought by federal civil servants, and though it produces suggestions on how to improve the civil service code, it does not operate as an oversight institution like the US Civil Service commission. Nor does it function as an ethics commission, because, in contrast to the arrangements for conflict-of-interest cases affecting MPs, ethical norms for the civil service are traditionally contained in the civil service code, which was broadened in 1998 in the context of growing concerns about public service corruption. Infringement of the code lays civil servants open to formal disciplinary measures by hierarchical superiors and in serious cases to be brought to disciplinary courts, which have recently been fused with administrative courts.

Parliamentary oversight of ministries and agencies takes the form of standing committees that shadow ministerial jurisdictions. Much of this oversight is relatively weak, but in the case of irregular operations MPs often put pressure on ministers to change policy, organization or personnel or even drive them to resign. The traditional waste-watcher is the Federal Court of Accounts (FCA), which has pre-democratic origins but now reports to parliament. Its president is elected by parliament, but up to now this office has been held by former top civil servants, albeit recently of the more politicized brand. Despite its aspirations to policy evaluation in the style of the American GAO, the FCA concentrates on traditional legality checks, focuses on cost-saving, and has only limited power to embarrass the federal government by giving ammunition to the taxpayers' union or the parliamentary opposition. Since 1969 the FCA president has also been regularly appointed as federal commissioner for economy in administration, but this involves periodic requests for reform recommendations rather than oversight of the individual behaviour of civil servants.

By contrast with mutuality, and to a lesser extent oversight, competition for office was traditionally not an especially well-developed mechanism for controlling the individual behaviour of higher civil servants. To be sure, elements of control through competition came in the form of fights over budget shares and rivalry for promotion and higher office that one would find in any career structure, but, as already noted, lateral entry has been limited and there has not been the highly institutionalized competitive examinations found in Japan and the UK, nor the necessity of going through a competitive and distinctive educational process as in France. But competition is built into federal relations as well as into the competitive party system. Opposition parties and factions are bound to go public when they discover weaknesses in government operations, and hence activate classical parliamentary oversight mechanisms. Moreover, in a federal system, the major opposition parties at federal level regularly hold power at *Land* government level and can make use of the bureaucratic expertise they accumulate there. This permits greater use of media than might be available to other monitors of the behavior of senior civil servants (and their political masters). Moreover, party competition and inter-bureaucratic competition may go hand in hand, since under coalition governments, each party needs to watch the moves of the others, for instance by installing a parliamentary state secretary in a department headed by a minister from another coalition party.

Randomness is not a form of control that is readily associated with the stereotype of orderly German bureaucracy, but a form of control through randomness can be identified in the way the political civil service functions, particularly when there is a change in government and about half the topmost civil service positions change hands, with an influx of senior civil servants of the appropriate party affiliation. Such changes are not frequent, but when they do occur the incoming group of top civil servants can scrutinize the quality and even the legality of the work of their predecessors. Control of this type is not of an everyday type, and arguably it is better suited to addressing major issues rather than numerous small issues.

2   Changes over Time

(a)   More central agencies and more political oversight

In addition to the traditional central ministries (Justice, Finance, Interior) whose agreement was needed before policy proposals in their domains reached the Chancellor's Office, two new ministries (for Environment and Women's Affairs) were created in the 1980s with cross-departmental responsibilities for policy oversight and scrutiny. Some would interpret such developments as (at best) co-ordination or a new form of mutuality rather than oversight in the strict sense, but they have produced new procedural hurdles for policy proposals to jump before they reach the Chancellor's Office. Examples of such developments over the past generation include checks for environmental compatibility, IT compatibility, cost and staffing implications, as well as the requirements for co-ordinating policy with EU developments, particularly since 1987 (see Derlien, 2000a). They have also produced more 'mirror' sections within ministries on issues such as environmental policy, though how far those units function as 'colonists' or 'buffers' is hard to determine.

Political oversight has also grown over the past 30 years. The number of political civil servants hardly grew over that period, but 'thickening at the top' (Light, 1995) took the form of increasing numbers of politicians in the ministries. Since the office of Parliamentary State Secretary was created in 1967, officially to alleviate ministers' burdens in communicating with parliament (or in the view of cynics, 'saving us the work we would not have to do if they did not exist'), the numbers of MPs holding such office has grown sharply, especially during the Kohl chancellorship in the early 1990s. This means that most ministries today have two 'junior ministers', who often belong to different coalition factions, to exercise direction and convey intelligence to that faction which does not run the ministry, exposing civil servants to an extra layer of oversight.

A comparable development is a growing number of federal government commissioners for special affairs, comprising both traditional functions such as US–German cultural affairs and more recent creations, such as human rights. This development has been much discussed from other perspectives, such as patronage and clientelism, but the effect of their existence and growth for control over higher civil servants is to expose the latter to another source of influence, since civil servants are expected to give such commissioners the opportunity to participate in decision-making in the revised interdepartmental government code. The more people hang around, the more noise in the marketplace.

(b)   Party politicization and its effects on mutuality and competition

In addition to the developments mentioned above, the cosy mutuality of the traditional German civil service could be weakened by increased party politicization of the federal ministries. The proportion of top civil servants with explicit party membership spiralled from 1970 to 1987 (Mayntz and Derlien, 1989) and reached 60 per cent in 1995. This development means that after a change of government, political purges (in the form of temporary political retirements) became ever more severe. It is possible that such changes may lead to mistrust between the followers of a new government and the irremovable party affiliates of the outgoing government further down the hierarchy, whose promotion chances will certainly be impaired. Nor is it clear how the party camps in the bureaucracy view the diminishing numbers of those belonging to no party, who were in the majority during the supposedly 'good old days' of the Adenauer government in the 1950s.

With an increased number of people reaching top positions allegedly owing to their party book, these state secretaries and division heads may be perceived as party commissioners in some cases, holding strong policy views in parliamentary committee statements, which would destroy their chances under a successor government of a different political stripe. Indeed, several of the political bureaucrats ousted by Chancellor Schröder after the fall of the Kohl government, continued their career as *Land* ministers (Derlien, 2001). It thus seems likely that control by mutuality in its traditional form may be weakened by the trend towards party-politically motivated appointments and dismissals, although the greater political homogeneity at the top may produce a different form of mutual controls. Moreover – perhaps paradoxically – control through competition may also be weakened by those developments, for in the battle for promotion those with the wrong party book do not count as serious competitors.

(c)   External waste-watchers and other overseers

In addition to the traditional waste-watcher, the Federal Court of Audit, a new form of influence over the operations of the civil service has come from the way that administrative modernization (including e-government) has developed into a multibillion dollar business in Germany (Derlien, 2000b), involving partnership between public authorities and commercial management consultants. Inside the federal bureaucracy, the Ministry of Interior, traditionally in charge of government organization, set up a staff unit on 'administrative modernization' in 1999. In 2000 one of its first achievements was a revision of the inter-departmental government manual, which deregulated some former procedural requirements while mandating the application of some modern management tools such as the duty to forecast financial and other consequences of new legislation. Benchmarking also became a growth industry at all levels of government (having originated from a public–private partnership organizing international 'beauty contests' of local government) but the element of control through competition inherent in benchmarking practices did not apply to the ministries themselves, but only to local authorities and subordinate agencies.

A further development in quasi-external oversight is the establishment of ethics commissions in some areas of public policy, notably where some sort of genetic manipulation is at stake. Such commissions normally take the form of regulation of behaviour of their members by professional associations, and their application to areas of public policy has been argued by some to be problematic on the grounds that ethical judgements should be left to parliament. Following the law of anticipation of external controls, these government commissions may be ways of anticipating external parliamentary or constitutional court oversight of policies, but none of them possesses hard weaponry. The same applies to international surveillance bodies such as Amnesty International or Transparency International, which can only have an effect if their reports are politicized by national political actors.

3   Summary

It can be argued that oversight is the dominant mode of control over the higher civil service at the federal level. A highly legalist political and administrative culture produces a set of rules to steer the bureaucracy, and these rules are also the reference point for ministerial accountability. In anticipating external oversight of all sorts, bureaucrats and politicians defend themselves by adhering to the rules of the game. This behaviour seems to be deeply imbedded in the bureaucracy and is reinforced by the legal training of most bureaucrats and executive politicians. But inside the federal bureaucracy, there is also some degree of 'mutuality in the shadow of hierarchy', as shown above.

Two features of control that changed during the last 30 years or so comprise growing numbers of internal 'mirror units' reflecting oversight ministries and more parliamentary politicians in the ministry and in government commissioners' offices, serving to complicate the arenas in which individual bureaucrats behave and to make them more political. The chains of interaction are longer than they were in the 1960s owing to more policy interdependencies and a broader field of external actors, in particular within a configuration of co-operative federalism and bureaucratic fusion of federal and EU bureaucracies (Wessels, 1998). It could be argued that the effect of such developments has been to change the 'village life' at the top of the federal bureaucracy from 'community' to 'society' in the sociological meaning of these terms. It seems likely that mutuality is no longer an encompassing mode of (self-) regulation but that it has turned more specific by being exercised primarily in functionally specific networks.

Certainly, more sophisticated tactical skills are required of a senior bureaucrat today than 30 years ago, including political skills. So it is hardly surprising that the political aspects of the role of a top civil servant were much more emphasized in 1987 than in 1970 when Robert Putnam carried out his survey in Bonn (Mayntz and Derlien, 1989). Another changing feature noted here, the rising incidence of 'party-book' bureaucrats, may ease the adaptation to these new requirements, but party politicization may also have contributed to the growing complexity of the world that higher bureaucrats have to operate in. In interpreting this new pattern, it is tempting to echo Norbert Elias who showed how 'civilized behaviour' developed in the absolutist courts when social and economic success and status no longer primarily depended on one's capability with a sword but increasingly required calculating consequences along the Byzantine chain of social interaction, anticipating behaviour and internalizing external social constraints.

4.6   THE NETHERLANDS: EDGING AWAY FROM PURE MUTUALITY?
Theo Toonen and Frits M. van der Meer

1   The Point of Departure: Control in Traditional Dutch Public Management

Control of the senior Dutch civil service a generation ago seems to have been an integrated mixture of hierarchy and mutuality, leaving a lesser role for competition and randomness. Indeed, the latter approaches were disliked in administrative doctrine and long relegated to the informal parts of Dutch public administration.

Formal regulation and oversight was shaped by the constitutional framework of a decentralized unitary state, embedded in a culture of proportionality, mutuality and consensus. The formal control framework was rooted in ministerial responsibility and followed a top-down pattern, with departmental inspectorates and many direct 'administrative' rules, procedures and regulations governing the day-to-day business of government.

Provinces were constitutionally entrusted with general oversight of local governments, but were never really able to exercise this function, except perhaps financial supervision for smaller municipalities. Their general administrative oversight functions were at best used for communication and for co-ordinating local and inter-municipal activities. The emphasis lay on the vertical policy sectors of the Dutch 'picket fence model'. The personal style of individual inspectorates was often experienced in terms of 'randomness' (van Twist, 1999), frequently resulting in a rather fatalistic attitude of part of those subject to such oversight.

Along with these trappings of formal regulation and oversight, however, mutuality prevailed at another level. The 'sociological federalism' of the Netherlands produced a pattern in which external groups, networks, an extended system of advisory bodies and informal power structures played a crucial role in controlling government. The unitary system of the Netherlands was administered not by 'bosses', but by collegial bodies, typically reflecting combinations of different administrative principles (Hendriks and Toonen, 2001). Different administrative rationales were mixed together into the key governing institutions throughout the system to produce a balance of public power and a system in which government was controlled by mutual dependence, collegiality and power-sharing.

Hierarchy had a place in traditional Dutch administration, but it was exercised in a political context with a strong institutional necessity for mutual consent. Many hierarchical elements of the constitutional structure were affected – and often perverted – by such mutuality. Secrecy was also a cultural rule in Dutch consociational politics and administration. The lack of transparency and independent external oversight meant that compliance within the bureaucracy was secured by formalized procedures, but the external social and political networks allowed all kinds of informal processes, making the traditional control system quite indefinite.

Moreover, formal government hierarchies covered only part of the public service delivery system. Many public services, notably in health, culture, welfare, social policy and education, were delivered through non-governmental institutions and many were jointly run and controlled by government and 'social partners'. The structure of pillarized mutuality constrained bureaucracy in many ways, but also provided a social constitution for public (though usually not transparent) control of associations, foundations and other not for profit organizations providing public services.

Once this structure weakened, partly due to historical development, many informal and previously 'trusted' systems of socialized public control gradually disappeared, leaving governmental organizations operated by professionals subject to little public control until it generally became clear that the Dutch welfare state was about to run 'out of control' and needed to be better managed to survive international developments from the late 1970s. With the quest for new and improved management of the public sector came the need to reinvent internal and external control.

2 Changes in Control Patterns: Denationalizing Public Administration

The Netherlands has an open economy and was therefore affected heavily by international developments over the last two decades. Strong mutuality in traditional control created control deficits in competition, contrived randomness and even oversight, and once the government system was opened to international standards, changes were inevitable. But at the same time, some institutional characteristics were reinforced, albeit modernized. For instance the mutuality of 'interactive governance' might be new to countries characterized by non-negotiable policy styles in relation to social interest groups, but it is deeply embedded in Dutch culture (Randaraad and Wolffram, 2001). What changed was the nature and the players in the game, both evolving away from 'groupism' towards more individualistic or fatalistic attitudes.

But the increased openness affected the non-competitive, non-hierarchical, consociational style of mutual control in government. The oversight function, as exercised by inspectorates, regional consultants and other actors, came to be separated from general administration. A 'control and compliance crisis', resulting from the unpleasant surprise of a series of incidents, disasters, fraud cases and administrative integrity debates, led to the conclusion that inspectorates did not meet public expectations. These expectations were based on a traditional image of inspectorates and other overseers as verifying, testing, checking and enforcing with legal or financial powers. But in fact most overseers, knowingly and willingly, did not operate like that, and in many cases, inspectorates had changed their attitude and role conception.

This style of hierarchical supervision produced conflicts between policy provision and policy oversight. Whistle-blowers, even if part of a formally institutionalized system of checks and balances, are not very popular in a 'mutual relations' regime. As a consequence, many inspectorates changed their behaviour into a more mutuality-based interpretation of their functions.

Later – from the late 1980s onward – a 'complementary' or mutual system of governance by inter-governmental bargaining developed. The Dutch system witnessed a virtual 'inter-governmental agreement explosion', beginning in 1987 with the agreement of the Lubbers II Government with the Association of Dutch Municipalities (VNG) over principles for national retrenchment and cutback policies. Given the important role of local governments in implementing government policies in the Netherlands, this agreement complemented the 1983 Wassenaar Agreement between government, employer organizations and labor unions, later identified as the beginning of the Dutch Polder Model (Hendriks and Toonen, 2001).

Bargaining-based systems need effective arenas and partners, as well as authoritative and independent officers who can evaluate agreements in terms of standards set, settle disputes and provide independent information on whether actual developments are in accordance with the standards. This was not a function the inspectorates and other existing supervisors could provide. In other words, the need for the traditional function of overseers as authoritative monitors has become more acute, but is not really performed any more by the inspectorates, whereas their more recently adopted role as regional consultants or ministerial advisers became less useful in the emerging governance model. Gradually, the traditional oversight institutions lost importance and disappeared into the deep background. Other institutions, organizations and techniques were introduced to fill the gap, but their core business was defined in terms of the immediate needs of governing (monitoring, policy evaluation, benchmarking, financial oversight) and the traditional functions of restraint and compliance were no longer well represented in the mainstream oversight bodies.

The development took place step by step and within sectoral boundaries, resulting in a differentiated and fragmented pattern of new-style controls. A proliferation of monitoring agencies, review boards, benchmarking institutions, evaluation and accreditation committees emerged (some of them engaged in certification and quality control activity of an at least nominally voluntary kind), but little attention was paid to the overall structure.

3   Oversight Bodies: Current Developments

(a)   Inspectorates
The Dutch government recently has paid considerable attention to oversight and supervision in the bureaucracy. The trend was to encourage 'Trust in Independence' of oversight bodies, as indicated in the title of a key report (Commissie Borghouts, 2001: 3–11). That report presaged a shift in attention from policy-making to policy implementation and policy review, together with more emphasis on transparency in administration.

Traditionally, independent inspectorates were not much favoured as an instrument of control over the civil service. Nearly all ministries had inspectorates, but as in France the inspectorates were tools of the minister to control the field, and therefore not independent at all. But at the time of writing various national ministries and other actors are engaged in creating new and sometimes independent inspectorates. For instance, in the area of social policy and social security in the early 1990s, an independent agency (*Centraal Toezichtsorgaan Sociale Verzekeringen – CTSV*) was created to review implementation of social security programs, partly in response to parliamentary investigations reflecting poor oversight in social insurance policy, social assistance policy and local employment policy.

Establishing CTSV as an independent agency soon created a political crisis, the result of the poor management of the agency by the parent department, and civil servants of the Social Affairs Ministry, used to having the inspection under their thumb, had difficulties dealing with a public inspectorate, reviewing both the field *and* the ministry. Despite the CSTV's 'independence', the principle of ministerial responsibility was invoked to hold the deputy minister responsible for the operation of the system.

Because of the false start in creating more independent oversight bodies represented by the CTSV fiasco, the movement towards creating such bodies did not pick up again until the late 1990s. The reform of the long-standing Educational Inspectorate from a subordinate Inspectorate in the Minister of Education into a statutorily independent oversight body was a turning point. Making this inspectorate more independent was a landmark that led to the consolidation, professionalization and strengthening of the inspectorates in numerous other ministries, including housing, planning, health and social policy, all of which represented an increasing emphasis on inspection and oversight.

(b) Auditors

The full thrust of institutional development in public audit on control of the civil service is hard to assess. Although there is general support for separating oversight from other administrative activity, and for trusting independent oversight bodies, there is also some backlash. Parliament and the media have come to associate 'independence' with lack of control, but this reaction is less directed against independent inspectorates, than against privatized or 'contracted out' services and independent executive agencies.

Parliament is not disposed to trust independent agencies and increasingly pursues information on government performance. Many policy domains over the past 15 years have seen a trend towards decentralization and off-loading of national responsibilities to local governments and regional authorities. Given that this decentralization seldom entailed total transfer of political responsibility, the logical consequence was that decentralization entailed a strategic bargain: more organizational autonomy and policy discretion in exchange for better and more centralized information on achievement and performance.

Since the logic of this movement underlies developments in many different policy domains, the overall result was an oversight explosion in terms of the monitors that national ministries have developed, often in collaboration with other levels of government. The Dutch parliament has also strengthened its oversight activity over ministries. The General Chamber of Audit (*Algemene Rekenkamer – AR*) developed into an independent auditing institution providing Parliament (in addition to its narrow tasks of reviewing departmental budgets), with all kinds of evaluations of government programmes.

The Chamber of Audit carefully guards its status as 'the only really independent budgetary review institution of Dutch government', but it is the tip of an iceberg. Many other institutions overseeing government and public services (including the long-standing food inspectorates, safety inspectorates and labour inspectorates) seem to have intensified their activities. Yet the fragmented nature of these various activities contributes to an image of limited effectiveness and efficiency in oversight.

(c)   External oversight
Parliament has also revitalized its oversight activities and during the past decade has increasingly exercised its traditional right to conduct independent investigations, for example in an annual review of governmental processes and policies within the regular budget cycle, first conducted in 2002 on the basis of a report by the *Algemene Rekenkamer*.

Such developments symbolize the Parliament's ambition to develop its oversight capacity over the administration, and similar developments took place in local and provincial government. Under the label of 'Dualization' a programme of local government reform developed which was intended to put municipal and provincial councils in the position of supervisor and overseer of (local) government, rather than that of local policy-maker. In exchange for the loss of legislative powers, councils were to obtain more powers in accounting, review and oversight.

The increase of legislative oversight at various levels of government is consistent with other developments aimed at strengthening traditional and even constitutional mechanisms to make government more responsible. In terms of grievance management, for example, the Ombudsman, an institution created in the 1980s, managed to occupy a very prominent position in overseeing government, albeit lacking formal powers to enforce his verdicts. The overall impression is of growth in external oversight, traditionally only limitedly developed in the Dutch administrative system.

4 Other Changes in the Control of the Higher Civil Service

As well as significant changes in oversight, there has been some change in the way mutuality and competition control government. In particular, the creation of a single employer, the ABD, for top civil servants created the equivalent of a *corps*. As well as answering to their minister, top civil servants are also responsible to ABD and are also linked with other top civil servants through this body. This change has been accompanied by the creation of a 'senior executive service' for this top cadre of government. Thus, senior civil servants have now been separated from the remainder of the service, a development that can both enhance their capacity to watch each other's actions in office, as well as enhance the ability to use competition in controlling them.

The ABD also sought to instil greater competition into the top rungs of Dutch public administration. In particular, it instituted performance contracting for top civil servants and sought to 'modernize' a system that had been governed largely by mutuality, with some touches of hierarchy. The creation of a cadre of senior managers also added an element of randomness to control, given that assignments may become more widely dispersed throughout the bureaucracy, and that randomness is reinforced by more aggressive auditing organizations. At the time of writing the success of these changes is hard to assess, but it seems likely to mark a shift in emphasis in controlling the bureaucracy.

Further, it is clear that the principle of collegial administration by a government of (political) equals, plays an important role in controlling the bureaucracy as an entity in itself, both at national and local and regional levels of the system. The Dutch civil service system at the core of the state involves the coexistence of 'multiple hierarchies'. Collegial administration within government brings a mixture of mutuality and competition to the overall control process of the core bureaucracy.

5 Summary

The traditional way of controlling the Dutch administrative system reflected the culture within which it worked, emphasizing mutuality and consensus. While those elements persist, there has been an increasing emphasis on strengthened oversight, along with the introduction of some elements of competition and randomness. Overall the system has perhaps not changed greatly, but the bureaucracy is not the autonomous actor it once was and is being exposed to greater oversight from above and greater competition within its own ranks.

4.7   NORWAY: MANAGERIALISM AND PARLIAMENTARY OVERSIGHT IN LOCK-STEP?
Per Lægreid

The Norwegian higher civil service functions within a small country with a history of effective and honest government. Some degree of regulation and control is necessary in any administrative system, as argued in the introduction to this chapter, but that need may be less manifest in Norway than in most others. Nevertheless, political and administrative leaders in Norwegian government have developed a full arsenal of oversight weapons to direct against their bureaucracy. Some of those tools have been available for decades, but others reflect the influence of the ideas of New Public Management (NPM) from the 1980s onward.

1   Oversight

The traditional oversight system in Norway was rather similar to that found in most parliamentary regimes. The fundamental principle was the parliamentary responsibility of ministers for the actions of their departments, with civil servants being largely protected from personal responsibility, at least at the political level. Their organizations may have been affected by parliamentary actions but the individuals were not exposed or directly accountable. Further, the system of administrative law was not well developed, so the burden of overseeing the executive and particularly the civil service fell on parliament. Moreover, the system seems to have been focused on routine oversight rather than concentrating on the more dramatic elements of scandal and the McCubbins and Schwartz 'fire alarms' approach to controlling bureaucracy.

There were, however, some distinctive features that amounted to early efforts at strengthening the parliament against the executive. First, Norway was one of the original countries to introduce ombudsmen as a way for parliament to supervise the civil service and correct malfeasance. Second, from the 1970s specialized committees developed in the parliament to mirror executive departments and provide closer parliamentary oversight over the bureaucracy. The Storting also later created a general scrutiny committee to oversee the executive branch of government: initial attempts to use this committee were largely unsuccessful, but it was revitalized in the NPM era. Finally, the audit function was moved in the 1970s from the executive to parliament, further strengthening the oversight capacity of the Storting.

In the NPM era several new oversight weapons have been added to the range of options available to would-be controllers, especially those in the Storting. The most important of these new instruments is management by objectives and results (MBOR), made mandatory in the public sector in 1991. Management by objectives and results is a variant of the now familiar performance management systems in government, though it seems to be used with somewhat greater vigour in Norway than in many other countries (Christensen, Lægreid and Wise, 2002). The guidance given to top administrative leaders for the performance of their organizations through the system has become central to the oversight process within government itself, and in relation to the Storting.

In addition to steering through objectives, during the NPM era Norwegian government added performance auditing and accounting. The Audit Office, like many of its counterparts in other countries, began to shift away from strictly financial accounting to greater concerns about efficient and effectiveness in government. This new-style auditing has provided the Storting with additional information and insights that it can use in its ongoing attempts to oversee the executive. In the process, the Audit Office may have in fact especially empowered the parliamentary opposition against the party in government and in the process, therefore, shifted some of the balance of power in the political system.

2 Mutuality, Competition and Randomness

The small size of the country, even when the rather active role of the state in society is considered, makes mutuality a natural form of control within the higher civil service. Although not working within a traditionally closed-career system, in contrast to many of the other cases in this study, the majority of the participants in the upper echelons of government in Oslo are likely to know one another and to have the opportunity to develop opinions about each other's capacity and suitability for high level employment. These links among people are likely to be long-standing, given the small number of universities and the common recruitment base for public and private employment. Proximity and frequent contacts are enhanced by the 'high cultural content', the egalitarian style of the society and polity, and more intuitive understandings about what it means to govern properly. Mutuality may have declined to some degree in the NPM era, at least relative to the use of other forms of control. And it is checked to some extent by the more lateral entry and some decentralization and deconcentration in governing.

Mutuality and co-operation dominate the operating style of the Norwegian public sector more than competition. Although any career system involves some level of competition for advancement, this element appears weak in Norwegian bureaucracy, in spite of the relative openness of the career structure and the significant involvement of Norwegian government in a range of market activities. Again, the egalitarian nature of the culture appears to blunt some competitive pressures in the public sector. The introduction of some elements of pay for performance into the public sector in the NPM years, along with performance management, have perhaps strengthened some aspects of competition, but competition nevertheless remains a minor part of the control system.

The Norwegian governing system appears to have relied little on contrived randomness to control the public bureaucracy, though in some ways the traditional parliamentary control system functioned randomly, given that MPs could intervene as and when they wished (Laegreid and Roness, 1999). However, the NPM period has added another mechanism that combines an element of randomness with parliamentary oversight. Prior to 1996, question time in parliament had involved providing a minister with prior notice of the questions to be asked. But since then the process has become unpredictable, with no prior notice of questions being required. While the original intent of this innovation had been to make the public more aware of politics (Nordby, 2000), the effect was also to make public servants (through their ministers) subject to more random scrutiny, and perhaps greater exposure of any failings.

3 Summary

The Norwegian government, despite the strength of mutuality and cultural controls, has invested a great deal of effort in developing effective oversight devices for the Storting. These oversight devices were already well developed before the NPM era, but have been strengthened by the managerialist changes from the 1990s onward. The principle of parliamentary control is central to governing in Norway, and it appears very clearly in the mechanisms used to control the higher bureaucracy.

4.8 THE UK AND AUSTRALIA: TWO WESTMINSTER-MODEL STATES COMPARED
Christopher Hood and Colin Scott

1 Differences and Similarities in the Control Context of Two Westminster-Model Bureaucracies

The UK and Australia both belong to the 'Westminster model' family of government, and the public bureaucracies in these two systems have important similarities. Both have a well-developed merit system for recruitment, but (increasingly) supplement that administrative core with some political appointees. Further, both have a penumbra of agencies and quangos whose boards may also be subject to political appointment. Both systems heavily stress the rule of law, albeit with a version of administrative law quite different from continental Europe, or their distant cousin the USA. Finally, mutuality – mutual checking among bureaucratic 'villagers' – has traditionally been stressed as much as formal oversight mechanisms in the control of the higher civil service in both cases.

Although similar in some fundamental ways, there are also important differences between these two systems. The UK has a tradition of elite recruitment for its top civil service, while Australia has no comparable 'administrative class' tradition. The UK civil service is constituted and employed through a mixture of royal prerogative power, general employment law and constitutional convention, whereas public services both at state and Commonwealth level in Australia were traditionally constituted by statute and overseen by statutory public service boards. Both operate under much debated conventions of ministerial responsibility for the activity of the departments they head, but in the UK ministers are traditionally physically located within their departments, whereas Australian ministers have traditionally had their offices within the parliament house, creating greater 'relational distance' with their departments and particularly with the official heads of their departments.

Nor do the important differences end there. The UK's Whitehall village was once the centre of a global empire and after that a 'public bureaucracy state' of massive scale. Canberra has no equivalent imperial baggage (Papua New Guinea perhaps excepted): it has a tradition of small government, albeit within what until recently was considered a 'developmental state' and the ambience of a 'bureaucrat city' physically far removed from Australia's commercial and industrial centres. The party-political context of government is different too, with majority-party government in the UK Westminster Parliament for most of the period since the Second World War but a permanently 'hung parliament' in the Australian Senate, the balance controlled by small parties elected through the PR system used for the upper house.

2   Mutuality

In both countries, mutuality appears to have traditionally been an important mechanism of control over the higher civil service, and arguably the most important one. A quarter of a century or so ago, Heclo and Wildavsky's (1974) famous study of financial control in Whitehall (echoing Finer's, 1950: 68, conclusions of a quarter of a century earlier) claimed that mutual control among senior civil servants, living and working together in a small geographical and social space over a long career, was more effective than any form of oversight. In Australia, too, relations between Commonwealth departments and agencies have traditionally been managed consensually and without extensive reference to rules and formal powers. Senior public servants, members of the Senior Executive Service (O'Faircheallaigh, Wanna and Weller, 1999: 151–5), have traditionally had common training and shared values. Like Heclo and Wildavsky's Whitehall villagers (arguably with an even more village-like life in a far smaller and more socially homogenous capital city) they operate in a limited space within Canberra, with frequent contacts.

These traditions have by no means disappeared in the New Public Management era. The upper echelons of the bureaucracy both in Whitehall and Canberra have suffered less change under the NPM revolution than have other parts of the public service. In the UK, Thatcherite threats to 'deprivilege the civil service' appear to have had the most impact on those parts of the civil service that were already the least privileged (Hood, 1995). In both cases senior officials responded to pressures for managerial effectiveness in delivering public services by a measure of 'dynamic conservatism' – that is, structural changes to preserve and refine the elite collegiality of the central departments. Those changes involved reducing the extent to which senior bureaucrats had to worry about managing operational and regulatory functions, many of which were given to semi-autonomous agencies for politicians and high civil servants to blame when things went wrong. Neither bureaucracy was subject to the same degree of 'contractualization' as their New Zealand counterparts, but tenure was removed from departmental heads in Canberra in the early 1980s, and greater lateral entry to the upper UK civil service in the 1980s and 1990s put pressure on assumptions of a closed-career corps relying on mutuality. The influx of lateral entrants, particularly into the headships of the 'executive agencies', was said to have created new pressures to codify unwritten rules and spell out what had hitherto been implicit aspects of the 'public service bargain' (Hood et al., 1999: 71). Accordingly, mutuality remains important, but there are signs of nibbling away at its edges, partly because changes in oversight mainly intended to affect other parts of the public service have 'boomeranged' on senior civil servants to at least some extent.

3   Oversight

Formal oversight applies to many aspects of the work of the higher bureaucracy in both countries, and occurs against the background of parliamentary oversight and legal adjudication. Parliamentary oversight of the bureaucracy in both countries is based overwhelmingly on the well-known fire-alarm approach (McCubbins and Schwartz, 1984), and in the UK attempts to strengthen parliamentary oversight after 1979 took the form of an extended set of select committees organized by department, with powers to hold hearings at which ministers and bureaucrats were expected to answer. In Australia the upper house has developed an expanded oversight role, supporting investigative work through the power to send for persons and papers, and linked that to regulatory initiatives over the bureaucracy.

The incidence of judicial review of government activity increased markedly in the UK in the later decades of the twentieth century (see Hood et al., 1999: 204), in contrast to an earlier period of judicial quiescence, and the significance of increased judicial activism is perhaps augmented by the tradition of comparatively high relational distance between bureaucrats and the judiciary. However, in spite (or maybe because of) a major revamp of Australian administrative law in the mid-1970s, no similar pattern of rising judicial review is detectable in Australia. That difference suggests that we need to be cautious about generalizing assumptions about a tidal wave of adversarial legalism affecting high bureaucracies.

A mixture of deregulation and re-regulation in oversight applied to both countries during the NPM era. The upper-level bureaucracy experienced some deregulation, especially over pay and staff management, described by a key player in Canberra as 'the removal of much of the central safety-net of prescribed rules and regulations' (Podger, 2002). Both countries introduced ombudsmen before the NPM era (the UK in 1967 and Australia in 1975) and both countries revamped their public audit systems in a similar direction during the NPM era. These changes created an audit office independent of executive government under an Auditor-General, who became an officer of Parliament with judicial tenure, and audit was extended to include performance and value for money as well as financial probity and legality. The upshot was to put more pressure on to senior civil servants over their own decision-making, in contrast with the older pattern in which the auditors' targets for financial mistakes tended to be individuals at the middle or lower levels of the bureaucratic food chain (see Hood et al., 1999: 87).

Among the spheres of bureaucratic behaviour covered by formal oversight, three are particularly important: financial probity and performance, administrative procedure, quality of service, and safety and security.

(a) Financial probity and performance

Both countries have a tradition of powerful finance ministries (the Treasury in the UK and the Department of Finance and Administration – DOFA – in Australia), whose roles have traditionally extended to policy co-ordination, leading some to portray those departments as super-regulators at the heart of central government (see Zifcak, 1994: 164–9). How far that characterization is accurate for either case is debatable. Both the UK Treasury and the DOFA have limited capacities for enforcing the standards they set and arguably the DOFA's capacities have been diminished since the publication of Zifcak's 1994 book. Indeed, budget group DOFA officials in interviews have portrayed themselves less as overseers of other departments than as filling the role of Chief Financial Planning Officer for the Commonwealth government.

In both cases budget oversight was traditionally exercised by a system that combined extensive authorization requirements with unpredictable questioning from the central financial ministry, allied with a public audit process focused on financial irregularities. In both cases subsequent change took the form of a revamped public audit system, with a broader scope of audit and greater independence from the executive, a system of budget allocation through general control totals for programmes and running costs rather than detailed authorization of 'line items', and a tendency to pass budget responsibility directly to agencies rather than routing it through the parent departments. Moreover, in both cases there was some subsequent rethink of the move away from detailed 'windows' for control (in the UK following the 1994 Fundamental Expenditure Review of the Treasury and in Australia following the 1997 Financial Management and Accountability Act). After 1997 in the UK the Treasury developed a detailed system of oversight (in the form of Public Service Agreements that gave targets to each department that in turn cascaded down to individuals' personnel assessments), but at the time of writing a strong backlash against 'targetry' is developing and some of the targets are being wound back.

Procurement regulation differs sharply between the two countries. In the UK, Treasury procurement rules had to be modified to reflect EU single-market procurement rules, requiring formal require notification in the official journal, and are justiciable in the European Court of Justice. In Australia, the procurement rules refer to money and competitive neutrality as general desiderata, but also instruct agencies to consider other matters, notably the development of Australian and New Zealand industry, the promotion of small and medium-sized enterprises and environmental policies (Department of Finance and Administration, 2002) and the Australian government has not signed up to the World Trade Organization (WTO) Agreement on Government Procurement.

(b)   Administrative procedure and quality of service
Despite their different bases of organization, the oversight machinery developed for administrative procedure has also changed in strikingly similar directions. In both cases there was a substantial deregulation of recruitment and staffing matters in the 1990s. 'Deregulation' amounted not only to removing what had once been a central system of managing recruitment and replacing it by regulatory rules, but also to an attempt to purge some of the accumulated detail from formal central personnel rules and replace them by what was described as a 'principles-based' regime (Australian Public Service Commission, 2001: 63). What that meant in the UK was a revamped Civil

Service Commission in the mid-1990s policing a general code through audits of departments carried out by private firms on a semi-random basis. In Australia it meant a new Public Service Act in 1999 declaring a set of 'Australian Public Service Values' (s. 10) and incorporating a Merit Protection Commissioner into the Public Service Commission, which developed as an agency for giving advice and monitoring agencies' staff management systems. These developments clearly parallel changes in financial controls, although at the very topmost levels of the civil service the UK Civil Service Commissioner has a direct role both in recruitment and (for the first time since 1995) promotion. Moreover, the package of changes introduced in the UK in the mid-1990s introduced a parallel process of 'merit oversight' for appointments to quangos, which previously had been subject to no specific oversight.

Neither country has a general US type Administrative Procedure Act, but in both countries, the ombudsmen established shortly before the NPM era continued to function as overseers of administrative procedure and quality, and in both cases produced guides to best practice that went beyond their traditional role as reactive grievance-handlers. In Australia the Commonwealth Ombudsman has been a key critic of public service reforms such as contracting out and privatization on the grounds that they weaken procedural protections for citizens (Fleming, 2000: 178–9). In both cases, too, the work of senior public servants was affected by new rules on access to official information. In Australia, freedom of information legislation was introduced for the Commonwealth government in the middle 1980s, under a regime overseen by a commissioner. In the UK, the traditional 1906 Official Secrets Act which all civil servants are required to abide by was seriously damaged by two major court actions in the 1980s, and a 1993 White Paper passed in 2000 heralded a regime of greater openness, overseen by the Ombudsman. New Labour promised a new Freedom of Information Act in its 1997 election manifesto, but the Act is only just coming into operation at the time of writing, and it was written in a restrictive way that makes it unlikely that the work of senior civil servants will be much affected, since civil service advice to ministers is exempted.

In both cases, too, new systems of oversight developed to cover regulatory rule-making by government, reflecting concerns with compliance costs and competitiveness. In the UK, a 'deregulation unit' was established in the Department of Trade and Industry in the mid-1980s, moved to the Cabinet Office in the early 1990s, and later was revamped (eventually as the Regulatory Impact Unit) under the Blair government, to promote guidelines for good regulation and to analyze 'regulatory impact assessments' that departments were required to produce when introducing legislation. Similarly in Australia, the Productivity Commission produced a general guide to regulation. The Commission contains a separate unit (the Commonwealth

Competitive Neutrality Complaints Office) for handling grievances over the conduct of business by the Commonwealth, while the Office of Regulation Review is a proactive overseer of rule-making, with powers extending beyond primary and secondary legislation to 'soft law' instruments coming from Commonwealth agencies and departments. In both cases the original impetus for such oversight arrangements was a concern with the impact of 'red tape' on business, but in the late 1990s the UK Regulatory Impact Unit extended its work to the oversight of public sector bodies such as universities, and in the early 2000s similar issues were being mooted for the activity of the Office of Regulatory Review.

For service quality the main new departure in oversight in both countries during the NPM era was the introduction – in the UK in 1992 and in Australia five years later – of service charters. The core idea was that agencies and departments should publish clear statements identifying their organization and its clients, their service standards and the rights and responsibilities of clients and customers, with attention to handling complaints and inquiries. In both cases, too, there was a central unit to promote and evaluate charters, linked with prizes and awards for excellence (but no brickbats for poor performance). In the UK oversight of the service charter regime was located initially in a unit in the Cabinet Office, and the programme survived the change of government from Conservative to Labour in 1997, albeit with a name change. In Australia responsibility for developing guidance and monitoring implementation of service charters was first in the Department of Finance and Administration, but in 2000 whole-of-government reporting was abandoned and responsibility shifted to the Public Services Commission. In both cases, however, the emphasis of the service charters was on the delivery of services to citizens rather than the policy-making activities of senior civil servants. In the UK the Service First programme explicitly excluded policy activity. Its Australian counterpart operated with a declared intention to include policy-making activity, but the award winners have in practice mostly been service delivery agencies, such as the Child Support Agency or Passports Australia.

(c) Security

Arguably one of the most important oversight systems for senior public servants, apart from those governing the use of information, is that associated with the security system, given that in both countries the security and intelligence services (MI5 and MI6 in the UK, together with police 'special branch' forces, and ASIO in Australia) are responsible for overseeing the activity of central government departments and for 'positive vetting' of those in a wide range of public offices. These organizations and their activity have always been important overseers of the higher public service in both countries and are not normally considered to be part of a putative 'oversight explosion', though in both cases they were themselves subjected to new oversight arrangements in the 1990s. The UK security services only acquired an official public identity in the early 1990s, being placed under a statutory oversight commission, and likewise in Australia the Inspector-General of Intelligence and Security developed as the only external inspectorate with a mandate over Commonwealth government agencies. However, in the nature of the case, regulatory scholars have not published contemporary studies of this very important field of public sector regulation in either country, so we cannot make definitive statements about whether this form of oversight over the high bureaucracies increased, decreased or maintained some constant level.

(d) Overall

This necessarily selective overview of oversight systems in the two countries suggests that the thrust of most of the oversight developments in the NPM era affected some parts of the public service more than others, though few upper-level public servants escaped the impact of those developments altogether. Changes in financial oversight – particularly new audit systems – may make higher civil servants answerable for their decisions in ways they were not previously, even though the new public audit offices were not always widely respected by higher civil servants in either country. High Australian public servants had to adapt to new statutory freedom of information legislation, while their UK counterparts were subject to pressures for greater openness, eventually culminating in a limited form of legislation. Their appointments and promotions and their role in hiring and promoting others was affected by a 're-regulated' oversight system in which central management and rule books were replaced by general principles linked to arm's-length monitoring. Club-like understandings of how business was properly done and where lines were drawn came to be written down into explicit codes of rules for the public service. And senior public servants could at least not wholly ignore regulatory impact assessments. Service charter arrangements applied more to the work of those heading service delivery units than those in general policy roles. The direction of change of security oversight is not known, even though such oversight arrangements are arguably more central to the work of the topmost levels of government than any other controls described here.

4 Competition

Competition traditionally figured in the control regimes for higher bureaucrats in the UK in several ways – including individual competition for appointment, promotion and political attention, and competition among agencies and departments for budget allocations and some types of policy responsibilities. In general, NPM reformers aimed to augment these traditional forms of bureaucratic competition with others, although arguably the most important aspect of competition – competition for entry to the higher civil service – if anything, tended to weaken. At the individual level, favoured methods of increasing competition included pay for performance to replace fixed-salary systems with incremental scales linked to seniority, and lateral entry to top positions to replace closed-career systems. At the institutional level, common recipes for increasing competition included 'market testing' (through invitations to tender for specified functions through auctions or other devices) and 'league tables' of saints and sinners setting out comparative performance even where market-testing methods of competition were not available.

At the high bureaucracy level in both countries, such standard institutional devices for increasing competition seem to have had much less impact than at lower levels or other parts of the public service. Market testing and league tabling were little applied to the functions performed by high bureaucrats (policy-making, regulation, resource allocation, advice and intelligence), and even the new-model public audit systems mentioned earlier made little use of this mechanism. However, outside of official reform programmes, it is arguable that the institutional competition to which high bureaucrats were exposed was augmented in at least two ways.

First, over the last two decades or so more use was made of policy think tanks and political consultants or spin doctors, replacing an earlier pattern in which such institutions were far from unknown but there were relatively fewer competitors to high bureaucrats in policy advice. Second, a small but significant 'political civil service' developed in both cases, which in principle could be seen as opening up more competition between regular 'merit' bureaucrats and political civil servants of various kinds. How far these changes contributed to a real increase in competition, however, is debatable and unknown. Political advisers and spin doctors often seem to have acted as gatekeepers to ministers rather than competitors to civil servants. The role of political and management consultants is poorly understood (in spite of an Australian senate inquiry into consultants in the early 1990s), but it is not clear that their rise has necessarily contributed to greater competition with the civil service over policy-making, or simply added another set of actors with symbiotic rather than rival relationships.

However, the high bureaucracy in both cases was exposed to NPM-type mechanisms for augmenting competition at the individual rather than institutional level. Lateral entry into top positions is more a feature of the UK story than the Australian one, and a major political battle over the ending of indefinite civil service tenure in the UK in the early 1990s resulted in a political compromise. That compromise, enshrined in a 1994 White Paper entitled *Continuity and Change*, provided for a mixture of lateral entry and career progression, and a mixture of short-term and indefinite contracts. There were more lateral entrants for the heads of executive agencies (introduced from the late 1980s in the UK but resisted for nearly a decade in Australia) than for the policy departments, and even then many of those entrants had some public service background in their careers. Performance pay in its modern form was originally introduced into the UK civil service for the upper-middle grades in 1984 on an experimental basis, coming only some years later to the topmost grades. Even then, the extent to which it represented a major new competitive instrument is debatable, since until the early 2000s it typically put less than 5 per cent of total pay at risk and at first there were no quotas on the proportion of staff that were permitted to receive performance supplements. However, over time the competitive element in performance-related pay for upper-level civil servants arguably increased, as quotas were imposed and the proportion of total pay that could be gained as a performance supplement grew to approximately 30 per cent.

Altogether, what happened to competition is far from clear. The evidence (for instance over distribution of performance pay supplements) is opaque, and opinions and interpretations vary. But it seems reasonable to conclude that, while higher level bureaucrats were not subject to such strong increases in organizational competition as were many service-delivery components of the public service, they were by no means exempt from increases in organizational competition and were more exposed to some forms of individual competition with the growth of performance pay and lateral entry combined with delayering of the upper-level ranks of the bureaucracy.

5 Randomness

In earlier work with colleagues, we argued (Hood et al., 1999) that the effect of NPM-era changes in the UK was somewhat to reduce the extent of control over bureaucratic activity through deliberate randomness. The argument was that the traditional architectonics of bureaucracy had stressed features such as relatively haphazard arrangements for posting individuals around a ramified structure, combined with 'dual key' arrangements, particularly for financial authorization, and unpredictable scrutiny from remote inspectors or budget controllers. Those features, the argument went, had been weakened both unintendedly (by downsizing, delayering and the splitting off of former field-office activity into separate organizations) and intendedly, particularly by the deliberate introduction of more transparent and predictable financial control systems and perhaps by concentration of formerly separate powers into 'hands-on' management responsibilities.

However, it could be argued that such features of contrived randomness were always more salient for middle and lower level bureaucrats than for the top-level villagers, who rarely had direct control over financial allocations and tended to move for most of their careers in 1 square mile of central London (a little more than that in less crowded Canberra). Arguably the element of randomness to which upper-level bureaucrats were exposed was the unpredictability of where in the bureaucracy the political and media spotlight will be directed at any one point, and – in spite of increasing investment in public relations and media relations – it is doubtful if this 'wild card' declined during the NPM era (many senior civil servants assert the opposite). Moreover, to the extent that lateral entry and the use of outside political consultants increased over that era (combined for the UK with the new demands of working with a changing and not always easily predictable cast of characters in the policy-making structures of the EU), it could be argued that some elements of randomness may have increased for the upper-level civil service while such elements may have declined elsewhere in the structure.

6   Conclusion

It is easy and tempting to focus on oversight over the high-level bureaucracy at the expense of other components, because oversight usually has institutional 'owners' – committees, commissioners or other office-holders – in a way that does not necessarily apply to other forms of control, and purposive control is often casually equated with oversight. Moreover, even though the way oversight works can be harder to pin down than appears initially, other apparently less tangible forms of control can be hard to identify and assess, even if they are as important in keeping the system within bounds.

Three related general conclusions can be drawn from this brief comparison. One – simple but important in the face of the 'control equals oversight' fallacy – is that both in 'traditional' controls and in the more recent NPM era, oversight is only one of a larger set of control mechanisms, and often not the most important one. Mutuality for the upper-level civil service may have diminished slightly in the more recent era, but has by no means disappeared. Competition was far from absent in the earlier pre-NPM era, and it is not clear that the traffic has been all one way. Deliberate randomness has declined in some ways, but it can come back in others, notably through contracting mechanisms. Indeed, oversight often becomes effective only when mated to some other form of control.

Second, the 'audit explosion' that Michael Power (1997) identified for a set of British institutions in the 1990s is not much in evidence for the higher bureaucracy in either of these Westminster model cases. What happened seems to have been more in the nature of a mild increase in oversight, sometimes as part of an unintended backwash or boomerang effect from oversight systems aimed primarily at other parts of the public service.

Third, despite the very different starting points of these two Westminster-family bureaucracies, their directions of change were relatively similar when viewed from our control perspective. There were certainly differences of timing and detail, but in spite of these differences, there was arguably a 'fly-paper effect' at work (Snodden and Wen, 1998) in that the two systems ended up in broadly similar places. It is sometimes claimed that Australia and the UK are moving apart as colonial ties (or 'cultural cringe') weaken, but there are strong similarities and even in places convergence in the way that controls changed over the NPM era.

PART III

Conclusions

5 Conclusion: making sense of controls over government

Christopher Hood

The issue was thus not one of interventionism versus laissez-faire, action versus inaction, authoritarianism versus liberalism, but of different forms of intervention, some more drastic and apparent, others more subtle . . .

(Baldwin, 1999: 535)

1 INTRODUCTION

In this chapter we offer three types of conclusions. First, we reflect on the idea that we introduced with a folk tale at the outset – and which is all too easily espoused by middle-aged professors facing new reporting and scrutiny regimes – that oversight and audit activity of various kinds over public services has grown dramatically over the last two decades or so, representing a new 'age of inspection' (Day and Klein, 1990: 4). There are cases and places that undoubtedly fit that pattern, as we have shown. But this study also shows that any such development has not been uniform across countries and policy sectors. We point towards a more nuanced conclusion of the type suggested by our epigraph, which is drawn from Peter Baldwin's historical study of the various ways that nineteenth-century European states responded to a common problem, namely, contagious diseases such as cholera, tuberculosis and syphilis.

This book shows that oversight explosions have taken place in some countries and policy domains but not in others. Some types and styles of oversight have declined as others have grown. And some of the most dramatic new developments in oversight described here, such as many of the university cases, have in fact been hybrid rather than 'pure' oversight. They link oversight with competition and mutuality, and may contain elements of randomness too. In that sense, they are what the cultural theorist Michael Thompson (2003) calls 'clumsy' solutions to the control of individuals and institutions. By 'clumsy' (a provocative term) Thompson means complex or culturally hybrid systems that cut across polar world views or pure institutional types such as the four control forms that we have used as the basis of our analysis. Thompson evidently sees those complex or hybrid systems as necessary for making institutional arrangements effective, on some variant of the cybernetic argument that high-variety systems can only be controlled by arrangements capable of marshalling at least equivalent complexity (Ross Ashby's, 1956, famous law of requisite variety). This study suggests that such 'clumsy' hybrids, cutting across the four polar types used in this analysis, are of central importance in controlling public services and government. But such control hybrids can have their limits. Indeed, as Thompson's 'clumsiness' metaphor would imply, such hybrids are not necessarily stable, and may break down under pressure, for instance as conflict between peer-group assessment and official regulation builds up in various professional groups.

Second, we reflect on what we have learned about the usefulness and limitations of the four-part optic (drawn from grid-group cultural theory), that we have used as a basis for our comparative exploration of control in and over government. This study has revealed multiple forms of each of the four 'primary' forms of control that we introduced at the outset and, as we showed in the opening chapter, how we characterize a country's control profile using the four-part optic depends in part on what institutional level or feature we look at. For instance, against the low-mutuality government-of-strangers features often said to apply to US executive government as a whole, particular bureaus may have very different features. As we saw in Chapter 2, the US Federal Prison Service is a bureau with a surprisingly high level of mutuality in the sense of reciprocal monitoring and influence by well-informed career-corps prison staff. By contrast, in what are traditionally regarded as the higher-mutuality public bureaucracies of the European states, we found a notable lack of connection between the operating level of prisons and the responsible government department in several cases, including Norway and the Netherlands. Similarly, as Guy Peters showed in Section 4.2, while mutuality may be low among Washington's transient political appointees considered as a group, those individuals are exposed to greater (and arguably increasing) mutuality controls in the form of the policy and party networks that monitor and evaluate them.

Such observations suggest that our analytic approach can be used to reach non-obvious conclusions about control of government if it is applied systematically and reflectively, avoiding the casual broad-brush characterization that can lead to 'degeneracy' in a research programme (to use the Lakatosian term applied by David Laitin, 1995: 168, to characterize what happened to the political culture approach in political science after Almond and Verba's famous *Civic Culture* of 1965). Our study has also shown some of the hybrids that have developed across the four 'primary' forms of control, underlining the conclusion that oversight of government is typically least effective when it is not linked to other forms of control. But that leaves us with a puzzle about why randomness seems to find so little favour in received prescriptions for increasing control over contemporary government.

Finally, we reflect on the link between changing control over government and the broader processes so much discussed by theorists of modernization and globalization. To what extent – in what policy domains and state traditions – are common functional pressures producing convergence of some kind in control styles? And what kind of convergence are we seeing?

2   OVERSIGHT IN CONTROLS OVER GOVERNMENT: DENSITY, STYLE AND GROWTH

On the first issue identified above, we find a mixture of commonality and diversity in the way oversight developed across our 24 cases (eight countries, three policy domains). There does seem to have been a widespread shift from the early 1970s to put more emphasis on output as well as to input and process as the object of oversight over many public services. That shift is much less marked for prisons than for universities, and, even for the latter, output-based oversight often tended to be laid on top of input-based and process-based oversight, rather than substituted for those other types in the way that the starrier-eyed advocates of New Public Management wanted. But exactly what that observation means for the widespread claims about the importance of varying state structures and traditions is hard to determine. On the one hand, supposedly 'gung-ho' reforming states such as the USA and Australia did not succeed in much more than symbolic 'bonfires' of many traditional oversight controls, but on the other hand the supposedly legalistic cultures of the continental European states did not prevent the addition of *ex post* output-based oversight to the traditional emphasis on input and process.

Turning from commonality to variety, we find that the 'oversight explosion' that undoubtedly affected the UK's 'old' universities in the 1990s (but not the ex-polytechnics, whose teaching programmes had always been closely regulated) was not repeated across all the cases. Our study shows that such changes in inspection, audit and the like were more dramatic in some policy domains than others and that they were more dramatic in some state traditions than others. Nor does it seem to have been just a case of convergent modernization, with the laggards catching up with more advanced players, since some domains and state traditions started low and finished low. Cultural and institutional variety still seems to matter, as in Baldwin's study of nineteenth-century state responses to disease. Table 5.1 aims to summarize some of that observed variety, examining degrees of change in oversight against variations in initial positions.

Table 5.1 The development of central oversight: points of departure and degrees of change, selected cases

		Intensity of formal oversight at point of departure		
		High	Medium	Low
Degree of expansion of oversight	High	UK new universities (ex-polytechnics) – research oversight added to teaching	German universities (research and teaching oversight on top of operational oversight)	UK old universities; ethics oversight for some high bureaucrats
	Medium	Extension of audit office scrutiny of high bureaucracy in many cases (e.g. Norway, UK)	French universities (*tutelle* retained, but contractual controls added); UK and Australian prisons (public private rivalry plus change in oversight)	Norwegian universities (some moves away from Humboldtian traditions of autonomy)
	Low	Security vetting of civil servants in the UK	Most prison cases	US universities (little appreciable growth in formal oversight)
Cases of reduction of oversight		Dismantling of formal central approval of individual salaries in several civil service systems	Dutch prisons (abandonment of inspection in the 1980s)	

From this set of cases, we do not have a clear case of a major domain of oversight that started from a low level of intensity and subsequently declined (the bottom right-hand cell of Table 5.1), and that may be a sign of the times. But we have enough cases to show that a high level of expansion of oversight is only one out of several patterns. We find numerous cases where only a low level of expansion of oversight took place and several in which oversight actually declined. But such cases tend to be given less attention than the dramatic cases of oversight expansion, even though the latter also appear to be the exception rather than the rule.

(a)   Variations across Policy Domains

Three features of oversight stand out in particular in comparative perspective. First, as Table 5.1 shows, from these cases there appears to be no uniform or universal trend to an explosion or dramatic growth in oversight of government. In none of our cases have prisons been exposed to the same degree of expansion in formal oversight over the last few decades as has applied to (old) university teaching and research institutions in many of our cases, and there has been no equivalent debate in the prison sector about some putative decline in professional autonomy. It is true that there has been some increase in international-level oversight of prison systems over a generation, but such oversight as yet amounts to little more than a conversation with states that have signed up to international human-rights treaties and conventions. At national or state government level there has been in many cases little dramatic change in prison oversight over 50 years or more – as far back as 1908 in the Japanese case, which has had several sets of bureaucrats responsible for inspecting its prisons for nearly a century. Indeed, in the Netherlands, the prison inspectorate was actually abolished in an apparently rather absent-minded way in the 1980s, meaning that formal central oversight declined rather than expanded. Moreover, many of our contributors have pointed to major limitations in the efficacy of traditional oversight systems, and such limitations can be severe for closed-world institutions like prisons. Nicole de Montricher and Marie Vogel in their contribution on France argue that the real impact of higher or external oversight bodies has long been almost of no account, and that conclusion was echoed by several of our other contributors on prisons.

The university sector, as we have seen, reveals in many cases a different story. Central oversight has not increased in all the countries in this study, but it has been a feature of many of our cases, with the UK 'old universities' exposed to particularly dramatic rises in external oversight from a very low base. However, the expansion of oversight in university systems has in all our cases been linked to competition in some form, whereas competition among institutions or individuals has been almost absent in the control arrangements applying to prisons.

Perhaps there is some modest pressure for national governments (at least those of a liberal rather than a populist political complexion) to avoid the embarrassment of being singled out by international prison inspectors and human rights, watchers as 'worst case' prison systems, and some mild satisfaction in being acclaimed, as Norway often is, as a shining example to others. But just how deep that embarrassment or satisfaction goes, and how far it links to any effective control at the field level, is at best debatable and probably variable. Moreover, where prisons are the responsibility of state governments in a federal system, as in Germany or (partially) the USA, competition among states may not necessarily work to drive up standards in the direction desired by humanitarian reformers. Having 'the worst (that is, toughest) prisons in the country' from the standpoint of prisoner conditions may be a badge of glory rather than of shame for state-level politicians of a certain hue, aiming for a tough-on-crime stance.

However, for those countries, notably Australia and the UK in our study, where there is some public–private competition ('metaphytic competition' in Corbett's, 1965, phrase) for the running of prisons, there does seem to be some evidence that such competition achieved what oversight alone could not do – creating pressures for higher and explicit standards at least for services like catering and laundry in the former exclusively public prison system. That is why those countries are classed in the medium-change category in Table 5.1 while most cases are classed in the low-change category.

It is not difficult, as we have argued earlier, to identify some features of the prison sector that might distinguish it from university-level teaching and research, though they share some common features too. Both are textbook cases of labour-intensive service industries, both have been subject to marked expansion in many countries and both are experiencing an internationalization of their clienteles in contrast to the greater national and cultural homogeneity of a generation ago (with non-nationals now approaching a majority of prisoners in German gaols, and coming close in numerous other cases). And, as we noted in Section 3.1, prisons have often – following Bentham (1931: 335) – been dubbed 'academies of crime' (though universities are less often called prisons of learning). But in many respects there are major social and political differences between the two sectors. The prison sector was never and nowhere a high-prestige or high-trust domain of state activity. Few middle-class children were encouraged by doting parents to dream of being prison officers when they grew up. The prison sector had no particular formal autonomy from the state apparatus, even though, like the police, it often seems to have had strong *de facto* autonomy as a uniformed service with a distinct administrative subculture. It was not central to economic management in most countries, although in the USA the traditionally very high levels of incarceration that we noted in Chapter 2 are often said to have had a dampening effect on unemployment figures, particularly for working-class African-American males, and also affected their franchise entitlements.

By contrast, university teaching and research in most cases was traditionally a domain for the upwardly mobile middle class, constituted a high-status and high-trusted profession aspired to by the ambitious and was separated from the state apparatus by conventions of academic autonomy (though those conventions were not always entrenched in law). There were notable cross-national variations in style and approach, including the French tradition of institutional separation of university teaching from research, the mass higher education approach of the USA with a multiplicity of institutions of varying quality competing for students, funds and attention, the markedly elite universities of England before the Second World War, and the French and German tradition of running universities as state organizations, albeit with some special legal provisions designed to guarantee academic freedom on the part of professors. But in all cases, the development of the much discussed 'information economy' in the late twentieth century and the expansion of university teaching and research made this sector more salient both in international competitiveness and in domestic politics. It is not difficult to see why older conventions of Humboldtian academic autonomy might have come under severe pressure in these conditions. But even for universities, as we have seen, the extent to which state oversight has expanded has varied markedly from case to case.

The higher civil service could be considered an intermediate and to some extent ambiguous case, between the prison and university sectors. In most cases it was traditionally a high-status sector with developed norms of operation, but by definition had no autonomy from the general state apparatus. But the starting points were very different, for example with 'lateral entry' competition traditionally adopted for the topmost positions in some civil service systems, including the Norwegian and US cases, but closed-career systems elsewhere. There are also notable variations in the linkage between civil servants and judges, with a markedly higher degree of 'relational distance' in the USA and the UK than in most continental European systems, common training and outlook in the German tradition, and civil servants operating as the top-level administrative-law judges in the French one.

But again these individuals have been subject to some common pressures, including the professionalization of domestic politics and the development of new demands coming from outside, including demands for greater transparency in policy originating from the original General Agreement on Tariffs and Trade in 1947 (requiring publication of information from governments on matters covered by the agreement) and other sources, notably the EU. The extent to which the work of higher civil servants has been exposed to greater litigation and judicial oversight has varied, but the development of ombudsman systems has been widespread and freedom of information legislation, originating in the Swedish press laws and the US Freedom of Information Act of 1966, has also extended to many other countries. In most cases the public audit offices that oversee the work of central government departments have expanded in size and scope, following the shift by the US General Accounting Office a generation ago from fiscal audit to value for money and performance audits. But that expansion of audit seems to have had less of an impact on the work of individual civil servants than the development of oversight in many of our higher education cases, both because it seems to have been less targeted on their individual work and because it is typically not linked to competition among organizations in the way that the expansion of oversight over higher education has been. In Thompson's analysis, outside audit of higher civil servants might be argued to be less 'clumsy' than oversight of university academics.

In short, what this discussion and Table 5.1 suggest is that changes in oversight can vary considerably by policy sector. Indeed, the features of an 'oversight explosion' (namely the top right-hand cell of Table 5.1, with a low initial level of external oversight followed by a sharp increase in such oversight with no compensating reduction in other types of oversight) are far from typical among the cases we examined, and seem to require a special combination of unusual initial conditions with dramatic cultural change.

(b)   Variations in State Traditions

The number of exceptions to general patterns noted above suggests a second conclusion, that the variations we have observed in control patterns are not all explained by differences in policy sector, any more than the state responses to nineteenth-century contagious disease (as in the study cited in the epigraph) varied only by the type of disease. Variations in state tradition evidently matter as well as policy domain in shaping how – or whether – central oversight develops, and also seem to matter in shaping the scope for alternative forms of control. For example, our examination of prison systems seems to show that the use of private firms to compete with state organizations in running prisons – probably the most significant step in the prison control story in the UK and Australia for half a century – appears to be more 'thinkable' in some state traditions than in others.

In the federal states in our study – the USA, Germany and Australia – the relevant oversight systems are partly to be found at the state rather than central government level, but even that seems to be quite variable. For example, in the German and Australian cases we have seen countrywide systems developing for oversight of the higher education sector, but wide variation among the states and the *Länder* in prison oversight. By contrast, the USA has a substantial federal-government prison sector, as well as an exotic variety of state government regimes, while its university sector is largely unregulated – yet ironically provides the benchmarks for university regulators in much of the rest of the world.

Applying the control analysis we have used in this study also leads us to question some of the standard stereotypes about 'state traditions' and public sector reforms. Various authors, notably Walter Kickert (1997) have claimed in comments on the New Public Management literature that there is an 'Anglo-American approach' to state administration that can be distinguished from a 'continental European' one and which generates doctrines for public service reform that are alien to the latter tradition. However that may be, what this study suggests is that, viewed in terms of control and oversight of public services, the putative 'Anglo-American' style is all too like Giovanni Sartori's (1994) famous cat-dog – a creature that does not actually exist. That is because the analysis of our three policy domains as well as the broader analysis of control styles and state traditions in the first chapter suggests that the UK style of controlling public services is at least as different from the US style as either style is different from the classical continental European state forms of France or Germany.

3   CONTROL OVER GOVERNMENT: DEVELOPING THE FOUR-PART OPTIC

We began the book by exploring controls over government operating through a quartet of mechanisms linked to grid-group cultural theory, and posing the question of how controls over government had changed across our set of countries during the recent era of government reform. We can conclude that none of the four primary forms of control disappeared from view, though in many cases they were considerably reshaped and several of our contributors asserted that randomness did not feature either in the traditional or contemporary forms of the systems they were trying to analyse. Moreover, this comparative inquiry helps us to distinguish some of the major sub-types and variants of the four control types in our initial scheme.

(a)   Reshaping Oversight of Government

This book shows that oversight activity figured large in many traditional systems of government, although the particular form it took varied widely across state traditions. The extent to which law courts and legislatures operated as effective external overseers of executive government varied across the state traditions in our study, as well as across domains (for instance, the law courts seemed to figure less heavily in control of German universities than of the other sectors). So did the extent to which the central level of government operated as an overseer of lower levels of government in the French *tutelle* tradition, and the extent to which there were central inspectors of public services.

Many of our contributors began by stressing and mapping out the official role of oversight in control of government, identifying the organizations and office-holders responsible for systems of authorization, evaluation, audit and adjudication. But – a point that applies to all the four control mechanisms discussed in this book – activity is not the same thing as achievement, and it remains quite debatable how far oversight activity amounts to effective *control* (keeping systems within bounds, checking deviation, moving objects of control in desired directions) and for what purposes. Indeed, many of the attempts to reform public services over the past few decades sprang from a perception or assertion of the futility or perversity of traditional forms of oversight and an attempt to reinforce or replace oversight with what were perceived as more effective controls, particularly new forms of competition.

Our ability to evaluate the effectiveness of such oversight systems is naturally limited and our analysis cannot escape being conditioned by observer bias (though the advantage of a team approach to analysing control is that such biases are less likely to go unchallenged). But some conclusions can be drawn with some confidence. For all the talk of deregulated and entrepreneurial government in the contemporary reform era, there is little evidence that oversight activity declined overall even in the most 'gung-ho' new public management states like the UK, even if some manifestations of oversight declined for some purposes (particularly in traditional central staffing control systems). But we can detect signs of a reshaping of oversight systems in at least three ways.

One, highlighted by many of our contributors, is that in several domains oversight shifted from an emphasis on detailed *ex ante* authorization to *ex post* appraisal and audit of activity and performance against general guidelines or principles – a shift that Fred Thompson (1993) has identified as central to the modern public management agenda and paralleling changing theories of effective management control in business. In this book we have seen such shifts in several contexts, including new arrangements for French and Japanese university administration that partly moved away from traditional civil service input controls, and the reshaping of staff management systems away from prior approval by central agencies to *ex post* audit. Whether that control shift amounts to a decline of 'rule-based administration' – something that is often loosely argued to be a feature or ambition of the New Public Management movement – is debatable, and turns on what exactly is meant by 'rules'. If the guidelines are more detailed than applied in an earlier era, as in the case of new 'ethics codes' in many cases, a shift from *ex ante* approvals to *ex post* evaluation may be part of a move towards more rule-based administration rather than less. Evidently, many of the public servants our contributors talked to did not perceive themselves as operating in a less 'rule-bound' context than in earlier times, though the nature of the rules may have changed.

A second conclusion is that where oversight expanded or was reformed, it often developed in new hybrid forms, particularly in competition-oversight and competition-mutuality mixes. Such mixes can be considered as instances of Thompson's 'clumsy institutions' hypothesis that we referred to earlier – namely that only combinations of the four pure types can form the basis of viable institutions. Figure 5.1 portrays some of those mixes diagrammatically, stretching the well-known three-circle Venn diagram form to four circles. The primary forms are labelled 1–4, with four two-part hybrids labelled 5–8, four three-part hybrids 9–12 and a single four-part hybrid labelled 13. For example, oversight-mutuality – a form of control much discussed in the burgeoning literature on 'enforced self-regulation' (Ayres and Braithwaite, 1992) and co-regulation – is a hybrid of type 6 in Figure 5.1. The combination of competition, mutual peer-group evaluation and oversight that has featured so large in the development of many control systems over universities is a case of a three-part hybrid of type 11 in that diagram. Figure 5.1 is not complete because it does not cover all the possible combinations, and it is intended to be illustrative rather than comprehensive.

Indeed, following the 'clumsy institutions' line of analysis, we conclude that oversight becomes more powerful precisely when it is linked to competition and mutuality, because (in cybernetic language) the competition provides powerful 'effectors' (what changes behaviour) and the mutuality provides powerful 'detectors' (what observes the true state of the system). In fact, as Figure 5.1 suggests, the pure form of scientific peer review amounts to a control system that is a four-part hybrid of type 13 – combining rivalry (for recognition of discovery) with mutuality (through review by peers), plus elements of randomness (through the unpredictability of which peers will review what) and oversight (in the sense of some hierarchy of certificated authority or levels of evidence). Arguably that is the difference between prison and university oversight in many of our cases.

A third and related conclusion is that new or at least revamped mechanisms and forms of oversight seem to have developed. For example, Ivar Bleiklie suggests that the vogue for targets and performance indicators in university government in Norway has been part of a broader shift in which a previous pattern of detailed central oversight over a limited range of activities or values has been replaced by less detailed oversight over a wider array of issues. Indeed, the scatter-gun approach of multiple targets and indicators may amount to a form of oversight that is a complex hybrid of oversight (in the

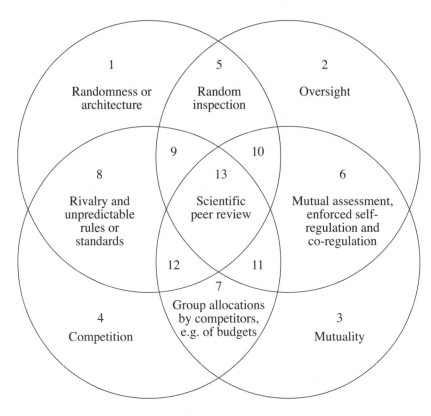

Figure 5.1   Control over government revisited: pure types and hybrids

setting and prescribing of targets and indicators), competition (among different values), mutuality (in the quasi-peer evaluations that produce the numbers) and unpredictability (in the shifting-sands political processes and changing casts of characters that constantly change the mix and weighting of indicators).

(b)   Mutuality, but Not as We Have Known It?

This book has shown that mutuality as a way of controlling government can take various forms and take place at several levels. As noted in the first chapter, we can distinguish between the degree of mutual accommodation that is designed into the formal or informal constitution of a state according to the number of 'veto players' it establishes (controlling those veto players by forcing them to do deals with one another, as in the classic 'pillarization' pattern of the Netherlands or the division of powers in the USA), and types of mutual control operating at a corporate rather than constitutional level, for example by systems of mutual surveillance within a group, as in the French *grands corps* or the Japanese higher civil service. There is little sign of any general decline in the first type of mutuality and, indeed, moves in the direction of more 'multi-level governance' (through developments in the EU, adoption of elected regional levels of government in traditionally unitary states such as France and the UK, and the much discussed phenomenon of increasing judicial activism within the UK and EU) might suggest that mutuality of this kind is more likely to have increased than decreased.

At the 'corporate' level of mutuality, many of our contributors and the interviewees they talked to began by interpreting changes in control over government in the New Public Management era as instances of mutuality in decline from some putative earlier era of higher trust in public sector professionals and informal group influence. However, the more we probed, the more we were led to the conclusion that in many cases it seemed to make more sense to identify the emergence of a different style of mutuality rather than the disappearance of mutuality *tout court*.

Types of mutuality that seemed to be in some decline included the old Dutch 'pillarization' model, the British 'Athenaeum Club' culture in the high civil service, and the informal mutual controls among the professoriat in Hans-Ulrich Derlien's perhaps idealized portrait of the traditional German university system. But in many cases reshaped or alternative types of mutuality seemed to be developing. For instance, in Chapter 2 Per Lægreid and Marjoleine Wik suggested that mutuality controls in Norwegian prisons seem to be moving from a single-profession (prison guard) mode to a multi-profession mode, reflecting the new specialities that have entered prison work, and even in the prison guard group, a substantial feminization of the guards over a generation has meant that the peer group has changed. Similar developments can be observed in several others of the prison cases. Indeed, in some cases we might plausibly argue that mutuality has increased in comparison to an earlier era. A case in point is the decline of the 1810 Humboldtian university ideal of a community of autonomous professors engaged in inextricably linked activities of teaching and research, as noted by Ivar Bleiklie and Hans-Ulrich Derlien in discussion of the Norwegian and German cases.

The replacement of that Humboldtian structure by departmental and faculty governance, plus a reshaping of traditional university senates, and separate evaluation of teaching and research is often loosely interpreted as meaning a loss of mutuality by scholars bewailing the decline of the old system. But it could just as well be interpreted either as an exchange of one form of mutuality for another, with a decline in mutuality in university governance but increased mutuality in the form of more peer review of performance in teaching and research or as a shift towards greater mutuality in the sense of more group control over the individual, and a move away from mere coexistence –

peaceful or otherwise – among autonomous scholars. So we might echo Horace (Epistles, Book 1): *Naturam expellas furca, tamen usque recurret.*

Much the same has been said about changes in the governance of health care (for instance in Michael Moran's [1999] comparative study of the USA, the UK and Germany), in attempts to describe and assess changes in the traditionally closed and 'private' world of medical self-government as different actors moved in. Whether this change amounts to an increase or decrease in overall mutuality is harder to assess than simple claims about the declining autonomy of the medical profession might lead us to think: Moran's own conclusion is that 'this new world of professional government is in some respects less penetrable by the agents of democratic politics than the old "private" world of professional government in the United States, precisely due to the extraordinary technical complexity of the policy language' (ibid. 125). Much the same might be said of changes in university autonomy, with the impenetrable and self-referential jargon that the new control professionals have introduced.

(c) Hyper-Competitive Public Services – or New Forms of Competition for Old?

As we suggested in the first chapter, those contemporary public sector reformers who speak and write as if they had invented competition as a way of controlling government are like teenagers who nurture the illusion that they are the first generation to have invented sex. This book has shown that competition was far from absent in the public sector in most countries in the days of those reformers' parents and grandparents. But, that aside, should we conclude that the recent past has seen a quantum increase in the degree of competition used to control public services? Are we seeing turbo-competition in government in an age of turbo-capitalism?

Only up to a point, it seems. Some forms of public-service competition might even be said to have weakened in recent decades. For example, an important element of competition might be said to have weakened, in so far as the declining attractiveness of public bureaucracy as a secure and respected career against other options during the long boom of the decades after the Second World War meant that the best and the brightest were less inclined to compete for traditional government work.

Moreover, from a consumer viewpoint, changes in public-service provision over recent decades have not necessarily seen an increase in competition in those services. The widespread notion that government should contract out public-service work to the private sector wherever it can (in every sphere from insurance to accounting) has undoubtedly in some cases led to a move from public monopoly to private monopoly, or at best oligopoly, for example in the case of automated data-processing or insurance. Indeed, in some cases competition declined, for instance in those cases where the once popular doctrine of 'metaphytic' competition in services like retail banking or airlines was replaced by a doctrine of unchallenged private sector provision, in rather the same way as tram and trolley-bus lines were torn up in many US and British cities after the Second World War to – literally – give a clear run to private cars.

In other cases and other forms, however, competition evidently increased. As we have shown, if the doctrine of 'metaphytic competition' went out of favour in some cases, it came back in others. Notably, it was applied to prisons in the UK and Australia and, as we showed earlier in the book, that increase in competition had major effects in giving private prison providers an incentive to comply with the demands of overseers, and gave those overseers a degree of extra leverage over the public prisons as well. And if the best and brightest emerging from college in the later decades of the twentieth century were less likely to compete for permanent jobs in the career bureaucracy than their counterparts in the hungry 1930s (or, indeed, much later in the case of Japan), new forms of competition were introduced in many bureaucracies.

Those new forms included more lateral entry for higher positions in previously closed-career structures, the addition of 'pay for performance' in several countries as a new forum for competition among bureaucrats on top of the traditional battle for promotion, the introduction of market testing in areas that were once the sole preserve of public organizations, increasing use of policy think tanks and political consultancies along with career civil servants in policy-making, and the widespread practice of higher level authorities 'top slicing' the budgets of lower level organizations to fund new initiatives over which the lower-level authorities were invited to compete. And if there has always to some extent been an 'invisible college' of peers controlling scientific reputations and career advancement, international competition for top students during the last few decades has undoubtedly increased in the university sector.

(d) Randomness: a Death that Has Been Much Exaggerated?

Contrived randomness could be considered as one of those dogs that did not bark in the night (recalling the famous Sherlock Holmes story of 'Silver Blaze'), since our contributors' first reaction in many cases was to dismiss it as an instrument of control in the traditional or contemporary era. But again on closer examination, randomness seems to be by no means absent from either traditional or contemporary controls over government. As suggested in the introduction to Chapter 4, we may have dismissed contrived randomness too hastily, because, like the proverbial drunk searching for the lost keys under the lamp-post, we were looking for it in the wrong place.

As with mutuality, this book has shown that randomness can work as a form of control at different institutional levels and in different ways. For example, moves to greater transparency (a doctrine of Jeremy Bentham's [Hume, 1981: 161] that came back into high fashion in the recent past as a recipe for 'good governance', with little critical scrutiny) can increase the exposure of individuals or groups to unexpected and unpredictable interventions by outsiders. Career unpredictability that makes it uncertain who an individual will be working with or for into the future (and thereby restricts the scope for some kinds of comfortable accommodation) can also be produced by a range of institutional processes. It is not only a product of the classic device of switching individuals around the various parts of a sprawling bureaucratic empire (much used in traditional field-service bureaucracies of the French type, as noted by Nicole de Montricher and also in the traditional posting system in the Japanese bureaucracy, as described by Takeshi Nishio).

We have seen numerous instances of randomness linked with oversight mechanisms, in a rough analogy with random audits by tax authorities or the 'snap inspection' beloved of military organizations. For instance, unexpected inspections of prisons have been part of the traditional tool kit of central authorities in Japan, the UK and some *Länder* in Germany, even though it apparently does not take place in France or the Netherlands. But in general, many of our contributors have exposed the difficulty that central authorities have found in using randomness effectively to control prisons, either by shuffling the deck of prison staff around establishments or by unexpected dawn raid-type inspections. Prison control generally seems to show a chronic randomness deficit and there is little sign of change.

In the world of university research, however, it could be argued that the element of randomness has increased in several ways, often in conjunction with other control modes. The 'globalization' of some aspects of university work means that the peer-reviewing system which controls many aspects of such work (for publications, grant funding, even review of institutions) may be becoming less predictable, particularly for senior academics, than the cosy world of more segmented national research communities of a generation ago in many subjects.

That does not apply in the same way to the world of higher bureaucrats, but even those individuals are exposed to a number of trends, some of them working in opposite directions. On the one hand, the downsizing or delayering of traditional bureaucracies, coupled with a higher incidence of outsourcing and outside consulting for many aspects of policy work, might be thought to reduce the random element of control built into rotation around bureaucratic systems over the course of a public service career. On the other hand, trends such as greater politicization (a key element of increasing randomness in the German case, as noted by Hans-Ulrich Derlien) and more career uncertainty for higher civil servants, plus the need to work with new partners of various kinds in policy or delivery, may well be increasing the element of random control rather than decreasing it for higher civil servants. In some cases, too, those individuals have been exposed to more randomness used by oversight bodies, as in the case of the Australian Independent Commissions against Corruption and in the UK by the private firms employed by the re-styled Civil Service Commission to audit compliance with merit appointment and promotion procedures.

Moreover, randomness forms a central component of a hybrid form of control that is applied to universities and many other kinds of public services today, which mixes an unpredictable and ever-changing array of output targets with competitive league tables, audit and inspection systems and some element of peer rating. That four-part hybrid is the type numbered 13 in Figure 5.1 – the 'clumsiest' possible kind of control system in our analytic scheme. Control of that type is far from the traditional stereotype of hierarchical oversight, and indeed looks more like the shifting-balances model of 'opposed maximizers' that Andrew Dunsire (1996) has labelled 'collibration'.

Altogether, we might echo Mark Twain (if less elegantly) in concluding that the idea of the death or even decline of randomness as a form of control over government may have been much exaggerated. It is true that randomness rarely seems to be used in a pure or primary form, but after all the same goes for oversight, mutuality and competition. What is puzzling is that randomness as a primary or hybrid form of control seems to find so little favour in most prescriptions for increasing controls over government, despite the theoretical importance of randomness for ideas about control of bureaucracy, as pointed out in Section 4.1. After all, we have an abundance of competition gurus, mutuality gurus and even oversight gurus. Where are the randomness gurus?

4   COMMON PATTERNS OF CHANGE IN CONTROL OVER GOVERNMENT?

Finally, we turn to some wider issues raised by this study. What general patterns can we detect, what are the various dynamics that seem to be going on and how do the control changes we have discussed in this book relate to all those much discussed processes of modernization and globalization?

Evidently, those processes form the backdrop to any study of changing controls in contemporary government systems. The so-called information age undoubtedly provides a different context for control over government than earlier technological eras. It is obvious that controls over government today take place in a world where ideas can travel fast, where developed states confront similar policy problems, and where bureaucrats, politicians and their advisers have ways of interacting with one another within and across state boundaries that were not available to their parents or grandparents.

But commonality of problems does not necessarily lead to commonality of response, as Baldwin showed in his study of how nineteenth-century states responded to cholera, tuberculosis and syphilis. Indeed, we can identify four broad patterns of change in control over government, which are summarized in Figure 5.2. One consists of little or no change, and our study revealed numerous instances of that. For instance, we need not expect any sudden or dramatic alteration in the effect of court oversight over German government or in the way mutuality works in the deeply entrenched French elite-cadre government structure. Against the case of relative stasis, we can divide patterns of change into those where the response to disturbances in the environment is to accentuate, reinforce or 'turbocharge' the distinctive features of each particular system and those where the response takes the form of some sort of convergence.

Cases of the reinforcement response are often found in public policy, and it is not difficult to see the mechanisms that can produce such a response

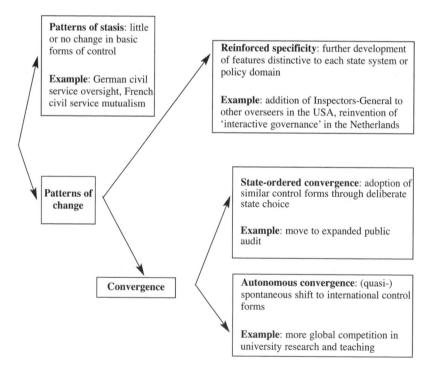

Figure 5.2   Control of government: four patterns of development

(institutional systems under pressure reinforce their established features because those features are familiar and the systems concerned are good at producing them). For instance, different developed states' initial responses to the AIDS epidemic that first broke in the 1980s are often cited as an example of such a process, since those initial responses tended to draw on different ways of dealing with contagious disease that had become established in the nineteenth century (see Baldwin, 1999; Freeman, 2000: 124–37). Examples of those nineteenth-century traditions that received reinforcement in the first throes of the AIDS epidemic included the British liberal-sanitarian approach and the Swedish tradition of compulsory treatment.

The US invention of Inspectors-General in the late 1970s (described by Guy Peters in Chapter 4) as yet another layer of oversight to add to an already oversight-heavy system might be considered as such a case, as might the Dutch tendency to add another form of 'interactive governance' to their traditional mutuality-suffused system in the contemporary reform era, as described by Theo Toonen. (A contrasting case, not discussed in this book, is the way the UK is often said to have extended its already elaborate oversight and monitoring of local government by central government in the 1980s and 1990s.)

However, in this study, we found few unambiguous cases of 'turbocharged specificity' in changes in control styles over government, and what we observed mostly looked more like either stasis or some form of convergence. But convergence itself can take at least two forms. One is the sort of convergence that consists of more or less consciously state-driven processes and preferences, and depends on the power and influence of states in agreeing and complying with international regimes or choosing to adopt similar principles and practices. Another is the sort of convergence that emerges largely through spontaneous interaction rather than state-driven change, producing something like an autonomous international domain. An example of the second kind of convergence is Gunther Teubner's (1997) account of the growth of the *lex mercatoria* as something that has developed in a relatively spontaneous way, and has only been limitedly shaped by the actions and preferences of states.

In general, dramatic convergence of either kind seems more obvious and easier to detect in the *substance* of what government does – from the software programs it uses, the contractors and consultants it employs, the particular technical policy standards it develops – than in the controls to which it is subjected, as conceived in this book, and it is important not to elide the substance of government activity with the way it is controlled, though the dividing line can certainly be hard to draw on occasion. When it comes to control the patterns of change described in this book fall mainly into three patterns – mainly stasis, a mixture of stasis and state-ordered convergence, and a mixture of state-ordered and spontaneous convergence.

Compared with the other sectors, stasis is the main story of what happened to prison controls in this study, together with a small element of state-ordered convergence, and we observed only minor variations according to state tradition. As already noted, there is a weak international human rights regime, in which the politics of compliance by states is the central element and the international regulators cannot do much more than enter into dialogue with states that are signatories to the international conventions, and cannot even do that for non-signatories (see Neary, 2001: introduction). Some globalization has taken place in the nature of the prison population in many states, as we saw earlier, but does not seem to have had the effect of augmenting international competition in the same way as greater internationalization of students has done in parts of the university sector. And the lack of effective competition – and consequent 'clumsiness deficit' – seems the most likely explanation for why oversight controls over prisons, however well-intentioned, are likely to remain relatively ineffective. The cases analysed in this book are consistent with the clumsiness hypothesis, in that racking up oversight without competition only seems to produce accountability overload without guaranteeing service quality or robustness.

By contrast, what happened to controls over the behaviour of higher civil servants looks more like a case that combines elements of stasis and state-ordered convergence, with considerable variation according to different state traditions. As noted earlier, some of the deeply entrenched forms of mutuality and oversight in this sector show little signs of change, but even the most hardened 'New Public Management sceptic' would be hard put to deny that there are signs of convergence over some forms of control, particularly as the 'Whitehall-model' states and those that resemble them come to adopt forms of control from other government systems. Whether that convergence amounts to a move towards 'clumsier' systems of control over higher civil servants is a topic that deserves more investigation.

When it comes to the university sector, stasis does not plausibly describe what happened to controls in any of the cases except (possibly) that of the USA, irrespective of state tradition. Rather, what characterizes that case is a pattern of change that combines elements of state-ordered and spontaneous convergence. Perhaps one of the reasons why academics have had so much to say about globalization over the past few decades is that they have personally been exposed to more global competition for faculty, students, the placing of publications in international peer-reviewed journals and related pressures to use English in research and, even, teaching.

As with many other instances of globalization, that development can be interpreted as reflecting the worldwide dominance of the US model of research and higher education, with states elsewhere tending to take the US model (or at least what they perceive that model to be) as the gold standard in the regulatory controls they impose on their university sectors. But it can also be argued, following Gunther Teubner's account of the growth of the *lex mercatoria*, that the sort of globalization that is at work in the university sector in part amounts to the development of a system that is not the intentional product of any state, with states picking up on those developments in their attempts to shape the system at the margin. Indeed, in some ways this development can be considered as 'back to the future,' in so far as it re-creates in a different way and on a far larger scale the sort of conditions that applied to Europe's universities in the pre-modern age, operating as they did with Latin as the lingua franca for scholars and with a common canon of received texts.

At the least, this book has shown there are substantial variations in control over government, and no more sign of a common worldwide response than there was a single response to cholera and other diseases in the nineteenth century. But will this variety continue? It seems unlikely to disappear entirely, not just because of institutional 'stickiness' – after all, that has not prevented university control systems from being reshaped in a generation, in very different state traditions – but because control is both inherently context-specific and dynamic in a Markovian sense. It can be self-disequilibrating as well as self-reinforcing, and indeed one of the analytic advantages of the grid-group framework is that it cuts across conventional clichés about state systems and allows us to make successively finer distinctions to track movement in control systems, rather like the way that micro-facial movements can be analysed with modern digital-picture techniques. As we have seen, the idea that viable control systems over government must have elements of 'clumsiness' in a cultural sense fits with much of our analysis in this book. There is much to be done before its full potential can be realized.

Bibliography

Abe, H. and M. Shindo (1994), *The Government and Politics of Japan*, trans. W. White, Tokyo: University of Tokyo Press.

Aberbach, J.D. (1990), *Keeping a Watchful Eye*, Washington, DC: Brookings Institution.

Aberbach, J.D. and B.A. Rockman (2000), *In the Web of Politics*, Washington, DC: Brookings Institution.

Administration pénitentiaire (2002), *Rapport d'activité 2000, Ministère de la Justice*, Paris: La documentation Française.

Ashby, R. (1956), *An Introduction to Cybernetics*, London: Chapman Hall.

Association of University Teachers (2001), 'UK academic staff casualisation 1994–95 to 2000–01', London: AUT.

Attali, J. (1998), *Pour un Modèle Européen d'Enseignement Supérieur*, Paris: Stock.

Aucoin, P. (1990), 'Administrative reform in public management – paradigms, principles, paradoxes and pendulums', *Governance*, **3**, 115–37.

Audit Victoria (1999), *Victoria's Prison System: Community Protection and Prisoner Welfare*, Melbourne: Victorian Auditor-General's Office.

Auditor-General (1998), *University of Western Sydney: Administrative Arrangements*, Sydney: AGNSW.

Auditor-General (2001), *Annual Report to Parliament*, vol. 7, Sydney: AGNSW.

Australian Bureau of Statistics (2000), 'Participation in education', Press Release 6272, Australian Bureau of Statistics, Canberra.

Australian Public Service Commission (2001), *State of the Service Report 2000–01*, Canberra: Commonwealth of Australia.

Australian Vice-Chancellors' Committee (2002a), *Forward from the Crossroads: Pathways to Effective and Diverse Universities*, Canberra: AVCC.

Australian Vice-Chancellors' Committee (2002b), *Specifications for Audit of Year 2001 Research Publications Data*, Canberra: AVCC.

Australian Vice-Chancellors' Committee (2003), 'Facts Card Canberra', AVCC, available at http://www.avcc.edu.au/news/public-statments/publications/facts03/facts_sheets.htm, visited 2 April 2004.

Ayres, I. and J. Braithwaite (1992), *Responsive Regulation: Transcending the Deregulation Debate*, Oxford: Oxford University Press.

Azuchi, S. (1988), *Unknown Rules of Prisons*, Toyko: Nihon Bungei Sha.

Baldwin, P. (1999), *Contagion and the State in Europe 1830–1930*, Cambridge: Cambridge University Press.

Barzelay, M. (1992), *Breaking Through Bureaucracy: A New Vision for Managing in Government*, Berkeley, CA: University of California Press.

Bauer and Bertin-Mourot (1994), *Les énarques en entreprises de 1960 à 1990*, Paris: CNRS-Boyden.

Baumgartner, F.R. and B.D. Jones (1993), *Agendas and Instability in American Politics*, Chicago: University of Chicago Press.

Becquart-Leclercq, J. (1978), 'Relational power and systemic articulation in the French local polity', in L. Karpik (ed.), *Organization and Environment*, London: Sage.

Bernelmans-Videc, M.-L., R.C. Risk and E. Vedung (eds) (1998), *Carrots, Sticks and Sermons. Policy Instruments and their Evaluation*, New Brunswick, NJ: Transaction Books.

Ben-David, J. and A. Zloczower (1991), 'Universities and academic systems in modern societies', in J. Ben-David (ed.), *Scientific Growth: Essays on the Social Organization and Ethos of Science*, Berkeley, CA, Los Angeles and London: University of California Press.

Bentham, J. (1791), *Panopticon or Inspection House*, London: Payne.

Bentham, J. (1931), *The Theory of Legislation*, ed C.K. Ogden, London: Routledge and Kegan Paul.

Better Regulation Task Force (2000), *Higher Education: Easing the Burden*, London: Cabinet Office.

Bleiklie, I. (1998), 'Justifying the evaluative state. New Public Management ideals in higher education', *European Journal of Education*, **33** (3), 299–316.

Bleiklie, I., H. Byrkjeflot and K. Østergen (2003), 'Innovation, politics and bureaucracy: a comparison of two large Norwegian public sector reforms', Stein Rokkan Centre for Social Studies, University of Bergen, paper prepared for presentation at the EGOS conference 2003.

Bleiklie, I., R. Høstaker and A. Vabø (2000), *Policy and Practice in Higher Education*, London and Philadelphia: Jessica Kingsley.

Bleiklie, I., P. Lægreid and M.H. Vik (2002), 'Changing government control in Norway: high civil service, universities and prisons', paper prepared for the workshop on regulating government in a 'managerial' age, London School of Economics and Political Science, 13–14 December.

Boer, H. de and J. Huisman (1998), 'The New Public Management in Dutch universities', in D. Braun and J.-X. Merrien (eds), *Towards a New Model of Governance for Universities? A Comparative View*, London: Jessica Kingsley, pp. 123–6.

Boin, A. (2001), *Crafting Public Institutions: Leadership in Two Prison Systems*, Boulder, CO: Lynne Rienner.

Boin, R.A. and M.H.P. Otten (1996), 'Beyond the crisis window for reform: some ramifications for implementation', *Journal of Contingencies and Crisis Management*, **4**, (3), 149–61.

Braun D. and F.X. Merrien (1999), *Towards a New Model of Governance for Universities? A Comparative View*, London and Philadelphia: Jessica Kingsley.

Brennan, J. and T. Shah (2000), 'Quality assessment and institutional change: experience from 14 countries', *Higher Education*, **40**, 331–49.

Bruneau, W. and D.C. Savage (2002), *Counting Out the Scholars: The Case Against Performance Indicators in Higher Education*, Toronto: James Lorimer.

Bureau of Prisons (2002), *State of the Bureau: Accomplishments and Goals*, Washington, DC: US Department of Justice.

Bureau of Justice Statistics (2002), *Census of Federal and State Correctional Facilities*, Washington, DC: Department of Justice.

Candy, P.C. and D. Maconachie (1997), *Quality Assurance in Australian Higher Education: A Recent History and Commentary*, Canberra: Australian Vice-Chancellors' Committee.

Canivet, G. (2000), *Amélioration du contrôle extérieur des établissements pénitenti-aires, Rapport au garde des Sceaux*, Paris: La Documentation Française.

Chevallier, J. (1986), *Réflexions sur l'institution des autorités administratives indépen-dantes*, Semaine juridique I (3254).

Christensen, T., P. Lægreid and L. Wise (2002), 'Transforming administrative policy', *Public Administration*, **80**, 153–70.

Christie, N. (1969), 'Modeller for fengselsorganisasjonen', in I. R. Østensen (ed.), *I stedet for fengsel*, Oslo: Pax.

Cohen, M., J. March and J.P. Olsen (1972), 'A garbage can model of organizational choice', *Administrative Science Quarterly*, **17**, 1–25.

Collins, W.C. (1998), *Jail Design and Operation and the Constitution*, Washington, DC: Department of Justice.

Commissie Borghouts (2001), Ambtelijke Commissie Toezicht (ACT), '*Vertrouwen in onafhankelijkheid*', Den Haag, 2001: 22

Congressional Digest (2002), 'Should the House pass the Homeland Security Act?', *Congressional Digest*, **81** (October), 238–57.

Corbett, D. (1965), *Politics and the Airlines*, London: Allen and Unwin.

Cornford, F. (1908), *Microcosmographia Academica, Being a Guide for the Young Academic Politician*, Cambridge: Bowes.

Council of Europe (2000a), 'Report to the United Kingdom government on the visit to the United Kingdom and the Isle of Man carried out by the European Committee for the Prevention of Torture and Inhuman or Degrading Treatment or Punishment (CPT) from 8 to 17 September 1997', Ref.: CPT/Inf (2000) 1 [EN], Strasbourg: Council of Europe http://www.cpt.coe.int/en/reports/inf2000-01en.htm (last accessed 28 August 2001).

Council of Europe (2000b), 'Response of the United Kingdom government to the report of the European Committee for the Prevention of Torture and Inhuman or Degrading Treatment or Punishment (CPT) on its visit to the United Kingdom and the Isle of Man from 8 to 17 September 1997', Ref.: CPT/Inf (2000) 7 [EN] http://www.cpt.coe.int/en/reports/inf2000-07en.htm (last accessed 28 August 2001).

Council of Europe (2001), 'European Convention for the Prevention of Torture and Inhuman or Degrading Treatment or Punishment', Strasbourg: Council of Europe, http://conventions.coe.int/treaty/EN/searchsig.asp?NI=126&CM=1&DF=(last accessed 28 August 2001).

Council of Europe (2003), 'Report to the government of the UK on the visit to the UK carried out by the CPT', Strasbourg: Council of Europe.

Day, P. and R. Klein (1990), *Inspecting the Inspectorates*, York: Joseph Rowntree Memorial Trust.

Degenne, H. (1975), 'Pérennité d'un corps de contrôle: l'Inspection générale de l'Administration du Ministère de l'Intérieur', *Administration*, numéro spécial consacré à l'Inspection Générale de l'Administration.

Department of Corrective Services (2001), *Annual Report 2000–2001*, DCS, NSW.

Department of Finance and Administration (2002), *World Trade Organisation Agreement on Government Procurement – Review of Membership Implications*, Canberra: DOFA.

Derlien, H.-U. (1988), 'Repercussions of government change on the career civil service in West Germany: the cases of 1969 and 1982', *Governance*, **1**, 50–78.

Derlien, H.-U. (1996), 'Germany: the intelligence of bureaucracy in a decentralized polity', in J.P. Olsen and B.G. Peters (eds), *Lessons from Experience*, Oslo: Scandinavian University Press, pp. 146–79.

Derlien, H.-U. (2000a), 'Germany. (Co-ordinating German EU policy) Failing Successfully?', in K. Hussein, B.G. Peters and V. Wright (eds), *National Co-ordination of EU Policy*, Oxford: Oxford University Press, pp. 54–78.

Derlien, H.-U. (2000b), 'Actor constellation, opportunity structure and concept feasibility in German and British public sector reforms', in H. Wollmann and E. Schröter (eds), *Comparing Public Sector Reform in Britain and Germany,* Aldershot: Ashgate, pp. 150–70.

Derlien, H.-U. (2001), 'Personalpolitik nach Regierungswechseln', in H.-U. Derlien and A. Murswieck (eds), *Regieren nach Wahlen*, Opladen: Leske and Budrich, pp. 39–57.

Digest of Educational Statistics (2001), Washington, DC: National Center for Educational Statistics.

Dill, D. (2001), 'The regulation of public research universities', *Higher Education Policy*, **14**, 21–35.

Dreyfus, F. (2000), *L'invention de la bureaucratie*, Paris: La découverte.

Dunleavy, P. (1991), *Democracy, Bureaucracy and Public Choice: Economic Explanations in Political Science*, London: Harvester.

Dunsire, A. (1996), 'Tipping the balance: autopoiesis and governance', *Administration and Society*, **28** (3), 299–334.

Dyson, K. (1980), *The State Tradition in Western Europe*, Oxford: Robertson.

Enders, J. (2001), 'A chair system in transition: appointments, promotions, and gate-keeping in German higher education', *Higher Education*, **41**, 3–25.

Engels, D. (2001), 'Bundespersonalausschuß und weisungsfreier Raum', in K.-P. Sommermann (ed.), *Gremienwesen und staatliche Gemeinwohlverantwortung*, Berlin: Dunker and Humblotd, pp. 69–88.

Faugeron, C. (1991), 'Les prisons de la V° République: à la recherche d'une politique', in J.-G. Petit, N. Castan, C. Faugeron, M. Pierre and A. Zysberg, *Histoire des Galères, Bagnes et Prisons, XIII°–XX° Siècles*, Privat.

Federal Ministry of Education and Research (2002), *Basic and Structural Data 2001/2002*, Berlin, available at http:/www.bmbf.de/pub/GuS2002_ges_engl.pdf visted 2 April 2004.

Feeley, M.M. and E.L. Rubin (1998), *Judicial Policymaking and the Modern State: How the Courts Reformed America's Prisons*, Cambridge: Cambridge University Press.

Fesler, J.W. and D.F. Kettl (1996), *The Politics of the Administrative Process*, Chatham, NJ: Chatham House.

Finer, H. (1940), 'Administrative responsibility in democratic government', *Public Administration Review*, **1** (4), 335–50.

Finer, S.E. (1950), *A Primer of Public Administration*, London: Frederick Muller.

Fischer, D.H. (1970) *Historian's Fallacies: Towards a Logic of Historical Thought*, London: Routledge and Kegan Paul.

Fleming, D. (2000), 'The diversification of administrative law' in G. Singleton (ed.), *The Howard Government: Australian Commonwealth Administration 1996–1998*, Sydney: UNSW Press.

Flügge, C. (2001), 'Von der Aufsicht zur Globalsteuerung', in C. Flügge, B. Maelicke and H. Preusker (eds), *Das Gefängnis als lernende Organisation*, Baden-Baden: Nomos Verlagsgesellschaft.

Foreign Press Centre (2004), 'Japan: a web guide', http://www.fpcj.jp/e/shiryo/pocket/education/education.html, visited 2 April 2004.

Foster, C.D. (1996), 'Reflections on the true significance of the Scott Report for government accountability', *Public Administration*, **74** (4), 567–92.

Franke, H. (1995), *The Emancipation of Prisoners: A Socio-Historical Analysis of the Dutch Prison Experience*, Edinburgh: Edinburgh University Press.

Freeland, R.M. and T.W. Hartle (2001), 'Stemming the rising tide of regulation', *Presidency*, **4**, 24–9.

Freeman, J.C. (ed.) (1978), *Prisons Past and Future*, London, Heinemann.

Freeman, R. (2000), *The Politics of Health in Europe*, New York: Manchester University Press.

Fridhov, I.M. (1994), *Nordisk fengselsforskning – ikke helt fraværende*, Oslo: Nordisk Samarbeidsråd for Kriminologi.

Friedrich, C.J. (1940), 'Public policy and the nature of administrative responsibility', in C.J. Friedrich and E.S. Mason (eds), *Public Policy: A Handbook of the Graduate School of Public Administration*, Cambridge, MA, Harvard University Press, pp. 3–24.

General Accounting Office (GAO) (1987), 'Senior executive service: executives' perspectives on the service', Washington, DC: USGAO, 15 May.

Gerken, J. (1986), *Anstaltsbeiräte*, Frankfurt: Peter Lang.

Goffman, E. (1961), *Asylums: Essays on the Social Situation of Mental Patients and Other Inmates*, New York: Anchor Books.

Grabosky, P. (1995), 'Counterproductive regulation', *International Journal of the Sociology of Law*, **23**, 347–69.

Group 4 Falck Global Solutions Limited (2002), *Annual Report 2002*, Copenhagen: Group 4 Falck.

Guilhot, B. (2000), 'Le contrôle de gestion dans l'université française', *PMP* **3** (18), 99–120.

Hall, C., C. Scott and C. Hood (2000), *Telecommunications Regulation: Culture, Chaos and Interdependence Inside the Regulatory Process*, London: Routledge.

Harding, R. (2001), 'Private prisons', *Crime and Justice: A Review of Research*. **28**, 265–346.

Heclo, H. (1977), *A Government of Strangers: Executive Politics in Washington*, Washington, DC: Brookings Institution.

Heclo, H. (1978a), 'Issue networks and the executive establishment', in A. King (ed.), *The New American Political System*, Washington, DC: American Enterprise Institute.

Heclo, H. (1978b), *A Government of Strangers*, Washington, DC: Brookings Institution.

Heclo, H. and A. Wildavsky (1974), *The Private Government of Public Money*, London: Macmillan.

Hendriks, F. and T. Toonen (eds) (2001), *Polder Politics in the Netherlands: Viscous State or Model Polity?* London: Ashgate.

Henkel, M. (1999), 'The modernisation of research evaluation: the case of the UK', *Higher Education*, **38**, 105–22.

Higher Education Funding Council for England (2002), 'Holdback of HEFCE Grant 2002–3', Bristol: HEFCE.

HM Chief Inspector of Prisons (2001), *Report of Her Majesty's Chief Inspector of Prisons*, Cm 548, London: The Stationery Office.

HM Prison Service (1999), 'HM Prison Service framework document', http://www.hmprisonservice.gov.uk/corporate/ (last accessed 28 August 2001).

HM Prison Service (2001), 'HM Prison Service contracts and competition group: privately managed prisons', http://www.hmprisonservice.gov.uk/corporate/. (last accessed 28 August 2001).

Hood, C. (1995), ' "Deprivileging" the UK civil service in the 1980s: dream or reality?', in J. Pierre (ed.), *Bureaucracy in the Modern State*, Aldershot: Edward Elgar, pp. 92–117.

Hood, C. (1996), 'Control over bureaucracy: cultural theory and institutional variety', *Journal of Public Policy*, **15** (3), 207–25.

Hood, C. (1998), *The Art of the State: Culture, Rhetoric, and Public Management*, Oxford: Clarenden Press.

Hood, C., C. Scott, O. James, G.W. Jones and T. Travers (1999), *Regulation inside Government: Waste-Watchers, Quality Police and Sleaze-Busters*, Oxford: Oxford University Press

House Committee on the Judiciary (2001), 'Statement of Kathleen Hawk Sawyer, Director Federal Bureau of Prisons May 3rd 2001', Washington, DC: USA House of Representatives, http://conventions.coe.int/treaty/EN/searchsig.asp?NT= 126&CM=1&DF= (last accessed 28 August 2001).

Huisman, J. (1997), 'De regulering van het opleidingenaanbod: Een slingerbeweging tussen overheidsplanning en zelfregulering', *Beleidswetenschap*, **11** (2), 122–42.

Huisman, J. (2003), 'Institutional reform in higher education: forever changes?', in S.A.H. Denters, Ov Heffen, J. Huisman and P.-J. Klok (eds), *The Rise of Interactive Governance and Quasi Markets*, Dordrecht: Kluwer, pp. 111–26.

Huisman, J. and I. Jenniskens (2000), *Nieuwe opleidingen in het HBO: het reguleren van zelfregie*, Tijdschrift voor Hoger Onderwijs 18–4, ISSN 0168–1095, pp. 267–78.

Hume, L.J. (1981), *Bentham and Bureaucracy*, Cambridge: Cambridge University Press.

IGAENR (2001), *Le Contrôle de Légalité des Etablissements Publics à Caractère Scientifique, Culturel et Professionnel*, Paris: Ministère de l'Education Nationale, Juin.

Ikenberry, S.O. and T.W. Hartle (2000), 'Where we have been and where we are going: American higher education and public policy', unpublished paper, ERIC database.

Illing, D. (2002), 'Slash tape, bureaucrat tells states', *The Australian*, 2 October, 32.

Independent Commission Against Corruption (2002a), *Degrees of Risk*, Sydney: ICAC.

Independent Commission Against Corruption (2002b), *Degrees of Risk: A Corruption Risk Profile of the New South Wales University Sector*, Sydney: ICAC.

Ingraham, P.W. and C. Ban (1984), *Legislating Bureaucratic Change: The Civil Service Reform Act of 1978*, Albany, NY: State University of New York Press.

Inspector of Custodial Services, WA (2002), *Annual Report 2001–2002*.

Inspector-General for Correctional Services, NSW (2001), *Annual Report 2000–2001*.

Ishida, T. (1983), *Japanese Political Culture: Change and Continuity*, Perth, WA: Transaction Books.

Ishizawa, Y. (1998), *The MOF*, Tokyo: Chuo-koron-sha (bunko).

Itoh, A. (2002), 'Higher education reform in perspective: the Japanese experience', *Higher Education*, **43**, 7–25.

James, O. (2000) 'Regulation inside government: public interest justifications and regulatory failures', *Public Administration*, **78** (2), 327–43.

James, O (2003), *The Executive Agency Revolution in Whitehall: Public Interest versus Bureau-shaping Explanations*, Basingstoke: Palgrave/Macmillan.

James, O. (2004), 'The UK core executive's use of public service agreements as a tool of governance', *Public Administration*, **82** (2), 397–419.

Jobert, B. and P. Muller (1988), *L'Etat en action*, Paris: PUF.

Johnsen, B. (2001), 'Sport, masculinities and power relations in prisons', PhD dissertation, Oslo: Norwegian University of Sport and Physical Education.

Joncour, Y. (1999), 'L'évolution des modes d'intervention des inspections générales: une diversification pour la performance', *PMP* (17), 3.

Kelke, C. (2000), *Nederlands detentierecht*, Deventer: Gouda Quint.

Kessler, M.C. (1986), *Les grands corps de l'Etat*, Paris: PFNSP.

Kickert, W.J.M. (1997), 'Public management in the United States and Europe', in W.J.M. Kickert (ed.), *Public Management and Administrative Reform in Western Europe*, Cheltenham, UK: Edward Elgar, pp. 15–38.

Kikuta, K. (2002), *Prisons in Japan*, Tokyo: Iwanami.

Kosky, L. (2002), *Victorian Higher Education*, Melbourne: Department of Education and Training.

Krugman, P. (2002), 'The payoffs from privatization', *New York Times*, 25 November.

Lægreid, P. and P. Roness (1999), 'Administrative reform as organized attention', in M. Egeberg and P. Lægreid (eds), *Organizing Political Institutions*, Oslo: Scandinavian University Press.

Laitin, D. (1995), 'The civic culture at 30', *American Political Science Review*, **89** (1), 168–73.

Law Society of England and Wales, and General Council of the Bar (2002), *The Academic Stage of Training for Entry into the Legal Profession in England and Wales*, London: Law Society and the General Council of the Bar.

Leroy, P. (1992), 'Contribution à une Réflexion sur le Pouvoir dans les Universités Françaises à Partir de la Réalité Grenobloise', in E. Friedberg and C. Musselin (eds), *Le Gouvernement des Universités*, Paris: L'Harmattan.

Leune, J.M.G. (1981), 'Besluitvorming in het onderwijsbestel', in J.A. v. Kemenade (ed.), *Onderwijs: Bestel en beleid*, Groningen: Wolters-Noordhoff, pp. 330–500.

Lichtbau, E. (2002), 'Bush restoring cash bonuses for appointees', *New York Times*, 12 April.

Light, P.C. (1993), *Monitoring Government: Inspectors General and the Search for Accountability*, Washington, DC: Brookings Institution.

Light, P.C. (1995), *Thickening Government: Federal Hierarchy and the Diffusion of Accountability*, Washington, DC: Brookings Institution.

Lijphart, A. (1969), 'Consociational democracy', *World Politics*, **21** (2), 207–25.

Maor, M. (1999), 'The paradoxes of managerialism', *Public Administration Review*, **59**, 5–18.

Marcou, G. (ed) (1983), *Le contrôle de l'administration pas elle-même*, Paris: CNRS.

Mathisen, T. and A. Heli (eds) (1993), *Murer og mennesker*, Oslo: Pax.

Mayntz, R. and H.U. Derlien (1989), 'Party patronage and politicization of the West German administrative elite 1970–1987 – towards hybridization?', *Governance*, **2**, 384–404.

Mayntz, R. and F.W. Scharpf (1975), *Policy-Making in the German Federal Bureaucracy*, Amsterdam: Elsevier.

Mayo, E. (1949), *The Social Problems of an Industrial Civilization*, London: Routledge and Kegan Paul.

McCubbins, M.D. and T. Schwartz (1984), 'Congressional oversight overlooked: police patrols versus fire alarms', *American Journal of Political Science*, **28**, 165–79.

McFarland, A.S. (1991), 'Interest groups and political time: cycles in America', *British Journal of Political Science*, **21**, 257–84.

Ménier, J. (1988), *Les inspections générales*, Paris: Berger-Levrault.

Ministère de la jeunesse, de l'éducation et de la recherché (2003), *Repères et references statistiques sur les enseignements, la formation et la recherche*, Paris.

Ministry of Education and Sciences (1985), *Higher Education: Autonomy and Quality*, The Hague: SDU.

Monnier, E. (1992), *Evaluations de l'action des pouvoirs publics*, Paris: Economica.

Montricher, N. de (2000), 'The prefect and state reform', *Public Administration*, **78** (3), 679–98.

Moran, M. (2003), *The British Regulatory State: High Modernism and Hyper-Innovation*, Oxford: Oxford University Press.

Moran, M. (1999), *Governing the Health Care State: A Comparative Study of the UK, US and Germany*, Manchester: Manchester University Press.

Musselin, C. (2001), *La Longue Marche des Universités Françaises*, Paris, PUF (coll. Sciences sociales et société).

Nakane, C. (1970), *Japanese Society*, London: Weidenfeld and Nicolson.

National Audit Office (2003), *The Operational Performance of Private Finance Initiative Prisons*, HC 700, Session 2002–3, London: The Stationery Office.

Neary, I. (2001), *Human Rights in Japan, South Korea and Taiwan*, London: Routledge.

Neave, G. and G. Rhoades (1987), 'The academic estate in Western Europe', in B.R. Clark (ed.), *The Academic Profession*, Berkeley and Los Angeles, CA: University of California Press.

Nelson, B. (2002a), *Higher Education at the Crossroads*, Canberra: Department of Education, Science and Training.

Nelson, B. (2002b), *Meeting the Challenges: The Governance and Management of Universities*, Canberra: Department of Education Science and Technology.

New South Wales Ombudsman (2001), *Annual Report 2000–2001*, Sydney: NSW Ombudsman.

Niklasson, L. (1996), 'Quasi-markets in higher education – a comparative analysis', *Journal of Higher Education Policy and Management*, **18**, 7–22.

Nishio, T. (1988), 'Jinji Gyosei Kikan' (The National Personnel Authority in a Historical Perspective), in NPA (ed.), *Komuin Gyoseino Kadai to Tenbo*, Tokyo: Gyosei.

Nishio, T. (1998), 'Arts and symbols in the Japanese public personnel management', *International Review of Administrative Sciences*, **64** (2), 261–74.

Niskanen, W.A. (1971), *Bureaucracy and Representative Government*, Chicago: Aldine Atherton.

Nitobe, I. (1969), *Bushido: The Soul of Japan* (first published in 1905), Rutland: Charles and E. Tuttle Co.

Nordby, T. (2000), *I Politikens Sentrum: Variasjoner i Stortingets makt 1814–2000*, Oslo: Scandinavian University Press.

Northcote Parkinson, C. (1961), *Parkinson's Law*, Harmondsworth, Penguin Books.

O'Faircheallaigh, C., J. Wanna and P. Weller (1999), *Public Sector Management in Australia*, South Yarra: Macmillan.

O'Neill, O. (2002), *A Question of Trust*, Cambridge: Cambridge University Press.

OECD (1992), *Education at a Glance: OECD Indicators 1992*, Paris: OECD.

OECD (1997), *Education at a Glance: OECD Indicators 1997*, Paris: OECD.

OECD (2000), *Education at a Glance: OECD Indicators 2000*, Paris: OECD.

OECD (2002), *Education at a Glance: OECD Indicators 2002*, Paris: OECD.

Osborne, D. and Gaebler, T. (1992), *Reinventing Government*, Reading, MA: Addison-Wesley.

PA Consulting (2000), *Better Accountability for Higher Education*, Bristol: HEFCE.

Penal Reform International (2001), *Making Standards Work: An International Handbook on Good Prison Practice*, London: Astron Printers.

Peters, B.G. (2002), 'The federal bureaucracy and public management', in G. Peele, C.J. Bailey, B. Cain and B.G. Peters (eds), *Developments in American Politics IV*, Basingstoke: Palgrave.

Peters, B.G. and J. Pierre (eds) (2001), *Politicians, Bureaucrats and Administrative Reform*, New York: Routledge.

Peters, G. (2001), *The Politics of Bureaucracy*, 5th edn, London: Routledge.

Phillips, F. (2001), *The Regulatory Environment Applying to Universities*, Canberra: Department of Education Science and Training.

Podger, A. (2002), 'The emerging framework of Australian government administration: efficient, agile and accountable', in CAPAM 2002 Biennial Conference.

Power, M.K. (1997), *The Audit Society*, Oxford: Oxford University Press.

Pressman, J.L. and A. Wildavsky (1973), *Implementation*, Berkeley, CA: University of California Press.

Prisons Ombudsman (2000), *Annual Report and Accounts 1999–2000*, Cm 4730, London: The Stationery Office.

Prisons Ombudsman (2001), *Annual Report and Accounts 2000–2001*, Cm 5170, London: The Stationery Office.

Prisons Ombudsman (1995), *First Six Months Report*, London: Prisons Ombudsman.

Quality Assurance Agency for Higher Education (2000), *Handbook for Academic Review*, Bristol: QAA.

Quinlan, J.M. (1990), 'What should the public expect from prisons: overcoming the myths', *Federal Prisons Journal*, **1** (4), 3–6.

Randaraad, N. and D. Wolffram (2001), 'Constraints on clientelism: the Dutch path to modern politics, 1848–1917', in S. Piattoni (ed.), *Clientelism, Interests and Democratic Representation*, Cambridge: Cambridge University Press, pp. 101–21.

Rapport de la Commission Sénatoriale Hyest (2000), Sénat Session Ordinaire 1999–2000 No. 449, Paris.

Ravneberg, B. (2002), 'Skolens funksjon i fengselet', working paper, Bergen: The Rokkan Centre.

Rhoades, G. and B. Sporn (2002), 'Quality assurance in Europe and the U.S.: professional and political economic framing of higher education policy', *Higher Education*, **43**, 355–90.

Rhodes, R.A.W. and P. Weller (eds) (2001), *The Changing World of Top Officials: Mandarins or Valets?*, Philadelphia, PA: Open University Press.

Rose, R. (1976), 'On the priorities of government: a developmental analysis of public policies', *European Journal of Political Research*, **4** (3), 247–89.

Rouban, L. (1994), *Les cadres supérieurs de la fonction publique et la politique de modernisation administrative*, Paris: Direction générale de l'administration et de la fonction publique.

Rynne, J. (2001), 'Protection of prisoners' rights in Australian private prisons', in D. Brown and M. Wilkie (eds), *Prisoners as Citizens: Human Rights in Australian Prisons*, Sydney: Federation Press.

Sakamoto, T. (2003), *The Prison Guard*, Keimukan: Shincho-sha.

Sartori, G. (1994), 'Compare why and how: comparing, miscomparing and the comparative method', in M. Dogan and A. Kazancigil (eds), *Comparing Nations: Concepts, Strategies, Substance*, Oxford: Blackwell, ch. 1.

Savoie, D.J. (1994), *Reagan, Thatcher, Mulroney: In Search of a New Bureaucracy*, Pittsburgh: University of Pittsburgh Press.

Schäfer, K.H. (1997), *Anstaltsbeiräte – die institutionaliserte Öffentlichkeit?* Heidelberg: CF Müller Juristischer Verlag.

Schelsky, H. (1971), *Einsamkeit und Freiheit. Idee und Gestalt der deutschen Universitäten und ihrer Reformen*, 2 Auflage, Düsseldorf: Bertelsmann Universitätsverlag.

Schick, A. (1966), *The Spirit of Reform: A Report Prepared for the State Services Commission and the Treasury*, Wellington: New Zealand State Services Commission.

Schuetze, H.G. and M. Slowey (2002), 'Participation and exclusion: a comparative analysis of non-traditional students and lifelong learners in higher education', *Higher Education*, **44**, 309–27.

Schultze, C.L. (1977), *The Public Use of Private Interest*, Washington: Brookings Institution.

Scott, C. (2002), 'Private regulation of the public sector: a neglected facet of contemporary governance', *Journal of Law and Society*, **29**, 56–76.

Scott, R. (1996), *Report of the Inquiry into the Export of Defence Equipment and Dual-use Goods to Iraq and Related Prosecutions*, London: HMSO (HC115 1995–6).

Snodden, T. and J.P. Wen (1998), 'A primer on intergovernmental grants: the flypaper effect', *Economics Working Paper Series*, Series 99–03 September 1998, London: Birkbeck College.

Spence, J.D. (1999), *The Search for Modern China*, 2nd edn, New York: Norton.

St.meld. nr. 104 (1977–78), *Om kriminalpolitikken*, Oslo: Ministry of Justice.

Statskonsult (2001), *Etatssutvikling i kriminalomsorgen*, Oslo: Statskonsult, Reprot 2001.

Stiles, D.R (2002), 'Higher Education Funding Council (HEFC) methods in the 1990s: national and regional developments and policy implications', *Public Administration*, **80**, 711–31.

Suleiman, E. (1974), *Politics, Power and Bureaucracy in France*, Princeton, NJ: Princeton University Press.

Suleiman, E., and H. Mendras (1995), *Le recrutement des élites en Europe*, Paris: La Découverte.

Sunstein, C.R. (1990), 'Paradoxes of the regulatory state', *University of Chicago Law Review*, **57**, 407–41.

Teubner, G. (1997), 'Global Bukowina: legal pluralism in the world society', in G. Teubner (ed.), *Global Law Without a State*, Aldershot: Dartmouth, pp. 3–28.

Thigpen, M.L., S.M. Hunter and A.Z. Thompson (1996), *Managing Staff: Corrections Most Valuable Resource*, Washington, DC: US Department of Justice.

Thoenig, J.C. (1987), *L'ère des technocrates*, Paris: L'Harmattan.

Thompson, F. (1993), 'Matching responsibilities with tasks: administrative control and modern government', *Public Administration Review*, July/August, 303–18.

Thompson, M. (2003), 'Clumsiness: it's as easy as falling off a log', paper for conference on 'Clumsy Solutions for a Complex World', Saïd Business School, University of Oxford, 4–6 April.

Thompson, M., R. Ellis and A. Wildavsky (1990), *Cultural Theory*, Boulder, CO: Westview.

Timmins, N. (2001), 'Bureaucratic overload is swamping governors', *Financial Times*, 20 June.

Tseblis, G. (2002), *Veto Players: How Political Institutions Work*, Princeton, NJ: Princeton University Press.

Twist, M.J.W. van (1999), 'Van sturing naar toezicht: De terugkeer van toezicht op de bestuurlijke agenda; horizontalisering vermomd als herstel van de hiërarchie?', in R.J. in 't Veld, *Sturingswaan & ontnuchtering*, Utrecht: Lemma.

UNESCO (1997), *Recommendation Concerning the Status of Higher Education Teaching Personnel*, Paris: UNESCO.

Vabø, A. (2002), *Mytedannelser i endringsprosesser i akademiske institusjoner*, Bergen: Dr. polit. thesis, University of Bergen.

Vagg, J. (1994), *Prison Systems: A Comparative Study of Accountability in England, France, Germany and the Netherlands*, Oxford: Clarendon Press.

Vasseur, V. (2000), *Médecin-chef à la Santé*, Paris: Le Cherche-Midi Editeur.

Vijlder, F.J. de (1996), *Onderwijs en natiestaat. Een essay over de erosie van de relatie tussen Westerse natiestaten en hun onderwijssystemen*, 's-Gravenhage: VUGA.

Vogel, M. (1998), *Contrôler les prisons. L'IGSA et l'administration pénitentiaire 1907–1948*, Paris: La documentation Française.

Vogel, S.K. (1996), *Freer Markets, More Rules: Regulatory Reform in Advanced Industrial Countries*, Ithaca, NY: Cornell Univerity Press.

Weaver, P.K. and B. Rockman (1993), *Do Institutions Matter? Government Capabilities in the United States and Abroad*, Washington, DC: Brookings Institution.

Weert, E. de. (2001), 'The end of public employment in Dutch higher education?' in J. Enders (ed.), *Academic Staff in Europe: Changing Contexts and Conditions*, Westport, CT: Greenwood, pp. 195–216.

Wessels, W. (1998), 'Comitology: fusion in action. Politico-administrative trends in the EU system', *Journal of European Public Policy*, **5**, 209–34.

Wettenhall, R. (2000), 'Public and private in the New Public Management state', paper presented to the Public Management and Governance in the New Millennium Conference, 10–11 January, City University, Hong Kong.

Wieringen, A.M.L. van (1996), *Onderwijsbeleid in Nederland*, Alphen aan den Rijn: Tjeenk Willink.

Wilson, J.Q. and P. Rachal (1977), 'Can government regulate itself?', *Public Interest*, **46**, 3–14.

World Bank (1999), *Civil Service Reform: A Review of World Bank Assistance*, Operations Evaluation Department Report no. 19599, Washington, DC: World Bank.

Wye, C. (2000), 'The evolution of a results-oriented management culture', *Public Manager*, **29** (3), 24–8.

Index